高等院校立体化创新经管教材系列

英语国家社会与文化
(第2版)

王 焱 杨 倩 主 编
孔宁宁 马晓奕 王晓雪 副主编

清华大学出版社
北京

内 容 简 介

本教材共分为六章，依次介绍了英国、美国、澳大利亚、加拿大、新西兰和爱尔兰等六个主要英语国家。每章分为地理位置与资源、历史与象征、教育与娱乐、政治与经济、文化与习俗、跨文化交际六个单元。课文中标记了英语四、六级词汇，便于学生了解使用。本书思政内容丰富，通过跨文化交际案例对中西文化进行对比，并增加了关于中国传统文化的英汉互译练习和关于当代中国的拓展阅读，以满足英语教学实践的需求。

本书封面贴有清华大学出版社防伪标签，无标签者不得销售。
版权所有，侵权必究。举报：010-62782989，beiqinquan@tup.tsinghua.edu.cn。

图书在版编目(CIP)数据

英语国家社会与文化/王焱，杨倩主编. —2 版. —北京：清华大学出版社，2024.4（2024.8重印）
高等院校立体化创新经管教材系列
ISBN 978-7-302-65841-2

Ⅰ. ①英… Ⅱ. ①王… ②杨… Ⅲ. ①英语—阅读教学—高等学校—教材 ②文化—概况—国外 Ⅳ. ①H319.37

中国国家版本馆 CIP 数据核字(2024)第 062018 号

责任编辑：陈冬梅
装帧设计：刘孝琼
责任校对：常　婷
责任印制：沈　露

出版发行：清华大学出版社
　　　　网　　址：https://www.tup.com.cn, https://www.wqxuetang.com
　　　　地　　址：北京清华大学学研大厦 A 座　　邮　编：100084
　　　　社 总 机：010-83470000　　　　　　　　邮　购：010-62786544
　　　　投稿与读者服务：010-62776969, c-service@tup.tsinghua.edu.cn
　　　　质量反馈：010-62772015, zhiliang@tup.tsinghua.edu.cn
　　　　课件下载：https://www.tup.com.cn, 010-62791865

印 装 者：三河市人民印务有限公司
经　　销：全国新华书店
开　　本：185mm×260mm　　　印　张：14.75　　　字　数：356 千字
版　　次：2019 年 1 月第 1 版　2024 年 5 月第 2 版　印　次：2024 年 8 月第 2 次印刷
定　　价：45.00 元

产品编号：101838-01

前　　言

《英语国家社会与文化(第 2 版)》以《大学英语教学指南(2020 版)》的培养目标、课程设置、教学要求和教学原则为指导，结合《普通高等学校本科专业类教学质量国家标准》，以辽宁省资源共享课平台和中国高校外语慕课平台为依托编写而成，旨在培养学生跨文化交际能力和思辨能力，提高学生文化自信。

一、教材特色

1. 线上与线下的融合

本教材主题契合学生要求和时代特点，利用教学案例，帮助学生拓宽视野，培养跨文化意识，选材内容适合线上教学模式或线上线下混合式教学模式。通过课前导学、线上自主学习、课堂讲授重点难点、课后夯实所学内容，满足不同层次学生的个性化学习需求，激发学生学习兴趣，优化学习效果。

2. 语言与内容的融合

本教材充分呈现课程的应用性、互动性和知识性，利用丰富的选材和重大历史事件，客观、如实地反映主要英语国家的地理位置与资源、历史与象征、教育与娱乐、政治与经济、文化与习俗、跨文化交际等。大量有关文化的词汇和主题篇章使学生置身于文化课堂的氛围之中，领略文化课堂的教学魅力，体会英美习俗和人文，在学习英语知识的同时感受文化的熏陶，有助于培养学生的跨文化交际意识和能力。

二、教材内容

本教材共分为六章，介绍了英国、美国、澳大利亚、加拿大、新西兰和爱尔兰等六个主要英语国家的最新国情，供一或两个学期使用。每章介绍一个国家，每个国家均按照地理位置与资源(Location and Resources)、历史与象征(History and Symbols)、教育与娱乐(Education and Recreation)、政治与经济(Politics and Economy)、文化与习俗(Culture and Customs)以及跨文化交际(Intercultural Communication)等六个单元设置。在主题篇章中，对四、六级词汇进行标记。在跨文化交际单元中，案例分析部分以各国相关的文化案例为主，通过具体案例，把抽象的理论形象化、具体化，使学生能够学以致用。

同时，根据线上网络课程同步配套习题。练习部分涵盖训练基础技能的简答和写作训练，并附有练习题的参考答案。

在再版过程中，我们对原版的内容进行了全面的修订和更新，以反映英语国家社会与文化的最新发展，修改并增补了关于各国国情的最新情况和数据，尽量使内容更加丰富和具有时效性。同时增加了一个新的章节——爱尔兰，并且在每一章新增了国家标志性词汇列表。在练习方面，除删除以往形式陈旧的阅读理解部分之外，在跨文化交际这一单元，增加了丰富的关于中国传统文化的英汉互译练习和关于当代中国的拓展阅读材料训练，以贴合思政内容的教学要求，从而引导学生进一步了解中国传统文化，增强民族自豪感，坚定文化自信，学会在新时代中国特色社会主义文化的背景下去理解和表达中华民族 5000 多年文明历史所孕育的中华优秀传统文化，帮助学生在掌握翻译技巧的同时，强化语言沟通能力。

三、使用说明

本教材大部分内容用英语编写，以满足培养复合型、应用型国际化人才的需要，可作为英语专业本科生及研究生必修课或选修课教材、非英语专业的后续拓展课程教材、通识教育课程教材，以及英语学习者了解中西方文化的自学材料。跨校修读学分高校可根据省级资源共享课的实际教学情况和教学目标选择使用。

本教材是辽宁省普通本科高等学校校际合作项目、国家级一流本科课程"中西文化对比"、省级一流本科课程"英语国家社会与文化"、"英语国家国情"、省级教改项目"新文科背景下跨校修读学分课程及其资源的完善与重构"等阶段性学术成果。

本教材编者均为从事英语教育多年并具有丰富教学经验的一线教师，希望本教材能对我国高校外语教学做出新贡献。对于本教材中的不足之处，敬请专家、学者、同行及使用本教材的师生不吝指正，以期不断完善。

编 者

目 录

Chapter One The United Kingdom of Great Britain and Northern Ireland 1

Unit 1 Location and Resources 3
    Vocabulary 3
    Geographical Location 3
    Weather and Climate 5
    Natural Resources 6
    Exercises 7
Unit 2 History and Symbols 8
    Vocabulary 8
    Historical Periods 9
    Historical Figures 12
    National Symbols 12
    Exercises 13
Unit 3 Education and Recreation ... 14
    Vocabulary 14
    School Education 15
    Famous Universities 16
    Cultural Life 17
    Exercises 19
Unit 4 Politics and Economy 20
    Vocabulary 21
    Political System 21
    Political Parties 23
    Economy 24
    Exercises 25
Unit 5 Culture and Customs 26
    Vocabulary 27
    Traditional Culture 27
    Literature Works 27
    Food Customs 29

    Exercises 30
Unit 6 Intercultural Communication 31
    Knowledge to Learn 31
    Cases to Study 31
    Translations on Traditional Chinese Culture 33
    Culture to Know 35
    Further Reading 37

Chapter Two The United States of America 39

Unit 1 Location and Resources 41
    Vocabulary 41
    Geographical Location 41
    Weather and Climate 43
    Natural Resources 43
    Exercises 44
Unit 2 History and Symbols 46
    Vocabulary 46
    Historical Periods 46
    Historical Figures 48
    National Symbols 49
    Exercises 50
Unit 3 Education and Recreation ... 51
    Vocabulary 51
    School Education 52
    Famous Universities 53
    Cultural Life 55
    Exercises 56
Unit 4 Politics and Economy 58
    Vocabulary 58
    Political System 58

Political Parties 59
  Economy 60
  Exercises 62
 Unit 5 Culture and Customs 64
  Vocabulary 64
  Traditional Culture 64
  Literature Works 65
  Food Customs 67
  Exercises 67
 Unit 6 Intercultural Communication 69
  Knowledge to Learn 69
  Cases to Study 69
  Translations on Traditional Chinese
   Culture 71
  Culture to Know 73
  Further Reading 74

Chapter Three Australia 77

 Unit 1 Location and Resources 79
  Vocabulary 79
  Geographical Location 79
  Weather and Climate 81
  Natural Resources 82
  Exercises 82
 Unit 2 History and Symbols 83
  Vocabulary 84
  Historical Periods 84
  Historical Figures 86
  National Symbols 87
  Exercises 88
 Unit 3 Education and Recreation 89
  Vocabulary 89
  School Education 90
  Famous Universities 92
  Cultural Life 93
  Exercises 95
 Unit 4 Politics and Economy 96

  Vocabulary 97
  Political System 97
  Political Parties 99
  Economy 100
  Exercises 102
 Unit 5 Culture and Customs 103
  Vocabulary 104
  Traditional Culture 104
  Literature Works 105
  Food Customs 107
  Exercises 108
 Unit 6 Intercultural Communication 109
  Knowledge to Learn 109
  Cases to Study 109
  Translations on Traditional Chinese
   Culture 111
  Culture to Know 114
  Further Reading 115

Chapter Four Canada 117

 Unit 1 Location and Resources 119
  Vocabulary 119
  Geographical Location 119
  Weather and Climate 121
  Natural Resources 122
  Exercises 123
 Unit 2 History and Symbols 124
  Vocabulary 124
  Historical Periods 125
  Historical Figures 126
  National Symbols 127
  Exercises 128
 Unit 3 Education and Recreation 130
  Vocabulary 130
  School Education 130
  Famous Universities 132
  Cultural Life 133

Exercises 134	Famous Universities 172
Unit 4　Politics and Economy 135	Cultural Life 173
Vocabulary 135	Exercises 175
Political System 136	Unit 4　Politics and Economy 176
Political Parties 137	Vocabulary 177
Economy 137	Political System 177
Exercises 139	Political Parties 179
Unit 5　Culture and Customs 141	Economy 179
Vocabulary 141	Exercises 181
Traditional Culture 141	Unit 5　Culture and Customs 182
Literature Works 143	Vocabulary 183
Food Customs 145	Traditional Culture 183
Exercises 145	Literature Works 185
Unit 6　Intercultural Communication 147	Food Customs 186
Knowledge to Learn 147	Exercises 186
Cases to Study 147	Unit 6　Intercultural Communication 187
Translations on Traditional Chinese	Knowledge to Learn 187
Culture 148	Cases to Study 188
Culture to Know 151	Translations on Traditional Chinese
Further Reading 152	Culture 189

Chapter Five　New Zealand 155

Unit 1　Location and Resources 157	Culture to Know 192
Vocabulary 157	Further Reading 193

Chapter Six　The Republic of
　　　　　　　Ireland 195

Geographical Location 157	
Weather and Climate 159	Unit 1　Location and Resources 197
Natural Resources 159	Vocabulary 197
Exercises 161	Geographical Location 197
Unit 2　History and Symbol 162	Weather and Climate 199
Vocabulary 162	Natural Resources 200
Historical Periods 163	Exercises 200
Historical Figures 166	Unit 2　History and Symbols 201
National Symbols 167	Vocabulary 202
Exercises 167	Historical Periods 202
Unit 3　Education and Recreation 169	Historical Figures 203
Vocabulary 169	National Symbols 204
School Education 169	Exercises 205

Unit 3 Education and Recreation 207	Vocabulary 216
Vocabulary 207	Traditional Culture 216
School Education 207	Literature Works................................ 217
Famous Universities 208	Food Customs 217
Cultural Life 209	Exercises 218
Exercises 210	Unit 6 Intercultural Communication 219
Unit 4 Politics and Economy 211	Knowledge to Learn 219
Vocabulary 211	Cases to Study 220
Political System 212	Translations on Traditional Chinese
Political Parties 212	Culture 221
Economy 213	Culture to Know 224
Exercises 214	Further Reading 225
Unit 5 Culture and Customs 215	**Reference** 226

Chapter One
The United Kingdom of Great Britain and Northern Ireland

英语国家社会与文化（第2版）

Contents

1. Location and Resources
2. History and Symbols
3. Education and Recreation
4. Politics and Economy
5. Culture and Customs
6. Intercultural Communication

Big Ben	大本钟	**Jubilee**	皇室庆典
Buckingham Palace	白金汉宫	**Loch Ness Monster**	尼斯湖水怪
Constitutional Monarchy	君主立宪制	**post box**	邮筒
cricket	板球	**Stonehenge**	巨石阵
double-decker bus	双层巴士	**the British Museum**	大英博物馆
English breakfast & tea	英式早餐和茶	**the Norman Conquest**	诺曼征服
fish and chips	炸鱼薯条	**the Union Jack**	米字旗
Greenwich Mean Time	格林尼治标准时间	**Tower Bridge**	伦敦塔桥
House of Lords	上议院	**University of Cambridge**	剑桥大学
Houses of Parliament	英国议会大厦	**University of Oxford**	牛津大学

Chapter One The United Kingdom of Great Britain and Northern Ireland

Unit 1 Location and Resources

Text Focus

1. Geographical Location
2. Weather and Climate
3. Natural Resources

1.1 Lecture1 Location.mp4

1.2 Lecture2 People.mp4

Vocabulary

1. consist	[kənˈsɪst]	v.	构成
2. occupy	[ˈɒkjupaɪ]	v.	占据
3. latter	[ˈlætə(r)]	adj.	后者的
4. respectively	[rɪˈspektɪvli]	adv.	分别地
5. metropolitan	[ˌmetrəˈpɒlɪtən]	adj.	大都市的
6. constitute	[ˈkɒnstɪtjuːt]	v.	构成
7. fluctuation	[ˌflʌktʃuˈeɪʃn]	n.	变化

The United Kingdom of Great Britain and Northern Ireland ***consists***[1] of three political divisions: England, Scotland and Wales on the island of Great Britain, Northern Ireland is the fourth region of the United Kingdom on the island of Ireland. With a maritime climate, the United Kingdom has a steady, reliable rainfall throughout the whole year. And the United Kingdom is rich in a mix of fossil fuels. Britain has a population of over 60 million and it is very unevenly distributed. London, as the capital city of England and the United Kingdom, together with Edinburgh, the capital city of Scotland, and Cardiff, Welsh capital city are major cities in the United Kingdom.

Geographical Location

The United Kingdom of Great Britain and Northern Ireland, commonly known as the United Kingdom (UK) or Britain, is a sovereign state located off the northwestern coast of continental Europe. It lies between the North Atlantic Ocean and the North Sea with the southeast coast coming within 35 kilometers of the coast of northern France, from which it is separated by the English Channel. The country ***occupies***[2] the major part of the British Isles and includes the island of Great Britain, the northeastern part of the island of Ireland and many smaller islands. Northern Ireland is the only part of the United Kingdom that shares a land border with another sovereign state—the Republic of Ireland. Apart from this land border, the United Kingdom is surrounded by the Atlantic Ocean, the North Sea, the English Channel and the Irish Sea. The capital, London, is situated on the River Thames in southeastern England.

The total area of the United Kingdom is approximately 244,100 square kilometers. It is a country in its own right and consists of four parts: England, Scotland, Wales and Northern Ireland. The *latter*[3] three of these are devolved administrations, each with varying powers, based in their capital cities Edinburgh, Cardiff and Belfast *respectively*[4]. The United Kingdom has 14 overseas territories. These are remnants of the British Empire which, at its height in 1922, encompassed almost a quarter of the world's land surface and was the largest empire in history. British influence can still be observed in the language, culture and legal systems of many of its former territories.

England is a constituent unit of the United Kingdom and the island of Great Britain. It shares land borders with Scotland to the north and Wales to the west; the Irish Sea is to the northwest, the Celtic Sea to the southwest, while the North Sea to the east and the English Channel to the south, separating it from continental Europe. Most of England comprises the central and southern part of the island of Great Britain in the North Atlantic. The country also includes over 100 smaller islands. England's terrain mostly comprises low hills and plains, especially in the central and southern England. However, there are uplands in the north and in the southwest. In geological terms, the Pennines, known as the backbone of England, are the oldest range of mountains in the country.

London is the capital city of England and the United Kingdom, the largest *metropolitan*[5] area in the United Kingdom. Located on the River Thames, London has been a major settlement for two millennia.

London is a global city, with strengths in arts, commerce, education, entertainment, fashion, finance, healthcare, media, professional services, research and development, tourism and transport all contributing to its prominence. It is the world's leading financial center alongside New York City and the largest in Europe. London has been described as a world cultural capital. It is the world's most-visited city and has the world's largest city airport system measured by passenger traffic. 43 universities in London form the largest concentration of higher education in Europe.

London has a diverse range of peoples and cultures, and more than 300 languages are spoken within its boundaries. London contains four World Heritage sites: the Tower of London, Kew Gardens, the site comprising the Palace of Westminster, Westminster Abbey, St. Margaret's Church, and the historic settlement of Greenwich. Other famous landmarks include Buckingham Palace, the London Eye, Piccadilly Circus, St. Paul's Cathedral, Tower Bridge, Trafalgar Square and Wembley Stadium. London is home to numerous museums, galleries, libraries, sporting events and other cultural institutions, including the British Museum, National Gallery, Tate Modern, British Library, Wimbledon and over 40 West End theaters. The London Underground is the oldest underground railway network in the world.

Scotland is a constituent unit of the United Kingdom and the island of Great Britain. Occupying one third of the island of Great Britain in the north, it shares a border with England to the south and is bounded by the North Sea to the east, the Atlantic Ocean to the north and west, and the North Channel and Irish Sea to the southwest. In addition to the mainland, over 790 islands *constitute*[6] Scotland. From a geological perspective, the country has three main subdivisions: Highlands and islands, Central lowlands and Southern uplands.

Edinburgh is the capital city of Scotland and the seat of the Scottish Parliament. It is the second largest city in Scotland. Located in the southeast of Scotland, Edinburgh lies on the east coast of the Central Belt, along the Firth of Forth, near the North Sea.

Edinburgh is the administrative, financial, legal, medical and insurance center of Scotland. It owns beautiful scenery and renowned architecture Edinburgh Castle.

There are two sides to Edinburgh: the historic Old Town with the medieval Edinburgh Castle and cobblestone alleys, and the elegant but classic Georgian New Town. Together, they create a dynamic and fascinating city which truly captures the magical spirit of Scotland.

Wales is a constituent unit of the United Kingdom and the island of Great Britain, bordered by England to its east and the Atlantic Ocean and Irish Sea to its west. The unit lies within the North Temperate Zone, and has a changeable, maritime climate.

Cardiff is the capital and the largest city in Wales. As Europe's youngest capital, the city is Wales' chief commercial center, the base for most national cultural and sporting institutions, the Welsh national media, and the seat of the National Assembly for Wales. Cardiff is a significant tourist center and the most popular visitor destination in Wales.

Cardiff was made a city in 1905, and proclaimed the capital of Wales in 1955. Since the 1980s, Cardiff has seen the significant development. A new waterfront area at Cardiff Bay contains the Senedd building, home to the Welsh Assembly and the Wales Millennium Center arts complex.

Northern Ireland is a part of the United Kingdom in the northeast of the island of Ireland. Northern Ireland shares a border with the Republic of Ireland to the south and west. Northern Ireland occupies about one sixth of the island of Ireland and is separated on the east from Scotland, another part of the United Kingdom, by the narrow North Channel. The Irish Sea separates Northern Ireland from England and Wales on the east and southeast, respectively, and the Atlantic Ocean lies to the north.

Weather and Climate

The climate varies greatly according to season and location, but on the whole, it can be described as temperate maritime, mild with few extremes and a relatively small *fluctuation*[7] in temperatures. Winters tend to be generally mild and cool. The main influence on the climate is Britain's close proximity to the Atlantic Ocean and the warming of the waters around the land by the Gulf Stream. The most typical feature of climate in Britain is that it is so changeable and unpredictable. The climate of Britain is also characterized by rainfall all year round. Rain is fairly well distributed throughout the year, with late winter and spring the driest period and autumn and winter the wettest.

English weather is diverse, with a generally mild but erratic maritime climate. Contrary to popular belief, it does not rain every day in England. However, it is always advisable to bring some type of waterproof clothing and keep yourself psychologically prepared as a result of the snag. The snag is that people never know what the weather will be like from one day to another. It can be sunny one day and rainy the next.

The climate of Scotland is temperate and oceanic, and tends to be very changeable. It is warmed by the Gulf Stream from the Atlantic, and has much milder winters than areas on similar latitudes.

Wales lies within the north temperate zone. It has a changeable, maritime climate. Welsh weather is often cloudy, wet and windy, with warm summers and mild winters. The long summer days and short winter days are due to Wales' northerly latitudes.

The whole of Northern Ireland has a temperate maritime climate, rather wetter in the west than the east, although cloud cover is persistent across the region.

Natural Resources

The United Kingdom has large deposits of coal, mined for more than 300 years. For most of the 19th and 20th centuries, coal was Britain's richest natural resource, meeting most of the nation's requirement for energy. Today, coal can be produced more cheaply in other countries, so many British factories and mines have been closed. Tin and iron ore deposits, once central to the economy, have become exhausted or uneconomical, and the coal industry, long a staple of the economy, began a steady decline in the 1950s that worsened with pit closures in the 1980s. Offshore petroleum and natural gas reserves are significant.

In the United Kingdom, the majority of electricity is generated by a mix of fossil fuels and nuclear power, releasing millions of tons of carbon dioxide into the environment. The business of generating electricity from the wind is growing fast as the world looks for cleaner ways to produce energy. Coal, oil and gas fired power stations could eventually be replaced by wind farms and other forms of renewable energy. Today, wind is used to generate electricity using wind turbines. Like windmills, wind turbines are mounted on a tower to capture the most energy.

The main commercial minerals are those used in the construction and building industries such as sand and gravel, limestone and gypsum. They are normally mined from the surface in

Chapter One The United Kingdom of Great Britain and Northern Ireland

quarries by using heavy machinery. Smaller quarries are also found across England and provide stone for the local building industry. This means that many parts of England have a distinctive appearance according to the local stone available.

Exercises

I. *Try to answer the following questions according to your understanding of the text.*

(1) How many parts does the United Kingdom consist of? What are they?
(2) What are the relationships among Northern Ireland, Ireland and the United Kingdom?
(3) What are those World Heritage sites in London?
(4) What are the major characteristics of the climate in the United Kingdom?
(5) What are the forms of generating electricity in the United Kingdom?

II. *Read the following passage carefully, and make a comment on it at the end of the passage in no more than 100 words.*

Edinburgh's population is largely a mixture of middle-class professionals and non-professionals. Both are more prosperous than their ancestors, most of whom emigrated from the surrounding countryside and small towns to provide the 19th century city with unskilled and semiskilled labour. The workforce has changed considerably since then, and now white-collar workers outnumber blue-collar workers. Most of the population is native to Scotland; about one in eight residents was born in England, representing the city's largest immigrant group by far. There are small percentages of Irish, Chinese, and South Asians, as well as a sprinkling of new immigrants from continental Europe. But the most striking element in the city's demographic composition is its student population. Edinburgh's universities enroll tens of thousands of students, many of whom come from overseas and contribute to the cosmopolitan character of the city. There are other unexpected features of life in Edinburgh. Edinburgh's white-collar workforce commutes both into the center of the city and out from the center to new virtual villages of suburban low-rise office blocks in places such as Gyle and Leith. The commuting belt extends well into Fife, across the Forth Estuary to the north, and as far west as Glasgow, resulting in overcrowded trains and highly congested roads.

A very different city from Scotland's largest city, the sometimes maligned Glasgow, Edinburgh is changing faster than Glasgow and has a more assured future, particularly since the late 1990s, when it regained its full status as a capital city. Edinburgh largely escaped the motorway schemes of urban planners beginning in the 1960s that proved detrimental to Glasgow's center. The two cities have a different historical legacy, too. Glasgow experienced a far greater influx of both Roman Catholic and Protestant immigrants from Ireland in the 19th century. As a result, at the turn of the 21st century Glasgow was split about evenly between adherents of Roman Catholicism and those of the Church of Scotland. In Edinburgh, by contrast, members of the Church of Scotland greatly outnumber Roman Catholics, though the proportion of those of all the main denominations who attend church regularly is quite low.

Comments:

In September 2014, voters in Scotland were asked in a referendum whether they wanted the nation to become independent from the rest of the United Kingdom. Finally, Scots voted against independence in a ballot sanctioned by the British government.

What do you think of the Scottish independence referendum in 2014?

Reference:

Argument:

(1) Being different from the existing political position

(2) Being one of the world's richest countries, aided by its oil wealth

(3) Taking charge of its own destiny, free from the shackles of a London-based parliament.

Counter-argument:

(1) United, Britain is one of the world's most successful social and political unions

(2) Weakened strength as a nation

(3) Causing chaos in different aspects, such as financial system, oil crisis and foreign affairs

Unit 2   History and Symbols

Text Focus

1. Historical Periods
2. Historical Figures
3. National Symbols

1.3 Lecture3 History.mp4

Vocabulary

1. characterize	[ˈkærəktəraɪz]	v.	具有……的特征
2. invade	[ɪnˈveɪd]	v.	侵略
3. eligible	[ˈelɪdʒəbl]	adj.	合格的
4. referendum	[ˌrefəˈrendəm]	n.	全民公投
5. devolve	[dɪˈvɒlv]	v.	移交
6. purity	[ˈpjʊərəti]	n.	纯洁

Chapter One The United Kingdom of Great Britain and Northern Ireland

The British history has witnessed intermittent periods of competition and cooperation between the people that occupied the various parts of this island, namely the Romans, the Celts, the Anglo-Saxons and the Vikings. The history of the United Kingdom as a unified sovereign state began in 1707 with the political union of the kingdoms of England and Scotland into a united kingdom called Great Britain. With a long history of more than 2,000 years, Britain has experienced significant changes in politics, economy, culture and science. After the rise and fall of Feudalism and the age of Empire, the United Kingdom of Great Britain and Northern Ireland came into being. This new kingdom plays an important role in the world ever since. Alfred the Great, William I, and Elizabeth I are all thought to be the greatest British rulers. The Union Jack represents the union of different countries and the growth of a family of nations whose influence extends far beyond the British Isles. The national anthem of the United Kingdom is *God Save the King*.

Historical Periods

Prehistoric Britain: The earliest settlers in Britain are the Iberians who came about 3,000 years ago from the Iberian Peninsular (now Portugal and Spain). The Beaker Folk, whose culture was ***characterized***[1] by bell beakers buried with their dead in round barrows, settled in Britain 1,000 years later. Both of these two groups were prehistoric people.

Roman Britain: The Romans were the first to ***invade***[2] Britain and came to Britain nearly 2,000 years ago. They changed the country. The Roman Empire made its mark on Britain, and even today, the ruins of Roman buildings, forts, roads, and baths can be found all over Britain.

Anglo-Saxon Britain: The Roman army left Britain about 410 AD. When they had gone, there was no strong army to defend Britain, and tribes called the Angle, Saxon, and Jute invaded. They left their homelands in northern Germany, Denmark and northern Holland and rowed across the North Sea in wooden boats.

Viking Britain: The Viking Age in Britain began about 1,200 years ago in the 8th century AD and lasted for 300 years. About the year 800, bands of fierce raiders began to attack the coasts. They were the Vikings. They came across the North Sea, just as the Anglo-Saxons had done 400 years earlier.

The Middle Ages-Medieval Britain: The Middle Ages in Britain covered a huge period. They took Britain from the shock of the Norman Conquest, which began in 1066, to the Black Death of 1348, the Hundred Years' War with France and the Wars of the Roses, which finally ended in 1485.

Tudor Britain: Henry Tudor emerged from the Wars of the Roses as the new King of England. Most of the Tudors are powerful kings—Henry VII, Henry VIII, Mary and Elizabeth I. They ruled England from 1485 to 1603—one of the most exciting periods of British history. The

English Reformation and Renaissance both came into being during this period.

Stuart Britain: Elizabeth I was followed to the throne by James VI of Scotland, who became James I of England. The relationship between early Stuart kings and Parliament was acrimonious, which finally resulted in the first English Civil War (1642—1646). Parliament drew most of its support from the middle classes, while the King was supported by the nobility, the clergy, and the peasantry. Parliamentary supporters were known as Roundheads while the king's army was known as Cavaliers. The Civil War ended up with the execution of King Charles I and the Regency of Cromwell(Fig. 1-1).

Fig. 1-1   Regency of Cromwell

Georgian Britain: In 1714, the British Queen Anne died without any heirs, and the throne was passed to George of Hanover, her nearest Protestant relative, who became George I of England. Under the reign of George I and his two successors, George II and George III, the very nature of English society and the political face of the realm changed—kings took little interest in politics and were content to let ministers rule on their behalf and the English political party system was formed into something resembling what the British have today.

Victorian Britain: Queen Victoria(Fig. 1-2) ruled for 64 years. The time of her reign (1837—1901) was a time of enormous change in this country, and was characterized as Britain's "Golden Years". Britain managed to build a huge empire during the Victorian period. While the empire was thrived on numerous bloody colonial expansion and plundered through almost all around the world. There was peace and prosperity, as the national income per person grew by half. Much of the prosperity was due to the increasing industrialization, especially in textiles and machinery, as well as to the worldwide network of trade and engineering that produce profits for British merchants and experts from across the globe. There was peace abroad, and social peace at home. Taxes were very low, and government restrictions were minimal. There were still problem areas, such as occasional riots, the housing and conditions of life of the working class in town and country. It was also a time of tremendous change in the lives of British people. In 1837, most people lived in villages and worked on the land. By 1901, most had lived in towns and worked in offices, shops and factories.

Fig. 1-2   Queen Victoria

Contemporary Era: In the 20th century, Britain experienced two World Wars and the cost was high for Britain to win the World War II. After the World War II, Britain no longer had the wealth to maintain an empire, so it granted independence to most of the Empire. The new states

Chapter One The United Kingdom of Great Britain and Northern Ireland

typically joined the Commonwealth of Nations. Even though the United Kingdom suffered from economic declines in the postwar era, stagflation in the 1970s and economic crisis in 2008, it still has been one of the leading economies in the world, a leading member of the United Nations and NATO(North Atlantic Treaty Organization), and gradually got recovered, which partially resulted from a British government's bank rescue package, and the government was to temporarily underwrite any *eligible*[3] lending between British banks.

The Scottish independence *referendum*[4]: On September 18, 2014, a referendum was held in Scotland on whether to leave the United Kingdom and become an independent country. Most people over the age of 16 who live in Scotland were eligible to vote. 84.6% of the electorate participated in this historic vote, and 55.8% of whom voted "No". The United Kingdom government believes that Scotland is better off in the United Kingdom and the United Kingdom is better off with Scotland in it. This referendum was a once-in-a-generation opportunity for people in Scotland to have their say about the country's future. It happened because the Scottish National Party, who campaigned for Scotland to be independent, won a majority at the last Scottish Parliament election. Even though Scotland chose to remain as part of the United Kingdom, extensive new powers for the Scottish Parliament are to be *devolved*[5].

Brexit, a portmanteau of the words "British" and "exit", is the withdrawal of the United Kingdom from the European Union. The United Kingdom voted to leave the European Union on the June 23, 2016 referendum. On March 29, 2017, the United Kingdom government invoked *Article 50 of the Treaty* on the European Union. The United Kingdom was thus due to leave the European Union on March 29, 2019. As a result, the UK legislated to withdraw from the European Union on January 31, 2020. An eleven-month transition period until December 31, 2020 follows the withdrawal, during which the United Kingdom and the European Union will negotiate their future trade relationship.

The year 2022 was an unforgettable one for the United Kingdom, with the death of Queen Elizabeth II(Fig. 1-3), three prime ministers and mass strikes across the country. On September 8, 2022, it was announced the Queen had died, aged 96. Her son became King Charles III. Born on April 21, 1926, Elizabeth II was proclaimed Queen after the death of her father, King George VI, on February 6, 1952. She was formally

Fig. 1-3 Queen Elizabeth II

crowned the monarch of the United Kingdom on June 2, 1953. Having ascended to the throne at age 25, Elizabeth became the United Kingdom's longest reigning monarch in September 2015 when she surpassed Queen Victoria's record of nearly 64 years. Elizabeth became the world's longest reigning monarch and head of state. Queen Elizabeth II's tenure as head of state spanned post-war austerity, the transition from empire to Commonwealth, the end of the Cold War and the

United Kingdom's entry into—and withdrawal from—the European Union. Her reign spanned 15 prime ministers starting with Winston Churchill, born in 1874, and including Liz Truss, born 101 years later in 1975. Her death marked the end of an era.

Historical Figures

Alfred the Great(Fig. 1-4)(849—899), was King of the southern Anglo-Saxon kingdom of Wessex and one of the outstanding figures of English history, as much for his social and educational reforms as for his military successes against the Danes. He is the only English monarch known as "the Great". Alfred successfully defended his kingdom against the Viking attempt at conquest. He had a reputation as a learned

Fig. 1-4 Alfred the Great

and merciful man of a gracious and level-headed nature who encouraged education, proposing that primary education be taught in English rather than Latin, and improved his kingdom's legal system, military structure and his people's quality of life.

William I(1028—1087), usually known as William the Conqueror, was the first Norman King of England, reigning from 1066 until his death in 1087. He was previously Duke of Normandy. In the 1050s and early 1060s, as a cousin of Edward the Confessor—the English king, William became a contender for the throne of England. When Edward the Confessor died childless, William built a large fleet and invaded England in September 1066. He was crowned king on Christmas Day 1066 in London and became William I.

Fig. 1-5 Elizabeth I

Elizabeth I(Fig. 1-5)(1533—1603) was Queen of England and Ireland from November 17, 1558 until her death and is thought to be one of the greatest British rulers. Single all her life, Elizabeth was also called "the Virgin Queen", and was the last monarch of the House of Tudor.

Elizabeth's reign is known as the Elizabethan era, which is famous for one of the greatest military victories in English history—England's defeat of the Spanish Armada in 1588, and for the English Renaissance, led by playwrights such as William Shakespeare and Christopher.

National Symbols

The flag of the United Kingdom is the Union Flag, which is also referred to as the Union Jack. It was first created in 1606 by the superimposition of the Flag of England on the Flag of Scotland and updated in 1801 with the addition of Saint Patrick's Flag. The national anthem of the United Kingdom is *God Save the King*, with "King" replaced with "Queen" in the lyrics whenever

Chapter One   The United Kingdom of Great Britain and Northern Ireland

the monarch is a woman. The Royal coat of Arms is the symbol of unity in the shape of a shield. The whole is encircled and is supported by a lion and a unicorn. The lion has been used as a symbol of national strength and of the British monarchy for many centuries. The unicorn, a mythical animal that looks like a horse with a long straight horn, has appeared on the Scottish and British royal coats of arms for many centuries, and is a symbol of ***purity***[6]. At the bottom, the motto of England is written in French, which means "god and my right". In the Royal Arms, three lions symbolize England, a lion rampant stands for Scotland, and a harp stands for Ireland.

Exercises

I. *Try to answer the following questions according to your understanding of the text.*

(1) Who were the invaders in the early history of Britain?
(2) What was the "Golden Years" like in Victorian Britain?
(3) What does "Brexit" mean?
(4) Why is King Alfred named as "Alfred the Great"?
(5) What does the Union Jack refer to?

II. *Read the following passage carefully, and make a comment on it at the end of the passage in no more than 100 words.*

Sir Winston Churchill, British statesman and author, had an unhappy childhood and was an unpromising student. After joining the 4th Hussars in 1895, he saw service as both a soldier and a journalist, and his dispatches from India and South Africa attracted wide attention. The fame as a military hero helped him win the election to the House of Commons in 1900. He quickly rose to prominence and served in several cabinet posts, though in World War I and during the following decade he acquired a reputation for erratic judgment.

In the years before World War II, his warnings of the threat posed by Adolf Hitler's Germany were repeatedly ignored. When the war broke out, he was appointed to his old post as head of the Admiralty. After Neville Chamberlain resigned, Churchill headed a coalition government as the prime minister. He committed himself and the nation to an all-out war until victory was achieved, and his great eloquence, energy, and indomitable fortitude made him an inspiration to his countrymen, especially in the Battle of Britain. Winston Churchill rallied the British people and led the country from the brink of defeat to victory. He shaped Allied strategy in the war. During the Battle of Britain, Churchill's speeches boosted the British morale during the darkest moments. With Franklin Roosevelt and Joseph Stalin, he shaped Allied strategy through the Atlantic Charter and at the Cairo, Casablanca, and Tehran conferences. Though he was the architect of victory, his government was defeated in the 1945 elections.

He led the Conservative Party back into power in 1951 and remained prime minister until 1955. He was knighted in 1953; he later refused the offer of a peerage. He was made an honorary

U.S. citizen in 1963. In his late years he attained heroic status as one of the titans of the 20th century.

Comments:

Winston Churchill is a controversial figure. Some think that he is often viewed as the best UK Prime Minister in history and his legacy is well deserved; while others think he is a conceited, warlike and overbearing Englishman.

What do you think of Winston Churchill?

Reference:

Argument:

(1) Being very determined and persistent

(2) Winning the Nobel Prize in literature

(3) Resisting Germany in World War II

Counter-argument:

(1) Misjudging many situations and ending up in disaster in some military campaigns

(2) Having weakness in his character

(3) Contributing to a period of economic crisis

Unit 3   Education and Recreation

Text Focus

1. School Education
2. Famous Universities
3. Cultural Life

1.4 Lecture4 Education.mp4

Vocabulary

1. alternative	[ɔːlˈtɜːnətɪv]	n.	可供选择的事物
2. comprehensive	[ˌkɒmprɪˈhensɪv]	adj.	综合性的
3. curriculum	[kəˈrɪkjələm]	n.	课程
4. guarantee	[ˌgærənˈtiː]	v.	保证
5. equivalent	[ɪˈkwɪvələnt]	n.	类似的事物
6. recruitment	[rɪˈkruːtmənt]	n.	招收

The British education system and academic research level are currently in the world's leading position. England, Northern Ireland, Scotland, and Wales have separate, but similar,

Chapter One The United Kingdom of Great Britain and Northern Ireland

systems of compulsory education. The world-famous education has a holy land at University of Cambridge and University of Oxford. Besides education, the British enjoy a wide range of colorful cultural life from movies to TV programs, from music to sports.

 School Education

The State System—11-year compulsory education: Education in the United Kingdom is compulsory. Children are legally obliged to attend school from the age of 5 to 16. State schools are funded by local and central government. About 93% of pupils receive free education from the public sector. The government also sometimes assists schools established by religious groups.

The Independent System—public schools: Parents can choose between sending their children to state schools or to private schools. In the private sector, there are independent schools which are commonly, but confusingly, called public schools. They are called public schools because they were originally seen as "public" *alternatives*[1] to having private tutors in aristocratic households. Independent schools receive their funding through the private sector and through tuition rates, with some government assistance. Independent schools are not part of the national education system. Parents choose to pay fees in order to send their children to these schools because the quality of education is such that their children have a better chance of getting into good universities and/or getting better jobs when they leave school. The most famous public schools are Eton, Harrow and Winchester. Take Eton as an example, the royal family thinks the school is just the place for Wills. In this self-contained world, titles confer no privileges, and the prince is probably not the only boy with a bodyguard. Foreign leaders' children and scions of Greek shipping magnates bring them along, too.

Pre-primary schooling: Up to the age of 5, children may have some pre-primary schooling in nursery schools, daycare, or play groups. The government has no obligation to provide such facilities and so many are private enterprise arrangements.

Primary schooling: From the age of 5 to 11, pupils mainly attend state sector primary schools. These schools are called co-educational or mixed schools because they admit both boys and girls.

Secondary schooling: From the age of 11 to 16, more than 80% of pupils in secondary schools in England and Wales attend mixed schools; 60% in Northern Ireland; Scotland, nearly all. About 90% of secondary schools are *comprehensive*[2] schools which admit children without reference to their academic abilities. Such schools provide a general education. Pupils can study everything from academic subjects like literature and science, to more practical subjects like cooking and carpentry.

Those children who do not attend comprehensive schools attend grammar schools instead. Grammar schools select children, usually at the age of 11, through an examination called "the 11-

plus". Those who show academic potential are admitted to the grammar schools where the emphasis is on advanced academic work rather than the more general ***curriculum***³ of the comprehensive schools.

Further education: At the age of 16, students can decide to quit school and find a job, or they can prepare to sit exams for university entrance, or they can concentrate on vocational training. Every 16-or 17-year-old is ***guaranteed***⁴ a place in full-time education or training. After five years of secondary education, English, Northern Irish and Welsh students sit their GCSE exams. GCSE exams are the main means of assessing pupils' progress in their final two years of compulsory education.

Pupils who hope to attend universities carry on their academic study in the sixth form for a further two years and then sit A-levels exams (General Certificate of Education Advanced Level). Most pupils try to achieve three or four A-levels in the subjects they are most proficient at. Since admittance to universities depends largely on A-level results, the two years spent in the Sixth Form are very important and often very stressful for British pupils. When first-year university students getting to know each other, the most common question after "What's your name?" and "Where are you from?" is "What A-levels did you take?"

Other pupils who decide not to go to universities may choose to take vocational training. The vocational ***equivalent***⁵ of A-levels are GNVQs (General National Vocational Qualifications), which provide a broadly based preparation for work or for taking further vocational education.

Higher Education: ***Recruitment***⁶ of universities is based on the grades of AS, A-levels, GNVQs, school references and the result of interview. British universities are public bodies which receive funds from central government.

Famous Universities

Higher education has a long history in the United Kingdom. The British education system is one of the world's most ancient education systems, which is famous for its higher education. Oxford and Cambridge date from the 12th and 13th centuries. The two universities are sometimes referred to collectively as "Oxbridge". British emphasis on education, is shown not only in gathering the famous and oldest schools and universities, but also in no shortage of new style and awareness of the innovative institutions. Higher education implements the two-track system, on the one hand, the autonomy of universities, on the other hand, public colleges and universities. The autonomy of universities refers to the classical universities, modern universities, Open Universities, and eight universities in Scotland; public colleges and universities refer to the multi-disciplinary Institute of Technology, Schools of Continuing Education and the Institute of Education. In Britain, degree titles are based on courses and credits. The most common titles for a first degree are Bachelor of Arts (BA) and Bachelor of Science (BS), granted to students who have passed examinations at the end of three or fours years of study. The second degree is Master, including Master of Arts (MA) and Master of Science (MS). The highest degree title is Doctor of Philosophy (PhD).

The University of Cambridge is a collegiate public research university in Cambridge, England. Founded in 1209, Cambridge is the second-oldest university in the English-speaking countries and the world's fourth-oldest surviving university.

Cambridge is formed from a variety of institutions which include 31 constituent Colleges and over 100 academic Departments organized into six Schools. The University also operates eight cultural and scientific museums, including the Fitzwilliam Museum, as well as a botanic garden.

The university has educated many notable alumni, including eminent mathematicians, scientists, politicians, lawyers, philosophers, writers, actors and foreign heads of state. Many important scientific discoveries and revolutions were made by Cambridge alumni. These include: Understanding the scientific method, by Francis Bacon; The Laws of Motion, by Sir Isaac Newton; Evolution by natural selection, by Charles Darwin; The structure of DNA, by Francis Crick and James D. Watson.

The University of Oxford(Fig. 1-6) is a collegiate research university located in Oxford, England. It is the oldest university in the English-speaking countries. Teaching existed at Oxford in 1096 and developed rapidly from 1167. It has a history as impressive as its alumni. The history and influence of the University of Oxford have made it one of the most prestigious universities in the world.

Fig. 1-6 Oxford Shield

The university is made up of a variety of institutions, including 36 colleges and three societies and four academic divisions. Being a city university, it does not have a main campus and instead its buildings and facilities are scattered throughout the city center.

The university operates the world's oldest university museum, as well as the largest university press in the world and the largest academic library system in Britain. Oxford has educated many notable alumni, including Nobel laureates, Prime Ministers of the United Kingdom and many heads of state and government around the world.

Cultural Life

Movies: A British organization that hosts annual awards shows for film, television, children's film and television, and interactive media. The British Academy Film Awards Ceremony is in February.

Sir Alfred Hitchcock is an English-American film director, screenwriter and producer. He began his career as a director in 1925 and became prominent with *The 39 Steps* and *The Lady*

Vanishes.

Colin Firth received the Royal Television Society Best Actor Award, who is best known for his successful role in *The King's Speech* and he received a BAFTA(British Academy of Film and Television Arts Awards) nomination for his role of Mr. Darcy.

Music: Britain is a nation of music. Britain gives much consideration to music education. There are important music festivals and music halls. The Royal Albert Hall in London hosts the biggest annual classical music festival, known as the Proms.

Fig. 1-7 The Beatles

Britain is more famous for pop music than it is for classical composers or jazz musicians. Names such as the Beatles(Fig. 1-7), the Rolling Stones, Elton John, George Michael and the Spice Girls are known worldwide, but little do people know of other British musicians not in the pop world. In Britain, many youths listen to punk, garage, house, rock, pop and R&B.

Media: The Newspapers are traditionally categorized into two types in the United Kingdom. Broadsheets which are larger in size and are seen as being more intellectual and upmarket; and tabloids which are smaller in size and seen as being more down market than broadsheets, containing more stories about celebrities or gossip. However, some broadsheet papers, such as *The Times* and *The Independent* have recently switched to a smaller size.

Internet now offered new opportunities. A newspaper was just that: news printed on papers. But the Internet now offered newspapers different places to publish, and on different media. Many newspapers now have podcasts and videos, and are beginning to compete with radio and television.

The most popular printed newspaper in the UK is *The Sun*. The mid-market audience mainly reads *The Daily Mail*. Of the quality newspapers, the most popular is *The Daily Telegraph*, followed by *The Times* and *The Guardian*.

The BBC (The British Broadcasting Corporation) channels offer a mixture of drama, light entertainment, films, sport, educational, children's and religious programs, news and current affairs, and documentaries. The BBC has national radio networks which together transmit types of music, news, current affairs, drama, education, sport and a range of feature programs.

Sports: Sport is a huge part of life in the United Kingdom. Numerous sports originated in the country, including cricket, tennis, and football, and the British are obsessed with the sporting life, because it is so easy to get involved, either through watching and supporting a sport, or playing it. Every week thousands of people across Britain participate in a wide variety of sports, playing at all levels or supporting their local team.

Chapter One The United Kingdom of Great Britain and Northern Ireland

Football, above all, has even been described as the "new religion" driven by the multimillion-pound clubs, like Manchester United, Arsenal, Newcastle United, Liverpool, etc. It is a huge industry in its own right with all the above clubs listed on the London Stock Exchange. Thankfully, now mostly free of the hooligan element and mob violence, the traditional working class interest in football has given way to a complete cross-cultural involvement.

Cricket is a serious game, which involves endurance, commitment, and application. Even so, it is actually meant to be fun too, because everybody in the team takes part in either batting or fielding, and usually everybody gets the chance to hit the ball and score runs. Cricket is also a game demanding fair play by the umpire and players.

Exercises

I. *Try to answer the following questions according to your understanding of the text.*

(1) How do you explain the compulsory education in the United Kingdom?
(2) What do you know about public schools in the United Kingdom?
(3) How many terms is the academic year divided into in the United Kingdom?
(4) What do you know about the famous bands in the music history of the United Kingdom?
(5) What are the most important scientific discoveries and revolutions made by Cambridge alumni?

II. *Read the following passage carefully, and make a comment on it at the end of the passage in no more than 100 words.*

A broadly comic show with a jarringly artificial laugh track that felt antiquated even in its own time. A show entirely focused on a jug-eared comedian with an unusually square face, sloping nose and beetle brows, a visage that could be alternately menacing and angelic.

Yes, the TV show is *Mr. Bean*.

It's not surprising, given that kind of social-media hegemony, that the awkward, arrogant, narcissistic naïf created 35 years ago by Rowan Atkinson is enjoying his fourth or fifth life.

The character has remained steadily popular in Britain, with Mr. Curtis and Mr. Atkinson producing sketches for Comic Relief fund-raisers and Mr. Atkinson appearing as Mr. Bean in the opening ceremony of the 2012 London Olympics.

Bean sketches follow a formula. The character is placed in an everyday situation—taking a test, shopping, packing for vacation—that disintegrates into a cascading series of predicaments and embarrassments. Mr. Bean responds with both prancing panic and a manic ingenuity that nearly always backfires.

The lack of dialogue is commonly cited as the main reason for his universal appeal. You don't need to know English to understand the sketch.

The ordinariness of the situations also plays a role—as crazy as the sketches get, the fundamental problems Mr. Bean faces are the ones we all encounter, like mistakenly ordering the steak tartare or picking up the wrong credit card. Of course, when we try to exchange cards with the man who picked up ours, we don't end up following him through the store and cowering behind him in a restroom stall while he sits on the toilet.

Mr. Atkinson feels that the most important factor is Mr. Bean's innocence. "There's always this sort of feeling of a childlike innocence combined with a childlike vindictiveness and selfishness and instinctive anarchy," he said. "I think I was considering him like an 11-year-old boy who's given the responsibilities of an adult but hasn't learned better. So what is funny about him is watching an adult behave in a way that adults are not supposed to behave."

Comments:

Mr. Bean is a famous British comedy character. Some describe him as "a child in a grown man's body", who is silly and hopeless in society; while others think he shows that British people are good at laughing at themselves.

What is your attitude towards Mr. Bean?

Reference:

Argument:

(1) Being funny to cause trouble everywhere

(2) Being a cultural icon

(3) Being brilliant for his humor

Counter-argument:

(1) Seeming ill at ease

(2) Causing inconvenience to others

(3) Being bizarre and stupid sometimes in the show

Unit 4　Politics and Economy

Text Focus

1. Political System
2. Political Parties
3. Economy

1.5 Lecture 5 Politics and Economy.mp4

Chapter One The United Kingdom of Great Britain and Northern Ireland

📖 Vocabulary

1. constitutional	[ˌkɒnstɪˈtjuːʃənl]	*adj.*	宪法的
2. legislation	[ˌledʒɪsˈleɪʃn]	*n.*	立法
3. coordination	[kəʊˌɔːdɪˈneɪʃn]	*n.*	协调
4. conservative	[kənˈsɜːvətɪv]	*adj.*	保守的
5. ideological	[ˌaɪdɪəˈlɒdʒɪkl]	*adj.*	意识形态的
6. offshore	[ˌɒfˈʃɔː(r)]	*adj.*	离岸的

The United Kingdom of Great Britain and Northern Ireland is fortunate in having a stable political situation and well-developed economy. On the one hand, the United Kingdom is a ***constitutional*** [1] monarchy, in which the most important real power is the choice of the Members of Parliament to form a government, but the Monarch follows the convention that this opportunity is granted to the leader of the political party with the most seats in the House of Commons or who stands the best chance of commanding a majority in a vote of confidence in the Commons. In addition, the United Kingdom of Great Britain is a major developed capitalist country, which has a "mixed economy" operated within the context of well-defined regulations and laws. The system makes the United Kingdom play an important role in the economic globalization and the British people live a high-quality life.

📖 Political System

In classical political theory, there are three arms of the state: the legislature, the judiciary, and the executive. The Monarch is the head of state and the Prime Minister of the United Kingdom is the head of government. The King/Queen's powers are largely traditional and symbolic. The governments at national and local levels are elected by the people and govern according to British constitutional principles.

The King/Queen is the Head of State in the United Kingdom, Head of the Armed Forces, Fount of Justice. As a constitutional monarch, His/Her Majesty does not "rule" the country, but fulfills important ceremonial and formal roles with respect to the Government.

The legislature is the British Parliament(Fig. 1-8), where laws are made. And it has three parts: the House of Commons, the House of Lords, and the Monarch. These three institutions must all agree to pass any given ***legislation*** [2]. The House of Commons is the most powerful part. It is where Members of Parliament sit. In modern times, all Prime Ministers and Leaders of the Opposition have been drawn from the Commons, not the Lords. The people who sit in the House of Lords are called peers: they are not chosen by the people. Most peers are now appointed by the government, either because they have inherited the seats from their forefathers or because they have been appointed by the sovereign, at the suggestion of the Prime Minister, such as certain bishops in the established Church of England, and the Judiciary.

Fig. 1-8　Palace of Westminster or Houses of Parliament

Scotland has its own devolved Parliament with power to make laws on things like education, health and Scottish law. Northern Ireland and Wales have their own devolved Assemblies which have some powers but less than the Scottish parliament. The United Kingdom Parliament remains sovereign and it could end the devolved administrations at any time.

The judiciary of the United Kingdom does not have a single legal system due to it being created by the political union of previously independent countries with the terms of *the Treaty of Union* guaranteeing the continued existence of Scotland's separate legal system. Today the United Kingdom has three distinct systems of law: English law, Northern Ireland law and Scots law. The Supreme Court of the United Kingdom came into being in October 2009, which took on the appeal functions of the Appellate Committee of the House of Lords. The Judicial Committee of the Privy Council, comprising the same members as the Supreme Court, is the highest court of appeal for several independent Commonwealth countries, the United Kingdom overseas territories, and the British crown dependencies.

The executive refers to the Ministers who run the country and propose new laws. Generally, the United Kingdom Government Ministers have to be a member of either the House of Commons or the House of Lords and every Government Department will have at least one Minister in the Lords, so that the Department can speak in either House as necessary.

The monarch appoints a Prime Minister as the head of His/Her Majesty's Government in the United Kingdom. Guided by the strict convention, the Prime Minister should be the member of the House of Commons, who is most likely to be able to form a Government with the support of

Chapter One The United Kingdom of Great Britain and Northern Ireland

that House. In practice, this means that the leader of the political party with an absolute majority of seats in the House of Commons is chosen to be the Prime Minister. If no party has an absolute majority, the leader of the largest party is given the first opportunity to form a coalition. To ensure good relations between the Crown and the Parliament, the King/Queen meets regularly with a group of important Parliamentarians, a group which is known as the Cabinet. And the Prime Minister is the most senior minister in the Cabinet, responsible for chairing Cabinet meetings, selecting Cabinet ministers, and formulating government policies. Cabinet meetings are typically held weekly, while Parliament is in session. Around 20 Members of Parliament in the governing party, who are chosen by the Prime Minister will become government ministers in the Cabinet. The Cabinet carries out the functions of policy-making, ***coordination***[3] of government departments and the supreme control of the government.

Political Parties

The idea of political parties first took form in Britain and the ***Conservative***[4] Party claims to be the oldest political party in the world.

There are three major political parties in the British parliamentary system. The Conservative Party and the Labor Party are the two biggest, and any general election is really about which of those two is going to govern. But there is also a third important party, the Liberal Democrats, which were the junior member of the Coalition Government of 2010—2015.

The Conservative Party is the center-Right party, the party that spent most time in power. In the post-1945 period, the party of government changed fairly frequently, as the Labor government was replaced by the Conservative and vice versa. The Conservative Party was in power for a long period. Basically, the Conservatives are seen as the party of the individual, protecting the individual's right to acquire wealth and to spend it the way they choose, and so favoring economic policies which businessmen prefer, such as low taxes.

The Labor Party is the center-Left party, created by the growing trade union movement at the end of the 19th century. Labor is a socialist party. That is to say, they believe that a society should be relatively equal in economic terms, and that part of the role of government is to act as a "redistributive agent": transferring wealth from the richer to the poorer by means of taxing the richer part of society and providing support to the poorer part of society.

The Liberal Democrats are the third biggest party, and to some extent may be seen as a party of the "middle", occupying the ***ideological***[5] ground between the two main parties. They emphasize the need for change in Britain's constitutional arrangements to make the government more democratic and accountable.

In addition to these parties, there are some smaller United Kingdom parties which operate specifically in Wales or Northern Ireland. Each political party chooses its leader in a different way, but all involve all the Members of Parliament of the party and all the individual members of that party.

Economy

National economies can be broken down into three main industries: "primary industries", such as agriculture, fishing, and mining; "secondary industries", which manufacture complex goods from those primary products; and "tertiary industries", often described as services, such as banking, insurance, tourism, and the selling of goods.

Britain's agricultural sector is small but efficient, producing 58% of the United Kingdom's food with only 2% of its workforce. Three quarters of Britain's land is used for agriculture, with about a quarter of that under crops—wheat and barley are the two commonest. The rest is for grazing animals, including cattle, though sheep are the most numerous type of livestock. The best agricultural land is in the southeast of England. The fishing industry provides 55% of the United Kingdom's demand for fish. Scottish ports land the majority of the fish caught.

British farming is intensive and highly mechanized, but the country is so heavily populated that it cannot supply its own food needs. The vast majority of imports and exports are with other Western European countries.

In the secondary sector of the economy, manufacturing industry remains important, producing 22% of national wealth. British companies are active in all major fields of manufacturing industries, but are particularly strong in pharmaceuticals, chemicals, aerospace and food and drink.

Energy production is an important part of the United Kingdom economy, accounting for 5% of the national wealth. Since the 1970s, when oil and gas were discovered under the North Sea, Britain has become a major oil and gas producer, in addition to its older coal mining industry, which now only accounts for about 25% of energy supplies, the rest being divided among oil, gas, and nuclear energy. This abundance of energy resources means that the United Kingdom has become an overall exporter of energy. The technology required to extract oil from the difficult *offshore*[6] conditions has given companies in the United Kingdom a strong position in the offshore oil industry around the world.

The United Kingdom is a developed country with the sixth largest economy in the world. It was a superpower during the 18th, 19th and early 20th century and was considered since the early 1800s to be the most powerful and influential nation in the world, in politics, economics and military strength. The United Kingdom continued to be the biggest manufacturing economy in the world until 1908 and the largest economy until the 1920s. The economic cost of the two World Wars and the decline of the British Empire in the 1950s and 1960s reduced its leading role in global affairs. The United Kingdom has strong economic, cultural, military and political

Chapter One The United Kingdom of Great Britain and Northern Ireland

influences and is a nuclear power. The United Kingdom holds a permanent seat on the United Nations Security Council, and is a member of the Commonwealth of Nations.

BP is a British multinational oil and gas company headquartered in London, England. Starting in 1909 with the discovery of oil in Persia, now it is one of the world's seven oil and gas "supermajors". It is a vertically integrated company operating in all areas of the oil and gas industry, including exploration and production, refining, distribution and marketing, petrochemicals, power generation and trading. It also has renewable energy interests in biofuels and wind power as the world moves into a lower carbon future.

Lloyd's of London, generally known simply as Lloyd's, is an insurance marketplace located in London, the United Kingdom. Lloyd's has been through the economic turmoil of the American Revolution, the Napoleonic Wars, the Civil War, World War I, the Great Depression, World War II and survived the credit crisis caused by other large insurance companies investing in subprime mortgages. It settled claims for the Titanic, the World Trade Center, and is the leader in aviation, space, and marine cargo insurance.

The market has its roots in marine insurance and was founded by Edward Lloyd at his coffee house on Tower Street in around 1686. Today, it has a dedicated building on Lime Street in the City of London financial district, which was opened in 1986.

Exercises

I. *Try to answer the following questions according to your understanding of the text.*

(1) What does constitutional monarchy mean?
(2) Who are called peers in the British parliament?
(3) How powerful is the Prime Minister in modern Britain?
(4) How important is the British agriculture?
(5) Why is BP one of the world's seven oil and gas "supermajors"?

II. *Read the following passage carefully, and make a comment on it at the end of the passage in no more than 100 words.*

The royal family is one of the most significant characters in the United Kingdom. With a history of over 300 years, the royal family is a symbol rather than a ruler nowadays. As is known to all, the political system in the United Kingdom is called the constitutional monarchy. However, the role of monarchy today is primarily to symbolize the tradition and the unity of the British state.

Due to the conservative character of the Englishmen, the monarchy is kept till now and serves as a tradition in the British society. The queen has no power while the prime minister is in charge of the whole country. So what do they do? Actually they are quite busy in some ways. For instance, the queen has to deal with some national affairs on behalf of the country's image. The lords have work to do in the parliament. Even the tourists will have a look at their everyday life.

So being a member of it is not easy anymore.

Since the monarch's job is symbolic, I don't really think it is necessary for the monarchy to exist. The Glorious Revolution is a partial success, which means it is a compromise between the royal household and the capitalist.

And today, the political system should be more efficient and those complex ceremonies should be simplified. The revenue is supposed to be invested to improve the living standards of the people rather than to support the extravagant lifestyle led by the royalty. Obviously, the British people don't agree with me. They keep the monarchy in modern time for a reason. The royal family has a spiritual power which unites the United Kingdom. Their ceremonies show their manner and politeness. The British speak to the world through the queen's words: they are making progress. So maybe after a hundred years, the monarchy will still exist. Don't be surprised. Just bow to them. It is the family that guards the United Kingdom and leads it to prosperity.

Comments:

As the younger generations' interest in the monarchy is dying out, the debate over whether to continue the monarchy becomes even more pressing. Some people are wondering whether they should continue the practice of royalty or abolish the thousand-year institution of the royal family after the Queen's death in the United Kingdom.

What is your opinion?

Reference:

Argument:

(1) Advocating the traditional moral values about family and community

(2) Adding color to the United Kingdom as a typical symbol

(3) Offering continuity to a country by Monarchy

Counter-argument:

(1) Being tired of the Royal family and establishing a Republic

(2) Being incompatible with democracy

(3) Causing financial burden on the British people

Unit 5   Culture and Customs

Text Focus

1. Traditional Culture
2. Literature Works
3. Food Customs

1.6 Lecture6 Customs.mp4

1.7 Lecture7 Culture.mp4

Chapter One The United Kingdom of Great Britain and Northern Ireland

Vocabulary

1. distinct	[dɪˈstɪŋkt]	adj.	不同的
2. commemorate	[kəˈmeməreɪt]	v.	纪念
3. compose	[kəmˈpəʊz]	v.	创作
4. depict	[dɪˈpɪkt]	v.	描述
5. conceive	[kənˈsiːv]	v.	构思
6. cereal	[ˈsɪəriəl]	n.	谷类

The culture of the United Kingdom is influenced by the history as a developed island country, and its composition of four units—England, Scotland, Wales and Northern Ireland—each of which has ***distinct*** [1] customs, cultures and symbolism. The wider culture of Europe has also influenced the British culture, and humanism and representative democracy developed from broader Western culture. Public holidays in the United Kingdom are days on which most business and essential services are closed. Legally defined holidays are usually called bank holidays in the United Kingdom.

Traditional Culture

Remembrance Day is on November 11th. It is a special day set aside to remember all those men and women who were killed during the two World Wars and other conflicts. By tradition, a two-minute period of silence is observed throughout the country at 11 a.m. At one time the day was known as Armistice Day and was renamed Remembrance Day after World War II. Remembrance Sunday is held on the second Sunday in November, which is usually the Sunday nearest to November 11th. Special services are held at war memorials and churches all over Britain. November is the time of the year when people wear a red poppy to ***commemorate*** [2] those who sacrificed their lives for the nation during wars.

Bonfire Night is a truly English holiday celebrated in November. It originates from the 1605 Gunpowder Plot—a plan to blow up the British Parliament, kill the Protestant King and replace him with a Catholic king. People celebrate it by having public bonfires and fireworks. A straw effigy called the "Guy", one of the conspirators—Guy Fawkes, is thrown on the bonfire. The biggest Bonfire Night celebration is held in Lewes.

Literature Works

Literature is a thriving, diverse, wide-ranging part of the United Kingdom cultural sector with a global reputation for excellence. It embraces everything from basic literacy and picture books to major literary works; from graphic novelists and emerging poets to renowned military historians. Those distinguished literature works are the cultural heritages in different periods of writing in the United Kingdom.

The Canterbury Tales, written by Geoffrey Chaucer, is a collection of stories in a frame story, between 1387 and 1400. It is the story of a group of 30 people who travel as pilgrims to Canterbury. The pilgrims, who come from all layers of society, tell stories to each other to kill time while they travel to Canterbury.

Geoffrey Chaucer, an English poet, was born in 1342. Known as the Father of English poetry for his heroic couplet, a master of realism, the founder of English literary language, he is widely considered as one of the greatest English poets of the Middle Ages.

While he achieved fame during his lifetime as an author, philosopher, and astronomer, **composing**[3] a scientific treatise on the astrolabe for his ten-year-old son Lewis, Chaucer also maintained an active career in the civil service as a bureaucrat, courtier and diplomat. Among his many works are *The Book of the Duchess*, *The House of Fame*, *The Legend of Good Women* and *Troilus and Criseyde*. He is best known today for *The Canterbury Tales*. Chaucer's work was crucial in legitimizing the literary use of the Middle English vernacular at a time when the dominant literary languages in England were French and Latin. Chaucer died in October, 1400 and was buried in Westminster Abbey in London. He was the first of those that are gathered in what we now know as the Poets' Corner in Westminster Abbey.

Fig. 1-9 *Great Expectations*

Great Expectations(Fig. 1-9) is the 13th novel by Charles Dickens and his penultimate completed novel; a bildungsroman that ***depicts***[4] the personal growth and personal development of an orphan nicknamed Pip. The novel is set in Kent and London from the early to mid-19th century and contains some of Dickens's most memorable scenes. *Great Expectations* is full of extreme imagery, poverty, prison ships and chains, and fights to the death, and has a colorful cast of characters who have entered popular culture. Dickens's themes include wealth and poverty, love and rejection, and the eventual triumph of good over evil. *Great Expectations*, which is popular with both readers and literary critics, has been translated into many languages and adapted numerous times into various media.

Charles Dickens, born in England in the year 1812, was an English writer and social critic. He created some of the world's best-known fictional characters and is regarded by many as the greatest novelist of the Victorian era. His works enjoyed unprecedented popularity during his lifetime, and by the 20th century critics and scholars had recognized him as a literary genius. His novels and short stories enjoy a lasting popularity. He wrote classic novels of the Victorian era

Chapter One The United Kingdom of Great Britain and Northern Ireland

like *David Copperfield*, *Oliver Twist* and *A Christmas Carol*.

Harry Potter is a series of fantasy novels written by British author J. K. Rowling. The novels chronicle the life of a young wizard, Harry Potter, and his friends Hermione Granger and Ron Weasley, all of whom are students at Hogwarts School of Witchcraft and Wizardry. The main story concerns Harry's struggle against Lord Voldemort, a dark wizard who intends to become immortal, overthrow the wizard governing body known as the Ministry of Magic, and subjugate all wizards and muggles, a reference term that means non-magical people.

As to the author of the children's fantasy *Harry Potter*, J.K. Rowling, born in 1965, is a British novelist, screenwriter, and producer. The books have won multiple awards, and sold more than millions of copies, becoming one of the best-selling book series in history. They have also been the basis for a film series, over which Rowling had overall approval on the scripts and was a producer on the final films in the series. She **conceived**[5] the idea for the *Harry Potter* series while on a delayed train from Manchester to London in 1990, and the first novel in the series, *Harry Potter and the Philosopher's Stone*, was published in 1997. There were six sequels, of which the last, *Harry Potter and the Deathly Hallows*, was released in 2007. Since then, Rowling has written four books for adult readers: *The Casual Vacancy*, *The Cuckoo's Calling*, *The Silkworm* and *Career of Evil*.

Food Customs

Fish and chips is England's traditional take-away food or as the Americans would say "to go". Fish and chips is not normally home cooked but bought at a fish and chips shop to eat on premises or as a "take away". British chips are usually significantly thicker than the American-style French fries sold by major multinational fast food chains.

Afternoon tea became popular about 150 years ago, when rich ladies invited their friends to their houses for an afternoon cup of tea. They started offering their visitors sandwiches and cakes, too. Soon everyone was enjoying afternoon tea(Fig. 1-10).

Most people around the world seem to think that a typical English breakfast consists of eggs, bacon, sausages, fried bread, mushrooms and baked beans all washed down with a cup of coffee. Nowadays, however, a typical English breakfast is more likely to be a bowl of **cereals**[6], a slice of toast, orange juice and a cup of coffee.

Many children at school and adults at work will have a "packed lunch". This typically consists of a sandwich, a packet of crisps, a piece of fruit and a drink. The "packed lunch" is kept in a kind of container.

Fig. 1-10 Afternoon tea

A typical British meal for dinner is "meat and two vegetables". The British put hot brown gravy on the meat and also on the vegetables. One of the vegetables is almost always potatoes.

Exercises

I. *Try to answer the following questions according to your understanding of the text.*

(1) Whom does Remembrance Day memorize?

(2) What is the story behind Bonfire Night?

(3) Who is the first group of occupants of the Poets' Corner in Westminster Abbey and why?

(4) Which book is your favorite in the *Harry Potter* series?

(5) What is the typical British food?

II. *Read the following passage carefully, and make a comment on it at the end of the passage in no more than 100 words.*

Gossip is an informal conversation, often about other people's private affairs. If you gossip with someone, you talk informally, especially about other people or local events. You can also say that two people gossip. If you describe someone as a gossip, you mean that they enjoy talking informally to people about others' private affairs.

Contrary to popular belief, researchers have found that men gossip just as much as women. The difference between men and women on gossip is that female gossip actually sounds like gossip.

Among the English, gossip about one's own private doings is reserved for intimates; gossip about the private lives of friends and families is shared with a slightly wider social circle; gossip about the personal affairs of acquaintances, colleagues and neighbors with a larger group; and gossip about the intimate details of public figures' or celebrities' lives with almost anyone. This is the distance rule. The more "distant" the subject of gossip from you, the wider the circle of people with whom you may gossip about that person.

The distance rule allows gossip to perform its vital social functions, social bonding, clarification of position and status, assessment and management of reputations, transmission of social skills, norms and values, without undue invasion of privacy. More importantly, it also allows nosey-parker anthropologists to formulate their prying questions in such a roundabout manner as to bypass the privacy rules.

If you want to find out about an English person's attitudes and feelings on a sensitive subject, for example, marriage, you do not ask about his or her own marriage, instead talk about someone else's marriage, preferably that of a remote public figure not personally known to either of you. When you are better acquainted with the person, you can discuss the domestic difficulties of a colleague or neighbour, or perhaps even a friend or relative. If you do not happen to have

Chapter One The United Kingdom of Great Britain and Northern Ireland

colleagues or relatives with suitably dysfunctional marriages, you can always invent these people.

Comments:

It is becoming more and more difficult to escape the influence of the media in our lives. Some suppose that people benefit a lot from the media, while others object to it.

What is your point of view?

Reference:

Argument:

(1) A need to communicate and to know what is going on in the world

(2) A desire to be entertained and a way to keep in touch with other people

(3) An immediate and portable way of using the Internet

Counter-argument:

(1) Preferring face-to-face communication to using technology

(2) Being lack of privacy

(3) Being overwhelmed by so many TV channels with poor quality

Unit 6 Intercultural Communication

 Knowledge to Learn

What Is Culture?

Culture refers to an appreciation of good literature, music, art, and food. There are three layers or levels of culture. The most obvious is the body of cultural traditions that distinguishes our specific society. The second layer of culture that may be part of one's identity is a subculture. The third layer of culture consists of cultural universals.

What Is Intercultural Communication?

Intercultural communication (ICC), a universal phenomenon, is defined as interpersonal communication between people from different cultural backgrounds, consisting of international, interethnic, interracial and interregional communication.

 Cases to Study

Case 1

Sophie and her baby came to visit her Chinese friend's family from England. The Chinese family invited her to have dinner outside in an open restaurant with clear air. The baby was so beautiful and attracted the attention of many Chinese people nearby. One elderly woman at the next table came directly to the baby, smiled at her and wanted to hug the baby. Sophie was frightened and even angry with that and refused the elderly woman very impolitely, which made the elderly woman very embarrassed.

What was the reason for the embarrassment?

Analysis

(1) In this case, the main conflict is whether the baby can be hugged by strangers.

(2) In China, people often fondle babies of their friends, and sometimes even strangers. Such behavior is merely a sign of affection and friendliness. Children and their parents will not mind at all.

(3) But in England, such action will be considered rude and offensive unless it is one of their most intimate relatives.

Case 2

Xiaomei, an exchange student from China, is studying in Nottingham. One day, she came across a British man at a narrow flight of stairs. The stairs are very narrow and only allow one person to go comfortably. Xiaomei was at the bottom of the stairs and about to go upstairs while that man was about to go downstairs. Xiaomei stepped on the stair after thinking twice, and the man stood at the other side waiting for her to pass. She was impressed by the man's gentility, and said "thank you" while passing him. After coming back, she told it to her British teacher as an impressive experience. But to her surprise, her teacher just smiled and said nothing. Xiaomei was confused, and then she remembered the strange expression on the gentleman's face when she smiled to him.

Is he a gentleman or not?

Analysis

(1) The conflict in the above case was caused by the misunderstanding of keeping space or being a gentleman.

(2) Actually, the reason why the man stood there waiting for Xiaomei to pass is that he didn't want others to invade his personal space. However, Xiaomei interpreted it as a behavior of a gentleman. So her "thank you" seems to be funny.

(3) For most Chinese, meeting other people in a narrow flight of stairs is nothing awkward. But for British people, to avoid awkwardness, most of them tend to let others go through first. In this way, they can keep away from others.

(4) From this case, we should know that the importance of informal space in daily life lies in that it includes the distances people unconsciously maintain when they are together. If we do ignore or misunderstand it, embarrassment may happen.

Chapter One The United Kingdom of Great Britain and Northern Ireland

Translations on Traditional Chinese Culture

Exercise 1

Translate the passage into English

中国位于亚洲东部、太平洋的西岸，是世界国土面积第三大国家。中国南北相距约 5500 公里，东西相距约 5200 公里，在地图上的形状像一只雄鸡。中国地势西高东低，地形多种多样。中国山区面积广大，几乎占陆地面积的三分之二，蕴藏着丰富的矿产资源。中国大陆海岸线长度约 18000 公里，沿海岛屿数量众多。台湾岛是中国最大的岛屿。

> **Translation Reference**
>
> Situated in eastern Asia, on the west coast of the Pacific Ocean, China is the world's third largest country by land area. Extending about 5,500 kilometers from north to south and about 5,200 kilometers from west to east, the shape of China on the map is like a rooster. Its terrain is higher in the west and lower in the east with great varieties of topographies. China's mountainous areas, broad and vast, occupy nearly two thirds of the land area and have abundant mineral resources. The mainland of China has a coastline of over 18,000 kilometers and a large number of offshore islands. Taiwan Island is the biggest island of China.

Translate the passage into Chinese

With a population of about 19 million, the Zhuang ethnic minority is the largest minority group in China. Over 90 percent of the Zhuang people live in Guangxi while the rest is distributed in southern provinces in China like Yunnan, Guangdong, Guizhou and Hunan. The Zhuang people have their own language which is mainly divided into southern dialect and northern one. The Zhuang people's agricultural products are tropical and subtropical crops such as rice and corn due to the mild climate and abundant rainfall in Southern China. The daily food of most Zhuang people is of little difference from that of the Han people.

> **Translation Reference**
>
> 壮族是中国人口最多的少数民族，约有 1900 万人。超过 90%的壮族人居住在广西，其余分布在云南、广东、贵州和湖南等南方省份。壮族人有自己的语言，主要分为南北两大方言。由于南方地区气候温和，雨量充足，壮族的主要农产品是热带和亚热带作物，如水稻和玉米。大多数壮族人的日常食物与汉族的并无多大差别。

Exercise 2

Translate the passage into English

书法在中国的传统艺术领域占有非常重要的位置。书法有着 2000 多年的历史。它有五种主要的书写方式，每种都有不同的书写技法。练习书法需要文房四宝。书法被认为是一种需要内心平静的艺术形式。今天，现代书写方式各种各样，但是书法仍然是很多人的一种业余爱好。书法在西方人中也越来越受欢迎。

> **Translation Reference**
> In China, calligraphy occupies a very important position in the field of traditional art. Calligraphy has a history lasting for more than 2,000 years. There are five main ways of writing and each needs different techniques. Practicing calligraphy requires the Four Treasures of the Study. Calligraphy is considered to be an art form requiring inner peace. Today, various modern ways of writing have come up, but calligraphy is still practiced by many people often as a hobby. Nowadays, it has also become more and more popular among Westerners.

Translate the passage into Chinese

Chinese characters were initially meant to be simple pictures used to help people remember things. After a long period of development, it finally became a unique character system that embodies phonetic sound, image, idea, and rhyme at the same time. Chinese characters are usually "round outside and square inside", which is rooted in ancient Chinese belief of "orbicular sky and square earth". During their long history of development, Chinese characters have evolved into many different script forms, such as the Seal script, Clerical script, Regular script and Running script.

> **Translation Reference**
> 汉字最初是人们用以记事的简单图画，经过长期发展，最终成为一种兼具音、形、意、韵的独特文字体系。汉字结构通常"外圆内方"，源于古人"天圆地方"的观念。汉字在其漫长的发展史中演化出许多不同的书写形式，例如篆书、隶书、楷书和行书。

Exercise 3

Translate the passage into English

儒家思想是中国影响最大的思想流派，也是中国古代的主流意识。自汉代以来，儒家思想就是封建统治阶级的指导思想之一。孔子是我国古代著名的思想家、教育家，儒家学派的创始人。相传孔子有弟子三千，贤者七十二人，孔子曾带领部分弟子周游列国 14 年。《论语》是儒家的经典著作之一，它是对孔子及其弟子的言行和对话的记录。《论语》一直极大地影响着中国人及其他亚洲国家人民的哲学观和道德观。

Chapter One The United Kingdom of Great Britain and Northern Ireland

> **Translation Reference**
>
> Confucianism is the most influential Chinese school of thoughts, and the mainstream consciousness of the ancient China. Confucianism has been one of the ruling ideology of the feudal ruling class since the Han Dynasty. Confucius is a famous ideologist, educator, and the founder of Confucian School in ancient China. It's said that he has 3,000 disciples, 72 out of whom are excellent ones, and he has led some disciples to visit various states for 14 years. *The Analects of Confucius* is one of the Confucian classics and is a record of the words and deeds of Confucius and his disciples, as well as the conversations they had. It has been heavily influencing the philosophy and moral outlook of Chinese people and that of the people of other Asian countries as well.

Translate the passage into Chinese

The Book of Songs is the earliest collection of poems in China. It contains 305 poems created over a period of some 500 years from the early Western Zhou Dynasty to the middle of the Spring and Autumn Period. At first, *The Book of Songs* was known as *Poems* or *Three Hundred Poems*. Confucius used it as a textbook for teaching his disciples. The ideological and artistic achievements of *The Book of Songs* have had great influences on the development of poetry of later generations.

> **Translation Reference**
>
> 《诗经》是中国最早的诗歌总集，收录了从西周初期到春秋中期约 500 年间创作的 305 首诗歌。最初，《诗经》被称为《诗》或《诗三百》。孔子以《诗经》作为教科书教授弟子，《诗经》的思想和艺术成就对后世诗歌的发展有极大的影响。

 Culture to Know

Culture Note 1

> **China,** a united multi-ethnic nation, is comprised of 56 ethnic groups. Among these groups, the Han nationality has the largest population, accounting for more than 91% of the total. The other 55 ethnic groups are traditionally referred to as ethnic minorities. The ethnic minorities, though with a considerably small population, are distributed far and wide in China, and mostly live in the northwest, southwest and northeast. Inner Mongolians, often called the "Grasslands Nationality", are mainly distributed on the Inner Mongolian Plateau. Tibetans distributed on the Qinghai-Tibet Plateau are often called the "Eagles of Plateau".

Culture Note 2

The oracle bone script is the earliest existing characters in China. These characters carved on tortoise shells or animal bones are quite mature. Before recognizing the oracle bone script, people regarded the shells and bones as medical materials. Accidentally, a scholar of the Qing Dynasty, Wang Yirong, discovered these tortoise shells and animal bones. After careful study, he believed that these signs were the characters of the Shang Dynasty more than 3,000 years ago. From these characters, people can roughly understand the daily life of the rulers at that time. The oracle bone script provides important materials for research into the origin of Chinese characters.

Culture Note 3

The Hundred Schools of Thought lasted from 770 BC to 221 BC. Known as the Golden Age of Chinese thought and the Contention of a Hundred Schools of Thought, the periods saw the rise of many different schools of thought. Great thinkers such as Laozi, Zhuangzi, Confucius, Mencius, Xuncius, Mocius and Han Feizi all lived in these periods. From different positions and perspectives, they made statements on the social issues, and gradually formed different schools. The emergence of various schools of thought and their exponents such as Laozi and Confucius occupy a very important position in the world history of philosophy.

Culture Note 4

Chinese Tea-Making Joins UNESCO List

The tea that has delighted and fascinated the world for millennia has finally received top-level global recognition as a shared cultural treasure of mankind. Traditional tea processing techniques and their associated social practices in China were added to UNESCO's Representative List of the Intangible Cultural Heritage of Humanity on November 29, 2022. The status was conferred by the Intergovernmental Committee for the Safeguarding of Intangible Cultural Heritage, hosted in Rabat, Morocco. According to UNESCO, in China, traditional tea processing techniques are closely associated with geographical location and natural environment, resulting in a distribution range between 18°-37°N and 94°-122°E. The inscription of the element is the 43rd entry from China on the Representative List of the Intangible Cultural Heritage of Humanity, whose total tops all other countries.

Chapter One The United Kingdom of Great Britain and Northern Ireland

Further Reading

Passage 1

China's Green Development in the New Era

A green and low-carbon economy and society are crucial to high-quality development. China must work faster to adjust and improve the industrial structure, the energy mix, and the composition of the transportation sector. China will implement a comprehensive conservation strategy, conserve resources of all types and use them efficiently, and move faster to put in place a system for recycling waste and used materials. Fiscal, taxation, financial, investment, and pricing policies and systems of standards will be improved to support green development. China will boost green and low-carbon industries and improve the system for market-based allocation of resources and environmental factors. China will accelerate the R&D, promotion, and application of advanced energy-saving and carbon emission reduction technologies, encourage green consumption, and promote green and low-carbon ways of production and life.

Passage 2

EVs to Increase in Public Transport

China aims to increase the share of electric vehicles(EVs) in the public transport system to 80 percent in key areas, including bus and taxi services, by 2025, as the country accelerates its steps to promote green transformation amid booming new energy vehicle development. According to a pilot plan of the Ministry of Industry and Information Technology and seven other ministries, China will speed up the full electrification of vehicles used in public transportation between 2023 and 2025, and the building of a charging and swapping infrastructure system that is "moderately advanced, well-balanced, intelligent and efficient". According to the development plan for the NEV industry from 2021 to 2035 approved by the State Council, the country's Cabinet, vehicles used in public transport will be completely electrified by 2035.

Chapter Two

The United States of America

英语国家社会与文化（第2版）

Contents

1. Location and Resources
2. History and Symbols
3. Education and Recreation
4. Politics and Economy
5. Culture and Customs
6. Intercultural Communication

Broadway	百老汇	the Empire State Building	(纽约)帝国大厦
diverse society	多元化社会	the Gold Rush	淘金热
Harvard University	哈佛大学	the Ivy League	常春藤联盟
Hollywood	好莱坞	the Melting Pot	大熔炉
KFC	肯德基	the Metropolitan Museum of Art	大都会艺术博物馆
McDonald's	麦当劳	the Statue of Liberty	自由女神像
motel	汽车旅馆	Wall Street	华尔街
NBA (National Basketball Association)	美国职业篮球联赛	the White House	白宫
Reader's Digest	《读者文摘》	Uncle Sam	山姆大叔
the Declaration of Independence	《独立宣言》	West cowboy	西部牛仔

Chapter Two The United States of America

Unit 1 Location and Resources

Text Focus

1. Geographical Location
2. Weather and Climate
3. Natural Resources

2.1 Lecture1 Location.mp4

2.2 Lecture2 People.mp4

Vocabulary

1. extensive	[ɪkˈstensɪv]	*adj.*	广阔的
2. latitude	[ˈlætɪtjuːd]	*n.*	纬度
3. deplete	[dɪˈpliːt]	*v.*	耗尽

The United States of America is located in the central part of North America, with the Atlantic Ocean to the east and the Pacific Ocean to the west, ranking fourth with 9.37 million square kilometers in the world. There are a lot of developed and major cities in the United States, such as Washington D.C., New York and Los Angeles. Owing to its large size, varied weather and climate present in the continent of the Untied States. It is a land rich in natural resources, such as water, iron ore, coal and oil, etc.

Geographical Location

The United States contains 48 contiguous states in North America. Hawaii, located in the central Pacific, is separated from continental United States.

The Atlantic Coast of the United States faces Western Europe, and its Pacific Coast and Hawaii give the nation an approach to the Far East and Australia. In the past, the Atlantic Ocean and the Pacific Ocean served as natural barriers between the United States and the rest of the world, which allowed the United States to grow and become strong with little outside interference. Later, the development of means of communication and transportation makes the United States well connected to the rest of the world.

The United States has ***extensive***[1] coastlines on both the Atlantic Ocean and the Pacific Ocean, as well as on the Gulf of Mexico. Rivers flow from far within the continent and the Great Lakes, five large, inland lakes along the United States border with Canada, providing additional shipping access. These extensive waterways have helped shape the economic growth of the country over the years and helped bind America's 50 individual states together in a single economic unit. So the location does quite a lot to the development of the United States. In the north, it connects with Canada and in the south, it faces Mexico and the Gulf of Mexico.

Washington D.C. is the capital city of the United States. "D.C." stands for "the District of Columbia", the federal district containing the city of Washington. The city is named after George Washington, the military leader of the American Revolution and the first President of the United States. The District of Columbia and the city of Washington are coextensive and governed by a single municipal government, so for most practical purposes they are considered to be the same entity. The District of Columbia, founded on July 16, 1790, is a federal district as specified by the United States Constitution. The United States Congress has ultimate authority over the District of Columbia, though it has delegated limited local rule to the municipal government. The land forming the original District came from the states of Virginia and Maryland. Nowadays, Washington D.C. serves as the headquarters for the World Bank, the International Monetary Fund, and the Organization of American States, among other national and international institutions. It is also the site of numerous national landmarks, museums, and sports teams, and a popular destination for tourists.

New York City(Fig. 2-1) is the most populous city in the United States, with an estimated population of nine million distributed over a land area of over 1,214 square kilometers. It is the most linguistically diverse city on the planet, with more than 800 languages spoken. The city is also the world's most ethnically diverse city. Located at the southern tip of the state of New York, the city is the center of the New York metropolitan area, one of the most populous urban agglomerations in the world. New York City exerts a significant impact upon commerce, finance, media, art, fashion, research, technology, education, and entertainment, and its fast pace defines the term of New York. Home to the headquarters of the United Nations, New York is an important center for international diplomacy and has been described as the cultural, financial, and media capital of the world. The Statue of Liberty is a sculpture in New York Harbor which was designed by Bartholdi in 1886, a gift from the people of France as an icon of freedom.

Los Angeles, officially called City of Los Angeles and often known by its initials L.A., is the cultural, financial, and commercial center of Southern California. It is the second most populous city in the United States and the most populous city in the state of California. Located in a large coastal basin surrounded on three sides by mountains reaching up to 3,068 meters, Los Angeles covers an area of about 1,215 square kilometers. Los Angeles, the center of the Los Angeles metropolitan area, is part of the larger designated Los Angeles-Long Beach combined statistical area. Another vibrant area of L.A. is Hollywood, the birthplace of the movie industry and still the center of the motion picture. Hollywood is a dream factory, the maker of "movie magic", offering people something to dream about. The cultural messages spread around by Hollywood are so penetrating and powerful that many Americans want their lives and love to be "just like in the movies".

Fig. 2-1   Night Scene of New York City

Weather and Climate

The weather and climate of the United States vary in different parts because of its vast size. In the middle latitudes north of the equator and in the northern temperate zone, the United States enjoys a continental climate. It varies from warm wet conditions of the Appalachian Mountains to the warm, dry conditions of some of the western states, and ranges from almost winterless climates in Southern Arizona and Southern Florida to long, cold winters in Alaska.

Determined by its *latitude*[2] and altitude, its vast size of territory and topography, and the different atmospheric circulations, there are extreme climatic variations in the United States—extreme variations of precipitation, and extreme variations of climatic types. It is almost impossible to make any generalization about the climate. Different climatic conditions divide the country into some climatic regions. All in all, it enjoys a continental climate in the northern zone, a humid subtropical climate in the south-eastern part, humid continental and humid subtropical climate in the central part and maritime climate in the Pacific Northwest.

Natural Resources

The natural resources of the United States are quite rich, such as water, iron ore, coal, oil, silver, and gold. The nation produces more than 80 million tons of iron a year. For many years, iron ore came primarily from the Great Lake Region of Minnesota and Michigan, but the mines were severely *depleted*[3] during the two World Wars.

Coal is another major natural resource found in large quantities in the United States which can last for hundreds of years. Coal deposits are widely distributed in the country. Most of the coal reserves are to be found in the Appalachians, the Central Plain, and the Rockies.

The United States, very rich in oil, was once the largest oil producing country in the world. The production, processing and marketing of such petroleum products as gasoline and oil make up one of the United States' largest industries. Most domestic production of oil and natural gas comes from offshore areas of Louisiana and Texas, and from onshore areas of Texas, Oklahoma, and California. Although the oil production in the United States is very large, the big consumption has made the United States insufficient in oil supply.

The United States enjoys abundant water resources. Today the rivers and streams of the United States furnish most of the water supply for cities, towns and farmlands. Water is also used by industry, and used to create electric power. Unlike some other countries, the United States as a whole has little trouble caused by the shortage of fresh water.

The United States also has plenty of fertile soil. Farmlands make up about 12% of the arable lands in the world, and they are among the richest and most productive. Of the 2.3 billion acres of land in the 50 states, an estimated 300 million acres are planted annually. The very large acreage of highly productive farmlands could be expected to continue to supply the nation generously, with substantial surplus for export.

 Exercises

1. *Try to answer the following questions according to your understanding of the text.*

(1) How much do you know about the location and size of the United States?

(2) What is the capital city of the United States?

(3) Which city is the second most populous one in the United States?

(4) How is the weather in the United States?

(5) What natural resources does the United States possess?

II. *Read the following passage carefully, and make a comment on it at the end of the passage in no more than 100 words.*

For a long time, most overseas visitors to the United States, whether on business or holiday, have arrived from Europe, but an increasing number of visitors today are coming from Asia, especially China. As to where overseas visitors go once they arrive in the United States, here are their top four destinations:

Los Angeles

Located in southern California and situated beneath a dramatic mountain backdrop, Los Angeles is famous for its "Mediterranean climate"—sunny, dry and warm weather all year round. The city's beaches and nearby Disneyland are tourist favorites. Los Angeles attracts film and TV

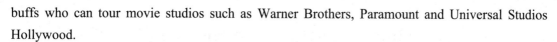

buffs who can tour movie studios such as Warner Brothers, Paramount and Universal Studios Hollywood.

Miami

The Port of Miami in southern Florida is the world's busiest cruise port. Overseas travelers hit Miami for the same reason as many Americans do: the beautiful beaches and warm weather, especially in December, January and February. The South Beach neighborhood is famous for its Art Deco architecture and Cuban cuisine.

Orlando

Orlando is a major city in central Florida, and is the county seat of Orange County. It is also the principal city of Greater Orlando. It is well known for the many tourist attractions in the area. Nearly 70 million tourists each year arrive in Orlando, with many hitting the Sea World, Universal Orlando Resort and the Walt Disney World Resort, which includes two water parks, Epcot and Disney's Magic Kingdom. Travelers to this central Florida destination also make trips to NASA's Kennedy Space Center to learn about America's space program, its astronauts and upcoming missions to explore deep space.

San Francisco

The Golden Gate Bridge in northern California is the city's most recognized landmark and one of the most famous spans in the world. Other legendary features of San Francisco include its trolley cars, steep hills, and neighborhoods such as Fisherman's Wharf and Chinatown.

Comments:

Traveling is very popular all over the world. Some people like traveling because it helps to relieve the stress from their work. Others dislike it because they worry about their safety or the environment.

How do you like traveling?

Reference:

Argument:

(1) Feeling relaxed and pleasant

(2) Getting a fresh start and making new friends

(3) Enriching one's experiences and broadening one's horizon

Counter-argument:

(1) Targets of muggings or being stolen

(2) Experiencing long flights or jet lag

(3) Leading to a tight budget

Unit 2 History and Symbols

Text Focus

1. Historical Periods
2. Historical Figures
3. National Symbols

2.3 Lecture3 History.mp4

Vocabulary

1. immigrant	[ˈɪmɪɡrənt]	n.	移民
2. persecution	[ˌpɜːsɪˈkjuːʃn]	n.	迫害
3. colonial	[kəˈləʊniəl]	n.	殖民地居民
4. hasten	[ˈheɪsn]	v.	加速
5. sympathize	[ˈsɪmpəθaɪz]	v.	同情
6. nuclear	[ˈnjuːkliə(r)]	adj.	原子核的
7. subsequent	[ˈsʌbsɪkwənt]	adj.	后来的

American history covers the development, struggle and experience of the United States from the history of early exploration through modern times, including European settlement, American Revolutionary War, the Civil War, the Great Depression, two World Wars and modern era improvement. Americans originally came from all over the world and formed much longstanding coexistence. They melt many different cultures, races and religions. A lot of American historical figures have played important roles in the development and improvement of the American history, such as George Washington, Thomas Jefferson, Abraham Lincoln, Martin Luther King, Jr., etc.

Historical Periods

European settlement began shortly after the first voyage of Columbus in 1492 and large-scale European colonization of the Americas started. Native people and European colonizers came into widespread conflict, and early European ***immigrants***[1] were often part of state-sponsored who attempted to found colonies in the Americas. Migration continued as people moved to the Americas to flee religious ***persecution***[2] or to seek economic opportunities. Millions of individuals were forcibly transported to the Americas as slaves, prisoners or servants. European colonists reached the Gulf and Pacific coasts, but the largest settlements were founded by the English on

Chapter Two The United States of America

the East Coast, starting in 1607, while in 1620 the Mayflower transported Pilgrims to the New World. With the 1732 colonization of Georgia, the 13 British colonies which would become the United States of America were established. By the 1770s, the 13 colonies contained 2.5 million people. With high birth rates, low death rates and steady immigration, the colonial population grew rapidly.

The American Revolutionary War was set off by tensions between American *colonials*[3] and the British during the revolutionary period of the 1760s and early 1770s and lasted from 1775 to 1783. Officially the United States began as an independent nation with the Declaration of Independence, drafted primarily by Thomas Jefferson on July 4, 1776. That date is now celebrated annually as the Independence Day of the United States.

The Constitution became the basis for the United States federal government in 1789, with war hero George Washington as the first president. The young nation continued to struggle with the scope of central government and with European influence, created the first political parties in the 1790s, and fought a second war for independence in 1812.

Slavery of Africans was abolished in the North, but the large quantity of demand for cotton in the world made slavery flourish in the Southern States. The 1860 election of Abraham Lincoln, who called for no more expansion of slavery, triggered a crisis as 11 slave states seceded to found the Confederate States of America in 1861. The American Civil War from 1861 to 1865 redefined the nation and remained the central iconic event. The South was defeated and, in the Reconstruction era, the United States ended slavery.

After the war, the assassination of Abraham Lincoln radicalized Republican Reconstruction policies which aimed at reintegrating and rebuilding the Southern States while ensuring the rights of the newly freed slaves. The territory of the United States expanded westward across the continent, brushing aside Native Americans and Mexico, and overcoming modernizers who wanted to deepen the economy rather than expand the territory. In the North, urbanization and an influx of immigrants from Southern and Eastern Europe *hastened*[4] the country's industrialization. The wave of immigration, lasting until 1929, provided labor and transformed American culture.

World War I broke out in 1914, and the United States initially remained neutral. Most Americans *sympathized*[5] with the British and the French although many opposed intervention. The United States declared war on Germany in 1917, and funded the Allied victory.

World War II broke out in 1939. After a prosperous decade in the 1920s, the Wall Street Crash of 1929 marked the onset of the decade-long and world-wide Great Depression. After the election as President in 1932, Franklin D. Roosevelt responded with the *New Deal*, a range of policies for relief, recovery, and reform, increasing government intervention in the economy, including the establishment of the Social Security System. After the Japanese attack on Pearl Harbor in December 1941, the United States was prompted to enter World War II alongside the

Allies and helped defeat Nazi Germany in Europe. The United States, having developed the first newly-invented ***nuclear***[6] weapons, used them on the two Japanese cities. Japan surrendered on September 2, 1945, which ended the war.

Contemporary era of the United States plays an important role on the stage of the world. The Cold War ended in 1991, leaving the United States to prosper in the booming Information Age. The economic expansion in the modern United States from 1993 to 2001 encompassed the Bill Clinton administration. After the 2000 presidential election, George W. Bush became president. International conflict and economic uncertainty heightened in 2001 with the September 11 attacks and ***subsequent***[7] wars on terror and the late-2000s recession. In response, the Bush administration launched a global War on Terror. In 2008, amid a global economic recession, the first African American president, Barack Obama was elected. Major health care and financial system reforms were enacted two years later. Donald Trump was elected in 2016 after he defeated Democratic nominee Hillary Clinton to win the presidency. And then Joe Biden won the US Presidential Election 2020. He took office as the 46th President of the United States in January 2021.

Historical Figures

George Washington(1732—1799) is often called the "Father of His Country". He was the military and political leader of the United States between 1775 and 1797. He led the American victory over Britain in the American Revolutionary War as commander-in-chief of the Continental Army. He also presided over the writing of the Constitution. He was unanimously elected as the first President of the United States. The president of the United States is head of state of the U.S., the chief executive of the federal government, and commander-in-chief of the armed forces. He built a strong, well-financed national government. He, along with Abraham Lincoln, had also become an icon of republican values, self-sacrifice, American nationalism, and the ideal union of civic and military leadership.

John Davison Rockefeller(Fig. 2-2)(1839—1937) was an American oil industry business magnate, industrialist and philanthropist. He is widely considered the wealthiest American of all time, and the richest person in modern history. Business was a big part of Rockefeller's life. But as big as that was, philanthropy was still as important to him if not more important. From the start, he gave 10% of his paycheck to his church. Later in his life he gave 80 million dollars to the University of Chicago. After he gave possibly his biggest donation of 250 million dollars

Fig. 2-2　John Davison Rockefeller

Chapter Two The United States of America

to his own foundation, the Rockefeller Foundation, in total, it is said that he had given away over 550 million dollars in his life. He was also the founder of both the University of Chicago and Rockefeller University and funded the establishment of the Central Philippine University in the Philippines.

Elvis Aaron Presley(Fig. 2-3)(1935—1977) was an American singer, musician and actor. Regarded as one of the most significant cultural icons of the 20th century, he is often referred to as "the King of Rock and Roll" or simply "the King". *Heartbreak Hotel* was released in January 1956 and became a No.1 hit in the United States. With a series of successful network television appearances and chart-topping records, he became the leading figure of the newly popular sound of rock and roll. Elvis Presley died at the age of 42 at his mansion in Graceland, near Memphis, shocking his fans worldwide. By the time of his death, he had sold more than 600 million singles and albums. Since his death, Graceland has become a shrine for millions of followers worldwide. Elvis Presley is the only performer to have been inducted into three separate music *Halls of Fame*. Throughout his career, he set records for concert attendance, television ratings and record sales, and remains one of the best-selling and most influential artists in the history of popular music.

Fig. 2-3 Elvis Aaron Presley

National Symbols

The national floral emblem of the United States is rose. The national bird is Bald Eagle. The national flag of the United States is the Stars and Stripes, which stands for the nation and history. The flag's 13 alternating red and white stripes represent the 13 original colonies. Its 50 white stars on a blue field represent 50 states. The red color on the flag represents valor and bravery, and the white color represents purity and innocence. The blue color on the flag represents vigilance, perseverance, and justice.

The Great Seal of the United States(Fig. 2-4) is the eagle with 13 arrows and olive branch. 13 arrows in the right talon and olive branch in the left talon symbolize that the United States has "a strong desire for peace, but will always be ready for war". The Great Seal is used to authenticate certain documents issued by the United States federal government. The phrase is used both for the physical seal itself, which is kept by the United States Secretary of State, and more generally for the design impressed upon it. The Great Seal was first used publicly in 1782.

Fig. 2-4 The Great Seal of the United States

Exercises

I. *Try to answer the following questions according to your understanding of the text.*

(1) When did European settlement begin?

(2) When and where did European colonists reach the New World?

(3) How much do you know about the Independence Day and its origin?

(4) Who is called "the Father of His Country"?

(5) What is Elvis Aaron Presley famous for?

II. *Read the following passage carefully, and make a comment on it at the end of the passage in no more than 100 words.*

Columbus and a crew of 88 men left Spain on August 3, 1492, in three ships. On October 12, they stood on land again on an island that Columbus named San Salvador.

He explored it and the nearby islands of what are now known as Cuba and Hispaniola. He believed they were part of the coast of East Asia, which was called the Indies. He called the people he found there Indians.

Columbus left about 40 men on the island to build a fort from the wood of one of the ships. He returned to Spain with captured natives, birds, plants and gold. Columbus was considered a national hero when he reached Spain in March, 1493.

Columbus returned across the Atlantic Ocean to the Caribbean area five months later. He found that the protective fort built by his men had been destroyed by fire. Columbus did not find any of his men. But this time, he had many more men and all the animals and equipment needed to start a colony on Hispaniola.

Seven months later, Columbus sent five ships back to Spain. They carried Indians to be sold as slaves. Columbus also sailed back to Spain. He made another trip in 1498, with six ships. This time he saw the coast of South America. But the settlers on Hispaniola were so unhappy with conditions in the new colony, Columbus was sent back to Spain as a prisoner. Spain's rulers pardoned him.

In 1502, Columbus made his final voyage to what some at that time were calling the New World. He stayed on the island of Jamaica until he returned home in 1504.

During all his trips, Columbus explored islands and waterways, searching for a passage to the Indies. He never found it. He also did not find spices or great amounts of gold. Yet, he always believed that he had found the Indies. He refused to recognize that it was really a new world.

Columbus's voyages, however, opened up the new world. Others later explored all of North America.

Chapter Two The United States of America

Comments:

Columbus discovered the New World. Some think that it is a great contribution to the world; while others believe that his discovery leads to the destruction of the American Indian civilization. What do you think of it?

Reference:

Argument:

(1) Establishing new trade routes

(2) Making the expansion of Europe possible

(3) Discovering some peculiar crops

Counter-argument:

(1) Occupying the living space of the native Americans

(2) Starting the slavery in the New World

(3) Bringing infectious diseases

Unit 3 Education and Recreation

Text Focus

1. School Education
2. Famous Universities
3. Cultural Life

2.4 Lecture4 Education.mp4

Vocabulary

1. compulsory	[kəmˈpʌlsəri]	adj.	义务的
2. institution	[ˌɪnstɪˈtjuːʃn]	n.	机构
3. diploma	[dɪˈpləʊmə]	n.	毕业证书
4. academic	[ˌækəˈdemɪk]	adj.	学术的
5. discipline	[ˈdɪsəplɪn]	n.	学科
6. generate	[ˈdʒenəreɪt]	v.	使形成
7. transform	[trænsˈfɔːm]	v.	转化
8. participatory	[pɑːˌtɪsɪˈpeɪtəri]	adj.	众人参与的

Formal education in the United States consists of elementary, secondary and higher education. Elementary and secondary education, which form public education, are free and *compulsory*[1]. Higher education in the United States has been developing for nearly 400 years from the founding of Harvard University. National basic values, especially the equality of opportunity are the representations of the educational *institutions*[2] in the United States. The goal of the American education is to teach students how to learn and to help them reach their maximum potentials, so American students are encouraged to express their own opinions in class and think for themselves. Recreational and cultural life of Americans is plentiful and colorful, including movies, television, music and sports etc.

School Education

Educational institutions in the United States reflect the nation's basic values, especially the equality of opportunity. From elementary schools through colleges, Americans believe that everyone deserves an equal opportunity to get a good education. In order to develop educated population, all the states have compulsory school attendance laws. These laws vary from one state to another, but they generally require school attendance from 6 to 16 years old. But most students attend school at least until high school graduation. About 80% of American children receive their elementary and high school education in public schools, which are supported by the state and local taxes and do not charge tuition. American public schools are locally controlled, and they are free and open to all at the elementary and high schools, but public universities charge tuition and have competitive entrance requirements. While other American children go to private schools, which charge tuition and are not under direct public control although many states set educational standards for them. To attend a private school, a student must apply first and be accepted.

Most children start school at the age of five, by attending kindergarten, or even at the age of three or four by attending pre-school programs. Kindergarten teachers have taken on the job of teaching literacy basics, such as teaching letters, numbers, colors and shapes. Still, there's a lot of time for playing games and fun. Then there are 6 years of elementary school and usually 2 years of middle school, and 4 years of high school. Not all school systems have kindergartens, but all do have 12 years of elementary, middle, and senior high school. School systems may divide the 12 years up differently.

After high school, the majority of students go on to college. Undergraduate studies lead to a Bachelor's degree, which is generally what Americans mean when they speak of a college *diploma*[3]. The Bachelor's degree can be followed by professional studies, which lead to degrees in professions such as law, medicine, and graduate studies which lead to master and doctoral degrees.

Higher education in the United States began with the founding of Harvard University in 1636. A university is much larger than a college. A university usually has several different colleges in it. Each college within a university has a special subject area. There may be a college of liberal arts where humanities, social science, natural science and mathematics are taught. There may be a college of education where students learn to be teachers. A university always has programs for advanced or graduate study in a variety of subjects. There may be a medical school, a law school, and other advanced programs.

A university program for undergraduates usually takes four years. In this way, a university and a college are alike. College students usually spend four years in school as well. A college, however, usually has only one or two kinds of programs. A college does not have graduate or professional programs in a variety of areas.

College students, like university students, usually have a high school diploma or its equivalent, when they enter college. Most students have completed regular high school programs. If a college student completes a course of study in the arts, he or she receives a Bachelor of Arts degree. In the sciences, the students receive a Bachelor of Science degree. If college students want to continue for a graduate or professional degree, they must go to a university.

Compared with universities and colleges, community colleges in the United States are quite different. The community college gives training for a variety of jobs, and also has an ***academic***[4] program. The programs of study in the community college usually last for only two years. The community college serves the community, and anyone who lives nearby may go there. When community college students complete a two-year program, they receive an Associate of Arts or Associate of Science degree. Community colleges are nearly always publicly funded by the state, country, or city government, but not usually funded by religious groups.

Famous Universities

Harvard University was established in 1636, which is the oldest institution of higher education in the United States. Harvard University, which is situated in Cambridge and Boston, has an enrollment of over 20,000 degree candidates, including undergraduate, graduate, and professional students. Harvard has more than 400,000 alumni around the world. Harvard University is devoted to excellence in teaching, learning, and research, and to developing leaders in many ***disciplines***[5] who make a difference globally. Harvard faculties are engaged with teaching and research to push the boundaries of human knowledge.

For students who are excited to investigate the biggest issues of the 21st century, Harvard offers an unparalleled student experience and a generous financial aid program, with over $160 million awarded to more than 60% of their undergraduate students. The University has 12 degree granting schools in addition to the Radcliffe Institute for Advanced Study, offering a global education.

Yale University(Fig. 2-5) is an American private Ivy League research university in New Haven, Connecticut. Founded in 1701, it is the third oldest institution of higher education in the United States and one of the nine Colonial Colleges chartered before the American Revolution.

Fig. 2-5 Yale University

Yale is organized into 14 constituent schools: the original undergraduate college, the Graduate School of Arts and Sciences and 12 professional schools. While the university is governed by the Yale Corporation, each school's faculty oversees its curriculum and degree programs. In addition to a central campus in downtown New Haven, the university owns athletic facilities in western New Haven, a campus in West Haven, Connecticut and forest and nature preserves throughout New England. The Yale University Library, serving all constituent schools, holds more than 15 million volumes and is the third-largest academic library in the United States.

Yale has graduated many notable alumni, including some United States Presidents, American Supreme Court Justices, living billionaires and many heads of states. In addition, Yale has graduated hundreds of members of Congress and many high-level U. S. diplomats. Some of the Nobel laureates, Fields Medalists, MacArthur Fellows, Rhodes Scholars and Marshall Scholars have been affiliated with the university.

Stanford University, officially Leland Stanford Junior University, is a private research university in Stanford, the heart of Northern California's Silicon Valley, 20 miles north of San Jose. Because of its academic strength, wealth, and proximity to Silicon Valley, Stanford is often cited as one of the world's most prestigious universities.

Stanford University was founded in 1885 by Leland Stanford and his wife Jane Stanford in memory of their only child, Leland Stanford Jr., who had died of typhoid fever at the age of 15 in 1884. Leland Stanford was a former Governor of California and the United States Senator, who made his fortune as a railroad tycoon. The school admitted its first students on October 1, 1891, as a coeducational and non-denominational institution.

Stanford University struggled financially after Leland Stanford's death in 1893 and again after much of the campus was damaged by the 1906 San Francisco earthquake. Following World War II, Provost Frederick Terman supported faculty and graduates' entrepreneurialism to build a self-sufficient local industry in what is later known as Silicon Valley. The university is also one of the top fund raising institutions in the country, becoming the first school to raise more than a billion dollars in a year.

The university is organized around three traditional schools consisting of 40 academic departments at the undergraduate and graduate levels and four professional schools that focus on graduate programs in Law, Medicine, Education and Business. Stanford's undergraduate program is one of the top three most selective in the United States.

 Cultural Life

The history of Hollywood(Fig. 2-6) is sometimes separated into four main periods: the silent film era, classical Hollywood cinema, New Hollywood, and the contemporary period. American film studios collectively ***generate***[6] several hundreds of movies every year, making the United States the third most prolific producer of films in the world. The major film studios of Hollywood are the primary source of the most commercially successful movies in the world, such as *Gone with the Wind*. The products of Hollywood today dominate the global film industry. To honor the outstanding film achievements of the film season, the first Academy Awards ceremony was held on May 16, 1929, and the Academy Awards honoring films is held every year.

Fig. 2-6   Hollywood

Americans are among the heaviest television viewers in the world. Even now, the most popular leisure-time activity is watching television. American TV programs consist mostly of game shows, talk shows, and never-ending soap operas. Evening entertainment consists mostly of sitcoms in a humorous way. There are also movies, adventure shows, dramas, and various weekly shows with the same cast of characters and general theme but a different story each week.

In general, more media, such as public television and radios, now provide Americans with news and entertainment than ever. Newspapers, magazines and traditional broadcast television organizations have lost some of their popularity. These public media receive money to operate from private citizens, organizations and government. Many of their programs are educational. At the same time, online and satellite media have increased in numbers and strength. The Internet has also changed American media.

Elements from folk idioms, such as old-time music, blues, were adopted and ***transformed***[7] into popular genres with global audience. Jazz was developed by innovators in the 20th century.

Country music developed in the 1920s, and rhythm and blues in the 1940s. In the mid-1950s, rock and roll became known to the Americans. More recent American creations include hip hop and house music. The history of country music is hundreds of years old. It is older than America itself. It begins with the immigrants from Scotland and Ireland who brought their traditional songs and instruments to the New World. There were new stories to tell, new troubles and heartaches to mourn. There were also new loves to sing about. New instruments started to be played too. In many ways, rock is a mirror of American culture. In 1955, rock and roll was born in America, when "Rock Around the Clock" was performed. So it was first known as "rock and roll" and then simply as "rock". So far, rock and roll has been popular not only in the United States, but all over the world as well. Rock and roll grew mainly out of rhythm and blues, and it was also influenced by country and western music. Rock and roll is a mixture of styles that work together, and it offers something to people of all ages.

Eight Olympic Games have taken place in the United States. International competition is not as important in American sports as it is in the sporting culture of most other countries.

The four most popular team sports are American football, baseball, basketball and ice hockey. The major leagues of these sports enjoy massive media exposure. As team sports, which appeal to American love of socializing and competing, they are both spectator sports and ***participatory*** [8] sports. Baseball is often called the "national pastime". It is likely that the average individual Americans will attend many times more baseball games in their lives than football games. American football has grown in popularity with the advent of television over the last several decades. Basketball and ice hockey are the country's next two leading professional team sports and basketball is also the world's most popular indoor sport.

Exercises

I. *Try to answer the following questions according to your understanding of the text.*

(1) What is the goal of the American education system?

(2) When do American children start their education?

(3) When did higher education start in the United States?

(4) How many famous universities do you know in the United States?

(5) How many periods is the history of Hollywood separated into?

II. *Read the following passage carefully, and make a comment on it at the end of the passage in no more than 100 words.*

Many studies have predicted there will be a great need for future workers skilled in jobs related to science, technology, engineering and math. In education, these areas of study are known as STEM.

Research suggests it is important to get students involved in STEM subjects as early as possible, starting in middle school or even before.

While STEM education programs have been increasing in many areas across the United States, there remains a lack of interest in the subjects by many younger students. The United States Department of Education has estimated that once students reach their last year of high school, only 16% are interested in a STEM career. A department study also found that even among those who do choose to study STEM subjects in college, only about half decide to work in a STEM-related job.

A survey released by Pew Research Center asked American adults why they believe many young people do not want to study math and science subjects. About 64% of those questioned said they think the main reason is that students consider STEM studies either too hard (52%) or too boring (12%). More than 20% blamed the lack of interest on the belief that a STEM degree might not be useful in the job market.

The study found about one third of Americans would tell a high school student seeking career guidance to study a STEM-related field. About 19% of them said they would suggest a health-related STEM career. And 14% would tell them to center on technology.

STEM careers made up about 13% of the total U.S. work force in 2016. However, the number of STEM-related jobs—especially in health and computer areas—has risen much faster than other areas for years.

Comments:

Some think that it is the right way to choose what you like as your major in university, while some think that the top university is the first choice but not your favorite major.

What's your point of view?

Reference:

Argument:

(1) The fame and the reputation of the university

(2) The value of diploma of the university

(3) The teaching qualities of the university

Counter-argument:

(1) Focusing on the interest first

(2) Focusing on the job potential

(3) Focusing on the future success

Unit 4 Politics and Economy

Text Focus

1. Political System
2. Political Parties
3. Economy

2.5 Lecture5 Politics and Economy.mp4

Vocabulary

1. dominate	[ˈdɒmɪneɪt]	v.	占主要地位
2. democratic	[ˌdeməˈkrætɪk]	adj.	民主的
3. enforce	[ɪnˈfɔːs]	v.	实施
4. liberal	[ˈlɪbərəl]	adj.	自由主义的
5. candidate	[ˈkændɪdət]	n.	候选人
6. headquarters	[ˌhedˈkwɔːtəz]	n.	总部
7. abundant	[əˈbʌndənt]	adj.	丰富的

The political parties in the United States are mostly **dominated**[1] by a two-party system, though the Constitution has always been silent on the issue of political parties since it was signed in 1787. The Constitution was adopted on June 21, 1788, which is the oldest written constitution still in use. The two major parties of the United States are the ***Democratic***[2] Party and the Republican Party. The United States has a capitalist mixed economy, which is fueled by rich natural resources, a well-developed infrastructure, and high productivity. It lays emphasis on private ownership and private businesses to produce most goods and services. A lot of top enterprises have emerged in the United States, such as Walmart, McDonald's, Amazon, etc.

Political System

The outline of the government of the United States is laid out in the Constitution. The government was formed in 1789, making the United States one of the world's first modern national constitutional republics. The United States is the world's oldest surviving federation. The government is regulated by a system of checks and balances defined by the Constitution of the United States, which is a constitutional republic and representative democracy. The Constitution is a basic law from which the government gets all its power. It is the law that protects those who live in the United States from unreasonable actions by the national government or any state government. The Constitution defines three branches of government. They are the legislative branch, which enacts laws; the executive branch, which *enforces*[3] those laws; the judicial branch, which interprets laws.

The legislative branch is called Congress, which is made up of two groups of legislators—the Senate and the House of Representatives. It makes federal laws, declares wars, approves treaties, as well as has the power of the purse and impeachment, by which it can remove sitting members of the government. A member of the Senate is addressed as the Senator. Members of the House of Representatives are called congressmen or congresswomen. The Senate is often referred to as the upper house, which has 100 members, two senators from each state. Both senators represent the entire state. Senators are elected to six-year terms. Every two years, one-third of all senators face election or reelection.

The lower house, which is called the House of Representatives, has 435 voting members, all of whom are elected every two years. The number of the representatives from each state is determined by that state's population. Seven states have the minimum of one representative, while California, the most populous state, has 53 representatives. For the purpose of electing representatives, each state is divided into congressional districts. The districts within a state are equal in population. One representative is elected from each district. One of a representative's major duties is to protect the interests of the people in that district.

The President is the nation's chief executive. The President is the commander-in-chief of the military and has the power to veto legislative bills before they become laws. Additionally, the President appoints the members of the Cabinet and other officers, who administer and enforce federal laws and policies. The President also spends much of his time making decisions about foreign policy. A very large number of advisers and other employees assist the President.

The judicial branch consists of the Supreme Court and lower federal courts, whose judges are appointed by the President with the Senate's approval, interprets laws and overturns those they find unconstitutional. Federal laws cannot violate the terms of the Constitution. As a matter of fact, federal laws are, in some way, controlled or affected by all three branches of the government—the Congress makes them; the President approves and enforces them; the courts determine what they mean and whether they are constitutional.

Political Parties

The modern political party system in the United States is a two-party system dominated by the Democratic Party and the Republican Party. These two parties have won every presidential election since 1852 and have controlled the Congress since 1856. Several other parties from time to time achieve relatively minor representation at the national and state levels.

At the time the Constitution was signed in 1787, there were no parties in the nation. Indeed, no nation in the world at that time had voter-based political parties. The need to win popular support in a republic led to the American invention of political parties in the 1790s. Americans were especially devising new techniques that linked public opinions with public policy through the party.

The Democratic Party is the oldest political party in the United States and among the oldest in the world. The Democratic Party, since the division of the Republican Party in the election of 1912, has consistently positioned itself to the left of the Republican Party in economic as well as social matters. It was once the largest political party, with 72 million voters claiming affiliation.

The Republican Party is often referred to as the Grand Old Party (GOP). Founded in 1854 by anti-slavery expansion activists and modernizers, the Republican Party rose to prominence with the election of Abraham Lincoln, the first Republican President. It is currently the second largest party with 55 million registered members.

Within American political culture, the Republican Party is considered center-right or conservative while the Democratic Party is considered center-left or *liberal*[4]. The states of the Northeast and West Coast and some of the Great Lakes states, known as "the blue states", are relatively liberal. The "red states" of the South and parts of the Great Plains and Rocky Mountains are relatively conservative.

In the early years of the United States, voting was considered a matter for state governments, and was commonly restricted to white men who owned land. Direct elections were mostly held only for the United States House of Representatives and state legislatures. Today, American citizens have almost universal suffrage from the age of 18, regardless of race, gender, or wealth, and both houses of Congress are directly elected.

The President serves a four-year term and may be elected to the office no more than twice. The President is not elected by direct votes, but by an indirect electoral college system in which the determining votes are apportioned to the states and the District of Columbia.

The President and the Vice President are elected together in a presidential election. The election is indirect, with the winner being determined by votes cast by electors of the Electoral College. In modern times, voters in each state select a slate of electors from a list of several slates, and the electors typically promise in advance to vote for the *candidates*[5] of their party. Presidential elections occur on the Election Day, Tuesday between November 2 and 8, coinciding with the general elections of various other federal, states and local races.

Economy

The United States has one of the world's largest national economy since at least the 1890s, compared with the European Union which has a larger collective economy, but it is not a single nation. The economy of the United States is a mixed economy and has maintained a stable overall GDP growth rate, a moderate unemployment rate, and high levels of research and capital investment. It is estimated that the US GDP is one of the highest in the world, thus making it one

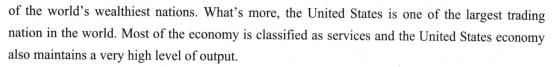

of the world's wealthiest nations. What's more, the United States is one of the largest trading nation in the world. Most of the economy is classified as services and the United States economy also maintains a very high level of output.

Agriculture is a major industry in the United States, which is a net exporter of food. Although agricultural activity occurs in all states, it is particularly concentrated in the Great Plains, a vast expanse of flat, arable land in the center of the United States and in the region around the Great Lakes known as the Corn Belt. Corn, turkeys, tomatoes, potatoes, peanuts, and sunflower seeds constitute some of the major holdovers from the agricultural endowment of the Americans.

The United States is one of the world's largest manufacturers. Many ***headquarters***[6] of the world's 500 largest companies are located in the United States. The labor market has attracted immigrants from all over the world and its net migration rate is among the highest in the world. The United States is one of the world's largest and most influential financial markets. China is the largest foreign holder of American public debt. About 60% of the global currency reserves have been invested in the American dollar, while 24% have been invested in the euro.

The United States has a capitalist mixed economy, which is fueled by ***abundant***[7] natural resources, a well-developed infrastructure, and high productivity. It lays emphasis on private ownership and private businesses to produce most goods and services. Two thirds of the output goes to individuals, while one third is bought by government and business.

Walmart Inc. was founded by American retail legend Mr. Sam Walton in Arkansas in 1962. Walmart has topped the Fortune 500 list several times. Walmart Inc. helps people around the world save money and live better in retail stores, online, and through their mobile devices. Walmart continues to be a leader in sustainability, corporate philanthropy and employment opportunity. Since the first Walmart store opened in 1962 in Rogers, Arkansas, Walmart has been dedicated to making a difference in the lives of the customers. The business is the result of Sam Walton's visionary leadership, along with generations of associates focused on helping customers and communities save money and live better. This rich heritage defines who we are and what we do today.

As a retailer, the company's legal name was changed from Walmart Stores, Inc. to Walmart Inc. on February 1, 2018. The name change demonstrates their determination to serve customers however they want to shop: whether in stores, online, on their mobile device, or through pickup and delivery. The company is committed to diversity, cultivating local talent, and women leadership. Walmart China opened the first Walmart Hypermarket and Sam's Club in Shenzhen in 1996. Since then, they have grown to operate hundreds of stores and multiple distribution centers in many cities nationwide.

McDonald's is an American fast food company, founded in 1940 as a restaurant operated by Richard and Maurice McDonald, in San Bernardino, California, the United States. They rechristened their business as a hamburger stand. The first time a McDonald's franchise used the

Golden Arches logo was in 1953 at a location in Phoenix, Arizona. In 1955, Ray Kroc, a salesman, joined the company as a franchise agent and proceeded to purchase the chain from the McDonald brothers. McDonald's had its original headquarters in Oak Brook, Illinois, but moved its global headquarters to Chicago in early 2018.

McDonald's is one of the world's largest restaurant chains by revenue. Although McDonald's is known for its hamburgers, they also sell cheeseburgers, chicken products, French fries, breakfast items, soft drinks, milkshakes, wraps, and desserts. In response to changing consumer tastes and a negative backlash because of the unhealthiness of their food, the company has added a lot to its menu, such as salads, fish, smoothies, and fruit. McDonald's restaurants offer both counter service and drive-through service, with indoor and sometimes outdoor seating.

Amazon.com, Inc.(Fig. 2-7), founded in 1994 by Jeff Bezos, is an American electronic commerce company with headquarters in Seattle, Washington. Bezos is said to have browsed a dictionary for a word beginning with "A" for the value of alphabetic placement. He selected the name Amazon because it was "exotic and different" and as a reference to his plan for the company's size to reflect that of the Amazon River, one of the largest rivers in the world.

Fig. 2-7　Logo of Amazon

Amazon is one of the big four technology companies in the United States, with the others being Meta(Facebook), Apple, and Google. In terms of revenue and market capitalization, Amazon is ranked as the world leader in cloud computing platform, artificial intelligence assistant provider, and e-commerce marketplace, as well as the largest Internet-based retailer in the United States. Amazon.com started as an online bookstore, but over the years, diversified by selling software electronics, jewelry, video games, toys, food, furniture, and apparel, among other items. The company also produces consumer electronics—notably, Amazon Kindle e-book readers, Fire tablets, Fire TV and Fire Phone—and is a major provider of cloud computing services. Amazon also sells certain low-end products like USB cables under its inhouse brand AmazonBasics. The company has individual websites, software development centers, customer service centers and fulfillment centers in many locations around the world.

Exercises

I. *Try to answer the following questions according to your understanding of the text.*

(1) What is the Constitution of the United States?

(2) What are the three branches of the Constitution?

(3) What are the two major political parties in the United States?

(4) Which party is considered center-right or conservative?

(5) How many top enterprises do you know in the United States?

Chapter Two The United States of America

II. *Read the following passage carefully, and make a comment on it at the end of the passage in no more than 100 words.*

The initiator of the AIDS Prevention Education Project for Chinese Youth and chairwoman of the Beijing Changier Education Foundation was recently awarded by the American Chinese United Association in recognition of her commitments to AIDS prevention, women empowerment and the improvement of youth education.

The AIDS-prevention project launched by the initiator has reached out to more than 1,200 universities, primary schools and middle schools across China, benefiting over 3.03 million people. The initiator also has traveled to Yunnan province, Sichuan province, Tibet autonomous region and some other remote places in China to help lift families out of poverty and bring local children easier access to quality education.

Additionally, the initiator and the foundation have been actively conducting collaboration with officials, scholars and educationists from different countries for creating a better environment for the growth of women and children, further protecting their rights. The awarding ceremony was held on the first day of the Chinese Lunar New Year, with 550 representatives of Asian communities in Massachusetts, Connecticut, and some other states, showing the strong cohesion within Chinese Americans from across the country.

Comments:

Some believe that charity organizations should help those who are in great need; some think that charity organizations should concentrate on those who live in their own country.

What is your point of view?

Reference:

Argument:
(1) Due to human's responsibility and obligation
(2) Promoting economic development and enhancing social harmony
(3) Being a reflection of moral obligation to cover a wide range of issues

Counter-argument:
(1) Helping local people more effectively
(2) Making a contribution to one's own country
(3) Enhancing harmony of the targeted community

Unit 5   Culture and Customs

Text Focus

1. Traditional Culture
2. Literature Works
3. Food Customs

2.6 Lecture6 Customs.mp4

2.7 Lecture7 Culture.mp4

Vocabulary

1. generalize	[ˈdʒenrəlaɪz]	v.	概括
2. dialect	[ˈdaɪəlekt]	n.	方言
3. patriotic	[ˌpeɪtriˈɒtɪk]	adj.	爱国的
4. distinguished	[dɪˈstɪŋgwɪʃt]	adj.	杰出的
5. controversially	[ˌkɒntrəˈvɜːʃəli]	adv.	有争议地
6. concern	[kənˈsɜːn]	n.	顾虑
7. obesity	[əʊˈbiːsəti]	n.	肥胖

The United States is probably most often ***generalized***[1] as a society of individuals and it has ethnically and racially diverse cultures because of large-scale immigration from different countries throughout the world, so American holidays can be secular, international, or uniquely American. Although the most commonly used language is English, people in the United States speak or sign more than 350 languages. The population is equivalent to less than 5% of the total world population and English is spoken widely as the official language throughout the country. In leisure time, Americans choose different kinds of recreational ways to rest and relax, including doing sports, reading, enjoying the cuisines, etc. A lot of popular literature works influence the life of Americans, such as *The Scarlet Letter*, *The Old Man and the Sea*, and *The Bluest Eye*, etc. Except for spiritual food, Americans also enjoy traditional cuisines, such as turkey, potatoes, corn, which were consumed by native Americans and early European settlers.

Traditional Culture

It is very difficult to define the general "American culture". Different situations require different responses, and different people from different ethnic, religious, and regional backgrounds have different values. America is probably most often generalized as a society of individuals. Americans are taught from a very young age to think for themselves, to form and express opinions, and to do things without help.

The United States is ethnically and racially diverse as a result of large-scale immigration from many different countries throughout its history. Its chief early influences came from English settlers of colonial America. In contrary to popular belief, American culture severely predates the signing of the Declaration of Independence, with the migration into the region that is today the continental United States, as well as with its own unique social and cultural characteristics such as ***dialect*[2]**, music, arts, social habits, cuisine and folklore. American culture includes both conservative and liberal elements, military and scientific competitiveness, political structures, risk taking and free expression, materialist and moral elements. It also includes elements which evolved from Native Americans and the culture of African Americans and different cultures from Latin America.

American holidays can be secular, religious, international, or uniquely American. But, not all Americans observe the same holidays, and there are many holidays which are not legal holidays. Also, some holidays are celebrated only by certain religious or cultural groups. Apart from some other common national observances, there are some major national legal holidays in the United States, such as New Year's Day, Memorial Day, Independence Day, and Labor Day.

New Year's Day is on January 1. The big celebration of this federal holiday begins at the night before New Year's Eve, when Americans gather to wish each other a happy and prosperous coming year. Many Americans make New Year's resolutions. The New Year is often "rung in" with bells and noisemakers. On New Year's Day itself, there are many parades and college football games on the television.

Memorial Day is a federal holiday observed on the last Monday of May. It originally honored the people killed in the American Civil War, which has become a day on which the American dead of all wars, and the dead generally, are remembered in special programs held in cemeteries, churches, and other public meeting places.

Independence Day is on July 4th. This federal holiday honors the nation's birthday—the adoption of the Declaration of Independence on July 4th, 1776. It is a day of picnics and ***patriotic*[3]** parades, and a night of concerts and fireworks.

Labor Day is on the first Monday of September. This federal holiday honors the nation's working people, typically with parades. For most Americans it marks the end of the summer vacation and the start of the school year.

Literature Works

The Scarlet Letter is a work of historical fiction by American author Nathaniel Hawthorne, published in 1850. Set in Puritan Massachusetts Bay Colony during the years 1642 to 1649, the novel tells the story of Hester Prynne, who conceives a daughter through an affair and then struggles to create a new life of repentance and dignity. Containing a number of religious and historic allusions, the book explores themes of legalism, sin, and guilt.

The Scarlet Letter was one of the first mass-produced books in America. It was popular when first published and is considered a classic work today. It inspired numerous film, television, and stage adaptations. Critics have described it as a masterwork and novelist D. H. Lawrence called it a "perfect work of the American imagination".

Nathaniel Hawthorne(Fig. 2-8)(1804—1864) was an American novelist, dark romantic, and short story writer. His works often focus on history, morality, and religion. Hawthorne's works belong to romanticism or, more specifically, dark romanticism, cautionary tales that suggest that guilt, sin, and evil are the most inherent natural qualities of humanity. Many of his works are inspired by Puritan New

Fig. 2-8 Nathaniel Hawthorne

England, combining historical romance loaded with symbolism and deep psychological themes, bordering on surrealism. His depictions of the past are a version of historical fiction used only as a vehicle to express common themes of ancestral sin, guilt and retribution. His later writings also reflect his negative view of the Transcendentalism movement.

The Bluest Eye is a novel written by Morrison in 1970. The novel was set in 1941 and centered around the life of an African-American girl named Pecola who grows up during the years following the Great Depression in Lorain, Ohio. Due to her mannerisms and dark skin, she is consistently regarded as "ugly". As a result, she develops an inferiority complex, which fuels her desire for the blue eyes she equates with "whiteness". The point of view of the novel switches between the perspective of Claudia MacTeer, the daughter of Pecola's foster parents, and a third person narrator with inset narratives in the first person.

Toni Morrison (1931—2019) is an American novelist, essayist, editor, teacher, and professor emeritus at the Princeton University. Morrison won the Pulitzer Prize and the American Book Award in 1988 for *Beloved*. The novel was adapted into a film of the same name, starring Oprah Winfrey and Danny Glover in 1998. Morrison was awarded the Nobel Prize in Literature in 1993. In 1996, the National Endowment for the Humanities selected her for the Jefferson Lecture, the United States federal government's highest honor for achievement in the humanities. She was honored with the 1996 National Book Foundation's Medal of **Distinguished**[4] Contribution to American Letters. Morrison wrote the libretto for a new opera, *Margaret Garner*, first performed in 2005. In 2016, she received the PEN/Saul Bellow Award for Achievement in American Fiction.

The Times They Are a-Changin' is a song written by Bob Dylan and released as the title track of his 1964 album of the same name. Dylan wrote the song as a deliberate attempt to create an anthem of change for the time, influenced by Irish and Scottish ballads. Released as a 45-rpm single in Britain in 1965, it reached number nine in the British Top Ten.

Bob Dylan (1941—) is an American singer, songwriter, author, and painter who has been an influential figure in popular music and culture for more than five decades. Much of his most celebrated work dates from the 1960s, when he became a reluctant "voice of a generation" with songs such as *Blowin' in the Wind* and *The Times They Are a-Changin'* that became anthems for the Civil Rights Movement and anti-war movement. In 1965, he ***controversially***[5] abandoned his early fan-base in the American folk music revival, recording a six-minute single, *Like a Rolling Stone*, which enlarged the scope of popular music. Bob Dylan has received many accolades throughout his long career as a songwriter and performing artist. Dylan's professional career began in 1961 when he signed with Columbia Records. 55 years later, in 2016, Dylan continued to release new recordings and was the first musician to receive the Nobel Prize in Literature. He won the Nobel Prize in Literature for having created new poetic expressions within the great American song tradition.

Food Customs

Traditional American cuisines use some ingredients, such as turkey, potatoes and corn, which were consumed by Native Americans and early European settlers. Wheat is the primary cereal grain. Slow-cooked pork and beef barbecue, potato chips, and chocolate chip cookies are distinctively American foods. Characteristic dishes such as apple pies, fried chicken, pizza, hamburgers, and hot dogs(Fig. 2-9) derive from the recipes of various immigrants. Americans generally prefer coffee to tea.

Fig. 2-9   Hamburger/Chips/Cola

The American fast food industry and fast food consumption have sparked health ***concerns***[6]. American frequent dining at fast food outlets is associated with what public health officials call the American "***obesity***[7] epidemic".

Exercises

I. *Try to answer the following questions according to your understanding of the text.*

(1) Why is the culture of the United States ethnically and racially diverse?

(2) How many major legal holidays are there in the United States and what are they?

(3) When is Memorial Day in the United States?

(4) How many distinguished American writers do you know?

(5) What is the primary cereal grain in the United States?

II. *Read the following passage carefully, and make a comment on it at the end of the passage in no more than 100 words.*

What do you think these names have in common? Royal, Charlie, Salem, Skyler, Justice, and Oakley. Well, in the United States, all of these names are considered fitting for girls and boys. They are considered gender-neutral. And modern American parents appear more willing than ever to consider the possibility of gender fluidity in their children.

Linda Murray is the head of BabyCenter.com. She told the AP(Associated Press), "This generation is truly interested in gender-neutral names." The Social Security Administration puts out a list of most popular baby names every year based on its registrations. Observers say the gender-neutral names have not made it into the top ten. However, they say such names are heavily represented in the longer list.

Younger parents seem especially likely to choose gender-neutral names for their babies. Pop culture and honoring family or religious history are important to baby naming. But more and more parents are choosing names that can be used for either sex. Some names just sound cool. Lori Kinkler, a psychologist in San Antonio, Texas, said she chose the gender-neutral name Riley for her daughter. She said if the 3-year-old does not identify as female later in life, she will not have to change her name. In Kinkler's words, "I like that she feels she has options and knows she'll be accepted by us."

Pamela Redmond Satran is a writer of *The Baby Name Bible* and *Cool Names for Babies*. She also writes about the subject online and is a founder of baby name site Nameberry.com. Satran says possible gender fluidity is not the only reason parents choose unisex names. She says, "A lot of people choose unisex names because they think they're cool or they're meaningful to themselves but they raise their kids in a very gender-specific way."

Comments:

Some people say the name is vital to a person; whereas some people hold the opposite opinion that names have no special meaning.

What is your point of view?

Reference:

Argument:

(1) Deciding whether a person will be successful or not

(2) Being easy to remember or not

(3) Bringing good luck to the family

Chapter Two The United States of America

Counter-argument:

(1) Being only a sign

(2) Being easily changed

(3) Having no special meaning

Unit 6   Intercultural Communication

Knowledge to Learn

What Is Communication?

Communication is related to both communion and community. It comes from Latin "communicate", which means "to make common" or "to share". The basic assumption is that communication is a form of human behavior derived from a need to connect and interact with other human beings. Therefore, communication can simply refer to the act and process of sending and receiving messages among people.

What Are the Features of Communication?

Interpersonal communication is a complex process. The following are some of the most distinctive features of communication.

Communication is dynamic, interactive, verbal and non-verbal, intentional or unintentional and rule-governed.

Cases to Study

Case 1

> A French woman who had just come to live in the United States said that she was really shocked by the way Americans behaved on the telephone. In some cases, when she attempted to converse with American acquaintances who answered her phone call, they would ask whom she wanted to speak with, and, without allowing her to continue, they would hand the phone over directly to the person she intended to speak with, as if they did not like chatting with her. On other occasions, she answered the phone, heard the voice of an acquaintance, and was surprised and hurt when the caller, instead of greeting and conversing with her, simply asked for somebody else. Apart from that, she sometimes felt a little annoyed because, unlike people in France, many American callers did not say anything to apologize for disturbing her.
>
> Why did the French woman feel shocked and hurt by the way Americans behaved on the telephone?

Analysis

(1) In France, it is required that all calls begin with an apology for disturbing the answerer.

(2) They are also expected to begin the phone call by checking that they have reached the right number, identifying themselves, and then chatting with whoever has answered the phone, if this person is known to them.

(3) Only after some conversations may callers indicate their wish to speak with the person they have actually called to or intended to speak to.

(4) In contrast, callers in the United States only apologize when they feel they have called at an inappropriate time. They often ask for the person they want without identifying themselves or conversing with the answerer, even when that person is known to them.

Case 2

> John Rohrkemper is an American professor. It was his first time to teach in a Brazilian university and he was quite excited about it. His two-hour class was scheduled to begin at 10 a. m. and end at noon. On the first day, to his surprise, there was no one in the classroom when he arrived on time. Many students came after 10 a. m.; several arrived after 10:30 a. m. Two students came after 11 a. m. Although all the students greeted him as they arrived, few apologized for their lateness. Dr. Rohrkemper was very angry about students' rude behaviors and decided to study the students' behaviors.
>
> What will Dr. Rohrkemper find in his study about Brazilian students' lateness?

Analysis

(1) In an American university, students are expected to arrive at the appointed hour. By contrast, in Brazil, neither the teacher nor the students always arrive at the appointed hour.

(2) Classes not only begin at the scheduled time in America, but also end at the scheduled time. In the Brazilian class, only a few students leave the class at noon; many remain past 12:30 to discuss the class and ask more questions. While people's arriving late may not be very important in Brazil, nor is staying late.

(3) People from Brazilian and North American cultures have different feelings about lateness. In Brazil, they believe that a person who usually arrives late is probably more successful than a person who is always on time.

(4) In fact, Brazilians expect a person with status or prestige to arrive late, while in the United States, lateness is usually considered disrespectful and unacceptable.

(5) Consequently, if a Brazilian is late for an appointment with an American, the American may misinterpret the reason for the lateness and become angry.

Chapter Two The United States of America

 Translations on Traditional Chinese Culture

Exercise 1

Translate the passage into English

中国有 5000 多年的历史，是世界上最古老的文明之一。从公元前 21 世纪的夏朝开始至清朝，中国历史上经历过几十个朝代的变更。每个朝代在政治、经济、文化、科技等领域都有独特的成就。汉朝时，中国是当时世界上最先进的国家。"汉族"这一名称就得名于汉朝。唐朝因统一时间长、国力强盛而被国人铭记，因此在海外的中国人自称为"唐人"。宋朝和明朝是经济、文化、教育与科学高度繁荣的时代。

> **Translation Reference**
>
> With a history of more than 5,000 years, China owns one of the oldest ancient civilizations of the world. From the Xia Dynasty in the 21st century BC to the Qing Dynasty, China experienced dozens of dynasties in history. Each dynasty achieved unique accomplishments in the fields of politics, economy, culture, science and technology etc. During the Han Dynasty, China was the most advanced country worldwide, which contributes to the formation of the name "the Han Nationality". The Tang Dynasty impressed the Chinese for its long-time unification and strong national power, so the overseas Chinese call themselves "the Tang people". The Song Dynasty and the Ming Dynasty were periods when economy, culture, education and science were highly prosperous.

Translate the passage into Chinese

Sanxingdui Sites are the largest sites of the ancient Shu Kingdom discovered so far in Southwest China. Sanxingdui Sites have also unearthed more than 10,000 cultural relics, all dating back to 5,000 to 3,000 BC. These cultural relics include gold, pottery and ivory products with exquisite craftsmanship and peculiar shapes. They are of great value to the study of the process of early countries and the development of religious consciousness, and occupy an important position in the history of human civilization.

> **Translation Reference**
>
> 三星堆遗址是迄今在中国西南地区发现的规模最大的古蜀国遗址。三星堆还出土了 10,000 多件文物，其历史均可追溯到公元前 5000 到 3000 年。这些文物包括制作精美和造型奇特的金器、陶器和象牙制品。对研究早期国家的进程及宗教意识的发展有重要价值，在人类文明发展史上占有重要地位。

Exercise 2

Translate the passage into English

丝绸之路是中国古代的一条商业贸易路线。丝绸之路以古代中国的政治、经济、文化中心——古都长安为起点，一直延伸至中亚、北非和欧洲。它最初的作用是出口中国生产的丝绸。"一带一路"倡议是共建"丝绸之路经济带"和"21世纪海上丝绸之路"的简称。面对困难和挑战，唯有加强合作才是根本出路，正基于此，中国提出"一带一路"合作倡议。

Translation Reference
The Silk Road is a trade route in ancient China. It started from the ancient capital Chang' an, the center of politics, economy and culture in ancient China, and stretched all the way to Central Asia, North Africa and Europe. Its original function was to export the silk produced in China. "The Belt and Road Initiative" is short for the initiative of jointly building "the Silk Road Economic Belt" and "the 21st Century Maritime Silk Road". Confronted with difficulties and challenges, closer cooperation is the fundamental solution. It is for this reason that China has proposed "the Belt and Road Initiative".

Translate the passage into Chinese

Dunhuang is a renowned tourist resort famous for the Mogao Caves. In ancient times, Dunhuang was the center of trade between China and its Western neighbors. With the flourishing of trade along the Silk Road, Dunhuang quickly developed into the most open area in international trade in Chinese history. Over 1,000 caves were cut out of cliffs in Dunhuang. The caves reflect the Silk Road civilization and important aspects of Chinese arts and customs. Mogao Caves have always been regarded as the national treasure of China.

Translation Reference
敦煌是以莫高窟而闻名的旅游胜地。在古代，敦煌是中国与其西方邻国之间的贸易中心。随着丝绸之路沿线贸易的蓬勃发展，敦煌迅速发展为中国历史上国际贸易最开放的地区。敦煌有1000多个石窟是在悬崖上雕刻出来的。石窟反映了丝绸之路文明和中国艺术与习俗的重要方面，莫高窟一直被视为中国的国宝。

Exercise 3

Translate the passage into English

中国的四大名著是指创作于明清时期的四部最伟大、最有影响力的小说，分别为《红楼梦》《三国演义》《西游记》和《水浒传》。四部巨著在中国文学史上的地位难分高低，都具有很高的艺术水平，可以帮助了解中国传统的社会、历史、地理、民俗和处世哲学。现在，四部小说都已被改编成电影或电视剧，受到很多观众的喜爱。

Chapter Two The United States of America

> **Translation Reference**
> The Four Great Classical Novels of China refer to the four greatest and most influential novels written in the Ming and Qing Dynasties, including *The Story of the Stone*, *The Romance of the Three Kingdoms*, *The Journey to the West*, and *Water Margin*. The position of them in the history of Chinese literature is difficult to distinguish. Being high in artistic level, they can acquaint people with traditional Chinese society, history, geography, folk customs and philosophy of life. Nowadays, the four novels have already been adapted into movies or TV series, favored by lots of audience.

Translate the passage into Chinese

The Four Great Inventions refer to the four inventions in ancient China that had great influences in the world. They are paper-making, printing, gunpowder and compass. Paper-making and printing led to the revolutionary progress in recording and transmitting information. The invention and spread of gunpowder changed the mode of war in the Middle Ages. And the compass greatly helped the European navigators to explore new routes. The Four Great Inventions are symbols of advanced science and technology in ancient China and of great significance in the development of Chinese and world civilizations.

> **Translation Reference**
> 四大发明是指古代中国对世界有巨大影响的四种发明,即造纸术、印刷术、火药和指南针。造纸术和印刷术使信息的记录和传播有了革命性的进步,火药的发明和传播改变了中世纪的战争模式,而指南针大大帮助了欧洲航海家探索新航路。四大发明是古代中国先进科学和技术的象征,在中国和世界文明发展中都有着重要的意义。

Culture to Know

Culture Note 1

Longmen Caves are located in the south of Luoyang city. Longmen Caves, Yungang Caves and Mogao Caves are regarded as three most famous caves in China. Lots of historical materials concerning art, music, religion, calligraphy, medicine, costume and architecture are kept in Longmen Caves. There are as many as 100,000 statues within the 1,400 caves, ranging from one inch to 57 feet in height. These works that are entirely devoted to the Buddhist religion, represent the peak of Chinese stone carving art.

Culture Note 2

Shennongjia Forestry District is located in the northwest of Hubei province, which is bounded by mountains, covering a total area of about 3,253 square kilometers. The forest fraction of coverage is 69.5%. It borders on Xiangyang, Shiyan, Yichang, and Wushan county of Chongqing city. The ridge extends from southwest to northeast over 3,000 square kilometers. Known as "The Oriental Botanic Garden" and the natural gene bank of biological species, Shennongjia shelters some of the world's rare or endangered plants and animals.

Culture Note 3

Before **printing** was invented, a scholar had to copy characters one by one if he wanted to publish a new book. During the Northern Song Dynasty, Bi Sheng invented the movable-type printing after many years of experimentation. He engraved the characters on small pieces of clay, and heated them until they became hard movable characters. When printing a book, people placed the moveable characters in order into a whole block and then ran off a print. After printing, they took the block apart and reused the characters later. This method was both economical and time-saving.

Culture Note 4

Oracle Bones Provide a Glimpse into History

In the Shang Dynasty, a lunar eclipse was observed, and the scene was engraved on oracle bones. Including this event, six solar and lunar eclipses, on oracle bones found in existence, have been deciphered by researchers. The inscriptions predominantly carved on tortoise shells, cattle scapula and other animal bones, progressed, and are today viewed as the earliest known form of Chinese characters. How people back then reacted to the celestial events is relatively unknown, although it is believed that Shang people began to learn more about observing eclipses. The recordings are helping researchers date the oracle bones and understand the course of the Shang Dynasty, and they can be used as references for further study of the Sun-Earth-Moon system.

 Further Reading

Passage 1

Pre-made Chinese Cuisine Finding Niche in Canada

People think of their faraway loved ones more than ever during festivals. For the Chinese,

Chapter Two The United States of America

festivals mean family reunions and delicious food. Now, pre-made Chinese cuisine—or ready-to-cook dishes—can cure overseas Chinese homesickness. Chinese pre-made cuisine industry has developed rapidly in the past few years with the formation of a group of powerful leading enterprises. The technologies and supply chains of these enterprises are already very mature, and in some fields, they have achieved international leadership. High-quality and cheap Chinese prepared dishes, especially Guangdong-prepared dishes with the most advanced technology and products, can greatly diversify Canadian meals.

Passage 2

China to Contribute 40% to Global Economic Growth, Economist Says

China's economy is expected to grow by 5.7% in 2023, contributing to around 40% of the global economic growth, said Robin Xing, Morgan Stanley's chief China economist. The world's second-largest economy will play a key role in boosting global economic growth this year, and China's growth prospects will have positive spillover effects for other economies in areas like trade and tourism, Xing told the media in Beijing. "Both the United States and Europe may face a year of subdued growth, and China, with an anticipated 5.7% growth in 2023, will benefit them a lot," Xing said. Looking ahead, Xing said China will likely set a 2023 GDP growth target of above 5%, with measures such as further waves of monetary and fiscal easing to support the rebound.

Chapter Three
Australia

Contents

1. Location and Resources
2. History and Symbols
3. Education and Recreation
4. Politics and Economy
5. Culture and Customs
6. Intercultural Communication

aborigine	原住民	**kangaroo**	袋鼠
Australia Day	澳大利亚日	**koala bear**	考拉熊
Australian Dollar	澳元	**Melbourne**	墨尔本
Australian Merino	澳洲美利奴羊	**Sydney Harbor Bridge**	悉尼海港大桥
Australian Open	澳大利亚网球公开赛	**Sydney Opera House**	悉尼歌剧院
Australian Rules Football	澳式足球	**the Governor-General of the Commonwealth of Australia**	澳大利亚总督
Boomerang	回飞镖	**the Great Barrier Reef**	大堡礁
Canberra	堪培拉(首都)	**The Twelve Apostle**	十二使徒岩
Gold Coast	黄金海岸	**Qantas**	澳洲航空
golden wattle	金合欢	**windsurfing**	帆板运动

Chapter Three Australia

Unit 1 Location and Resources

Text Focus

1. Geographical Location
2. Weather and Climate
3. Natural Resources

3.1 Lecture1 Location.mp4

3.2 Lecture2 People.mp4

Vocabulary

1. approximately   [əˈprɒksɪmətli]   adv.   大约
2. territory   [ˈterətri]   n.   领地
3. temperate   [ˈtempərət]   adj.   温和的
4. sub-zero   [ˌsʌbˈzɪərəʊ]   adj.   零下的
5. distribute   [dɪˈstrɪbjuːt]   v.   分布

Australia, officially Commonwealth of Australia, is the smallest continent and the sixth largest country (in area) on Earth. Surrounded by the Indian Ocean and the South Pacific, Australia is the only nation in the southern hemisphere to occupy an entire continent. Owing to its location, its climate is notably affected by ocean currents. Australia has rich deposits of minerals, such as coal, natural gas, uranium ore, iron ore, nickel, zinc and gold. Canberra, Australia's capital city, is roughly half way between the two largest cities Melbourne and Sydney.

Geographical Location

Australia is located in the southern hemisphere and it occupies the smallest one of the seven continents. Lying between the Indian and Pacific oceans, the country is ***approximately***[1] 4,000 kilometers from east to west and 3,600 kilometers from north to south, with a coastline 36,735 kilometers long, and it is also an island of around 7,690,000 square kilometers, the sixth largest country(in area), smaller than Russia, Canada, China, the United States and Brazil, roughly four fifths of the size of China.

Australia has three major physiographic regions. More than half of its land area is on the Western Australian plateau, which includes the outcrops of Arnhem Land and the Kimberley region in the northwest and the Macdonnell Ranges in the east. The second region, the Interior Lowlands, lies east of the plateau. The Eastern Uplands, which include the Great Dividing Range, are a series of high ridges, plateaus, and basins. The country's highest point is Mount Kosciuszko in the Australian Alps, and the lowest is Lake Eyre. Major rivers include the Murray-Darling system, the Flinders and Swan rivers, and Cooper Creek. There are many islands and reefs along the coast, including the Great Barrier Reef, Melville Island, Kangaroo Island and Tasmania.

Politically, Australia is divided into six states and two ***territories***[2]. The six states include New South Wales, Victoria, Queensland, South Australia, Western Australia and Tasmania. The two territories are the Northern Territory and the Australian Capital Territory.

Canberra in aboriginal language means a meeting place and it is the capital city of Australia. Being Australia's largest inland city, it is located at the northern end of the Australian Capital Territory(ACT), about 280 kilometers southwest of Sydney, and 660 kilometers northeast of Melbourne. As the seat of the government of Australia, Canberra is the site of Parliament House, the High Court and numerous government departments and agencies. It is also the location of many social and cultural institutions of national significance. The city's design was influenced by the garden city movement and incorporates significant areas of natural vegetation that have earned Canberra the title of the "bush capital".

Sydney(Fig. 3-1), Australia's largest and oldest city, is also an increasingly international metropolis and the host city to the 2000 Sydney Olympic Games. It was founded in 1788 as a penal colony and quickly became a major trading center. It is built on low hills surrounding one of the world's finest natural harbors, which supports extensive port facilities. It is dominated by Sydney Harbor Bridge, one of the biggest single-span bridges in the world, and the Sydney Opera House. Sydney has an area of more than 12,000 square kilometers. It has taken over from its closest rival, Melbourne, as the financial center of the country, and likes to think of itself as the more worldly capital. After all, it has beaches, rugby, and Rose Bay Bridge, Queen Victoria building, and so on. The city is widely known for its water sports, recreational facilities, and cultural life. It is the site of the Universities of Sydney and New South Wales and Macquarie University.

Fig. 3-1 Sydney

Melbourne is located in the southeast of Australia, capital city of the Australian state of

Victoria, and is known as the "Garden State." It was the financial center of Australia and now is considered as the cultural center, and more Victorian in attitude and style than Sydney. This city has attracted travelers from all over the world, reasons range from the country's glorious history of human culture to its tempting entertainment and food.

Weather and Climate

The majority of Australia experiences ***temperate***[3] weather for most of the year. The northern states of Australia are typically warm all the time, with the southern states experiencing cool winters but rarely ***sub-zero***[4] temperatures.

Snow falls on the higher mountains during the winter months, enabling skiing in southern New South Wales and Victorian ski resorts, as well as the smaller resorts in Australia's island state, Tasmania. Most of Australia is warm and dry, and the southern part is the most comfortable, with temperatures in Melbourne averaging 9℃ in July, to 20℃ in January.

Due to the country's vast size, the climate in Australia varies tremendously with different climate zones. The center of Australia, which is the largest part of the island, has a warm desert climate and is surrounded by a large zone of warm steppe climate. Much of the northern part of the country has a tropical predominantly summer rainfall climate. The southwest corner of the country has a Mediterranean climate. Much of the southeast is temperate. Because Australia is located in the southern hemisphere, seasons are exactly opposite of ours. When winter falls in China, summer will start in Australia and the other way around.

Because Australia is close to the equator, it's a relatively warm country. In the northern part temperatures will still be above 20℃ during the winter. Only in some southern parts will there be a slight chance of frost or snow. Australia is also rather dry. Over half of the country gets less than 500 millimeters of rain a year.

Australia's size gives it a wide variety of landscapes, with subtropical rain forests in the northeast, mountain ranges in the southeast, with the oldest and least fertile soils; desert or semi-arid land commonly known as the outback makes up by far the largest portion of land. As the driest inhabited continent, only its southeast and southwest corners have a temperate climate.

The climate of Australia is significantly influenced by ocean currents, which is correlated with periodic drought and the seasonal tropical low pressure system that produces cyclones in northern Australia. These factors induce rainfall to vary markedly from year to year. Rainfall in Australia has slightly increased over the past century. Water restrictions are frequently in place in many regions and cities of Australia in response to chronic water shortages due to urban population increases and localized drought. Throughout much of the continent, major flooding regularly follows extended periods of drought, flushing out inland river systems, overflowing dams and inundating large inland flood plains.

Natural Resources

Australia is well endowed with an abundance of both fossil and renewable fuels. It is estimated that Australia has over 147 billion tons of coal reserves, over one quarter of which is black coal deposited in Permian sediments in the Sydney Basin of New South Wales and in Queensland. Brown coal suitable for electricity production is found in Victoria. Australia meets its domestic coal consumption needs with its own reserves and exports the surplus.

Natural gas fields are liberally distributed throughout the country and now supply most of Australia's domestic needs. There are commercial gas fields in every state and pipelines connecting those fields to major cities. All in all, Australia has trillions of tons of estimated natural gas reserves trapped in sedimentary strata ***distributed***[5] around the continent.

Australia has rich deposits of uranium ore, which is refined for the use of fuel for the nuclear power industry. Western Queensland near Mount Isa and Cloncurry, contains three billion tons of uranium ore reserves. There are also uranium deposits in Arnhem Land in far northern Australia, as well as in Queensland and Victoria.

The Western Australian Shield is rich in nickel deposits and zinc reserves. Besides, gold production in Australia, which was substantial earlier in the century, has declined from a peak production of four million fine ounces in 1904 to several hundred thousand fine ounces. A vast diamond deposit was found in Western Australia in 1979.

Exercises

I. *Try to answer the following questions according to your understanding of the text.*

(1) What is Australia like in terms of land area, compared with other countries like China?

(2) Why is Canberra entitled the "bush capital"?

(3) Which city is the host to the 2000 Summer Olympic Games?

(4) What are the effects of the factors mentioned in the text on the climate of Australia?

(5) What kinds of natural resources is Australia rich in? Where can they be found?

II. *Read the following passage carefully, and make a comment on it at the end of the passage in no more than 100 words.*

Australia has some of the oldest geological features in the world with the oldest known rocks dating from more than 3,000 million years ago and rare zircon crystals dating back 4,400 million years located in much younger rocks. The zircons evolved very soon after the planet was formed. These ancient features compare with the oldest known rock on Earth in northwestern Canada. Scientists say that rock was formed 4,031 million years ago.

Some areas of Victoria and Queensland are geologically much younger as a result of volcanic activity which last erupted a few thousand years ago. Australia's youngest mainland volcano is

Mount Gambier in South Australia which last erupted only about 6,000 years ago. Formed more than 2,700 million years ago, Wave Rock is 14 meters high, and 110 meters long. The granite cliff resembling a wave about to break is on the northern face of a large erosional remnant called Hyden Rock. This curved cliff face is 15 meters high and 110 meters long which has been rounded by weathering and water erosion, undercutting its base and leaving a rounded overhang. It was formed by water dissolving and redepositing chemicals in the granite as it runs down the cliff face.

In recent years, the advent of improved technology and more extensive geological exploration has resulted in a greater knowledge of the age of rocks in Australia. It has resulted also in an increased ability to better understand the continent's past. This has been achieved by combining exploration methods such as deep seismic surveys with geochronology methods, including use of equipment such as the Sensitive High-Resolution Ion Microprobe, or SHRIMP. This equipment uses uranium and lead isotopes from tiny portions of zircon crystals which have been extracted from rock samples to calculate the age of the crystal based on the natural decay rate of uranium to lead. The SHRIMP is central to Geoscience Australia's geochronology program.

Comments:

Australia is rich in fossil fuels and deposits. And what is your point of view in exploiting those natural resources?

Reference:

Argument:

(1) Meeting the needs of human for natural resources

(2) Promoting economic development

(3) Creating employment opportunities

Counter-argument:

(1) Destroying the ecological environment

(2) Causing resource waste without a proper plan

(3) Exacerbating resource shortages

Unit 2　History and Symbols

Text Focus

1. Historical Periods
2. Historical Figures
3. National Symbols

3.3 Lecture3 History.mp4

Vocabulary

1. aborigine	[ˌæbəˈrɪdʒəni]	n.	土著居民
2. convict	[kənˈvɪkt]	n.	罪犯
3. conscription	[kənˈskrɪpʃn]	n.	征兵
4. outbreak	[ˈaʊtbreɪk]	n.	爆发
5. context	[ˈkɒntekst]	n.	背景

Australia's first inhabitants were the aboriginal people. Its history began when the European explored this country. In the century that followed, the British established colonies on the continent, and the European explorers ventured into its interior. Modern Australia came into being in 1901 and then was greatly affected by the two World Wars. Many well-known historical figures showed a great influence on the history of Australia, such as Edmund Barton, John Monash and Catherine Helen Spence. The Commonwealth Coat of Arms is one of Australia's national symbols, reflecting different aspects of its history.

Historical Periods

The first inhabitants of Australia were the *aborigines*[1] (Fig. 3-2), who are believed to have arrived in Australia 40,000 to 60,000 years ago from Southeast Asia. They developed a hunter-gatherer lifestyle, established enduring spiritual and artistic traditions, and used stone technologies.

Fig. 3-2 Aborigines

The period of European discovery and settlement began with Dutch, Portuguese, and Spanish ships sighting Australia in the 17th century. The British arrived in 1688, but it was not until Captain James Cook's voyage in 1770 that Great Britain claimed possession of the vast island, calling it New South Wales. A British penal colony was set up at Port Jackson (what is now Sydney) in 1788, and about 161,000 transported English *convicts*[2] were settled there until the system was suspended in 1839. Free settlers and former prisoners established six colonies: New South Wales, Tasmania, Western Australia, South Australia, Victoria and Queensland.

The Australian colonies of New South Wales, South Australia, Tasmania, and Victoria achieved self-government during 1855 and 1856. Queensland received a constitution similar to that of New South Wales when it was separated from the latter and established as a new colony in 1859. Western Australia remained under the old system owing to its small population and limited economic growth. Democratic political practices developed rapidly after the new constitutions came into force. The 1870s and 1880s were decades of great economic development in the

Australian colonies. Gold rushes and agricultural industries brought prosperity.

The Commonwealth of Australia was established on January 1, 1901. After approval of a draft constitution by Australian voters, the British Parliament had passed legislation in 1900 to enable the commonwealth to come into existence. The constitution gave the commonwealth, or federal government, certain defined powers—all residual powers were given to the governments of the six colonies, which were renamed states.

World War I had a devastating effect on Australia. There were less than three million men in 1914, and around 420,000 of them volunteered for service in the war. An estimated 60,000 died and tens of thousands were wounded in action. In response, the Australian Government established the "Soldier Settler Scheme", providing farmland and funds to returning soldiers. When the Great Depression hit in 1929, social and economic divisions widened and many Australian financial institutions collapsed.

During **World War II**, Australian forces made a significant contribution to the Allied victory in Europe, Asia and the Pacific. In February of 1942, the largest single attack ever conducted by a foreign military power on Australia took place in Darwin. The generation who fought in the war and survived came out of it with a sense of pride. When World War II ended in 1945, hundreds of thousands of migrants from across Europe and the Middle East arrived in Australia, with many finding jobs in the booming manufacturing sector.

In **the post-World War II era**, Australians were swept up in the revolutionary atmosphere of the 1960s. Australia's new ethnic diversity and increasing independence from Britain contributed to an atmosphere of political, economic and social change. In 1972, the Australian Labor Party under the idealistic leadership of Gough Whitlam was elected to power, ending the post-war domination of the Liberal and Country Party coalition. Over the next three years, his new government ended ***conscription***[3], abolished university fees, introduced free universal health care, abandoned the White Australia policy, embraced multiculturalism and introduced no-fault divorce and equal pay for women. However, by 1975, inflation and scandal led to the Governor-General dismissing the government. In the subsequent general election, the Labor Party suffered a major defeat and the Liberal-National Coalition ruled until 1983.

Between 1983 and 1996, the Hawke-Keating Labor governments introduced a number of economic reforms, such as deregulating the banking system and floating the Australian dollar. In 1996, a Coalition Government led by John Howard won the general election and was re-elected in 1998, 2001 and 2004. The Liberal-National Coalition Government enacted several reforms, including changes in the taxation and industrial relations systems. In 2007, the Labor Party, led by Kevin Rudd, was elected with an agenda to reform Australia's industrial relations system, cut greenhouse emissions and implement a national curriculum in education. Three years later, Rudd was challenged by Julia Gillard who was to become the first female Prime Minister of Australia. In 2013, the new Coalition government was sworn in, led by Tony Abbott. In September, 2015,

Abbott was defeated in a leadership ballot by Malcolm Turnbull, who was re-elected in a general election in July 2016. In May, 2022, Anthony Albanese has claimed victory for his Labor Party after Prime Minister Scott Morrison conceded defeat in Australia's 2022 federal election.

Historical Figures

Edmund Barton(Figure 3-3) (1849—1920) was the first Prime Minister of Australia and a founding member of the High Court of Australia. In the late 1870s, Barton's attention turned to politics, elected to the seat of University of Sydney in the state legislative assembly in 1879 after two unsuccessful attempts. In 1882, he became Speaker of the assembly. Through the late 1880s Barton sat in the Legislative Council. For much of 1902, Barton was in England for the coronation of Edward VII—the trip was also used for the negotiation of a permanent British naval presence. In 1903, Barton left Parliament to become one of the initial group of judges of the High Court of Australia. In 1911, he was acting chief justice. Barton died suddenly of heart failure at Medlow Bath in the Blue Mountains on January 7th, 1920.

Fig. 3-3　Edmund Barton

Fig. 3-4　John Monash

John Monash(Fig. 3-4) (1865—1931) was a civil engineer and an Australian military commander of World War I. He commanded the 13th Infantry Brigade before the war and then, shortly after its ***outbreak***[4], became commander of the fourth Brigade in Egypt, with whom he took part in the Gallipoli campaign. In July 1916, he took charge of the newly raised third division in northwestern France and in May 1918 became commander of the Australian Corps, at the time the largest corps on the Western Front. The successful Allied attack at the Battle of Amiens on August 8th, 1918, which expedited the end of the war, was planned by Monash and spearheaded by British forces including the Australian and Canadian Corps under Monash and Arthur Currie. Monash is considered one of the best Allied generals of World War I and the most famous commander in Australian history.

Catherine Helen Spence(Fig. 3-5) (1825—1910) was one of the most prolific Australian authors who drew a vivid picture of South Australia through her writings and lectures. She won reputation as a literary critic and social reporter and her articles were published in many South Australian newspapers and magazines. She was also a famous suffragist and Australia's first female political candidate to run for the elections. She was 67 when she started her campaign but her enthusiasm was that of a young woman. She represented the Federal Convention at Adelaide though unsuccessfully. Catherine Helen Spence contributed to the accomplishment of the women's suffrage movement. Spence dedicated her life for the education of girl children and betterment of the poor. Miles Franklin called her the "Greatest Australian Woman". On her 80th birthday, the image of this "Grand Old Woman of Australia" was placed on the Federation Australian five-dollar note. As a sign of her ever-present influence, Adelaide's daily newspaper *The Advertiser* included her name in its list of the ten greatest South Australians of the 20th century. Spence described herself as "a clear-brained commonsense woman of the world".

Fig. 3-5 Catherine Helen Spence

National Symbols

Australia has no official animal symbol. Its national floral emblem is the Golden Wattle, and its national gemstone is the opal. The tune of *Advance Australia Fair* has been Australia's official national anthem since April 19, 1984. The national flag itself features the Southern Cross, a constellation often related to Australia. The stars of the Southern Cross represent Australia's geographic position in the Southern Hemisphere. The large Commonwealth star symbolizes the federation of the states and territories, and the Union Jack reflects Australia's early ties to the Great Britain. Green and gold, long associated with Australian sporting achievements, hold a treasured place in the Australian imagination.

The Commonwealth Coat of Arms(Fig. 3-6) is the formal symbol of the Commonwealth of Australia and its ownership and authority. Symbols of Australia's six states appear together on the shield, which are the central feature of the coat of arms. In the top half, from left to right, the states represented are: New South Wales, Victoria and Queensland. In the bottom half, from left to right: South Australia, Western Australia, and Tasmania. The border of the shield symbolizes federation. A gold Commonwealth Star sits above the shield. Six of the star's points represent the Australian states. The seventh point represents the combined territories. A wreath of gold and blue sits under the Commonwealth Star. The kangaroo and the emu are the native animals that hold the shield with pride. Its background is wreath of Golden Wattle, the official national floral emblem. At the bottom of the coat of arms is a scroll that contains the name of the nation.

These formal symbols have assisted in the establishment of a national consciousness. Flora and fauna native to the continent, such as the kangaroo, koala, emu, and wattle, are symbols of the national ethos, especially in national and international ***contexts***[5], although this is also the case for unique buildings such as the Sydney Harbor Bridge and the Sydney Opera House.

Fig. 3-6　The Commonwealth Coat of Arms

Exercises

I. *Try to answer the following questions according to your understanding of the text.*

(1) What was the life of the aborigines like?

(2) Did six Australian colonies achieve self-government at the same time? Why or why not?

(3) Why is John Monash regarded as one of the best Allied generals of World War I?

(4) What is the Commonwealth Coat of Arms made up of?

(5) What are the national symbols related to and what national symbols can you think of when it comes to Australia?

II. *Read the following passage carefully, and make a comment on it at the end of the passage in no more than 100 words.*

At a time when Australia was not yet a nation but still a number of separate British colonies, gold was discovered in a number of places, and the gold rush that followed changed its history. In the early days, traces of gold had been found but were hushed by the government, in fear that convicts and settlers would abandon the settlements to seek their fortunes. However, in February 1851, a man named Hargraves found gold in near Bathurst, New South Wales, and words quickly spread. Within a week there were over 400 people digging there for gold, and by June there were 2,000. They named the goldfield Ophir after a city of gold in the Bible. The Australian gold rush had begun!

People came from all over the world, intending to strike it rich and return home to their own countries. For many, the journey to Australia took seven or eight months, and on the cheapest fares, conditions were tough. There were many epidemics of illness on the ships, and those who survived the journey arrived at the goldfields weak and unfit for the hard life on the diggings.

Fresh food at the diggings was limited, and the basic diet was mutton, damper and tea. Clean water was in short supply because the diggers muddied the creeks, so cleanliness was difficult. Sewerage was not disposed of in a sanitary fashion, and disease was common. There were a few doctors or chemists at the diggings, but not all were qualified. Many people died of diseases such as dysentery or typhoid.

At the diggings, the gullies were filled with claims, and so the higher ground nearby soon became huge campsites. People lived in tents at first, but later on huts made from canvas, wood and bark were built. Gradually, there were stores and traders and other amenities, but life remained hard. Food and other goods had to be brought in by cart and so were very expensive. The settlements were all rather makeshift and temporary. Gold buyers and traders set up stores. Hotels and boarding houses were established, built of wood and lined with calico.

Comments:

What are the positive and negative influences brought by the gold rush in Australia?

Reference:

Argument:

(1) Changing the course of Australian history

(2) Expanding Australia's population

(3) Boosting economy

Counter-argument:

(1) Leading to the emergence of a new colony

(2) Starting a series of rushes that transformed the nation

(3) Being greedy and lured by gold

Unit 3 Education and Recreation

Text Focus

1. School Education
2. Famous Universities
3. Cultural Life

3.4 Lecture4 Education.mp4

 Vocabulary

1. relatively	[ˈrelətɪvli]	adv.	相对地
2. syllabus	[ˈsɪləbəs]	n.	教学大纲

3. certificate	[səˈtɪfɪkət]	n.	证书
4. faculty	[ˈfæklti]	n.	系
5. philosopher	[fəˈlɒsəfə(r)]	n.	哲学家

Education in Australia is primarily the responsibility of the states and territories. Each state or territory government provides funding and regulates the public and private schools within its governing area. The education system in Australia provides primary, secondary and tertiary education. Compulsory education in Australia starts at around the age of five or six, with minor variations between the states and territories. There are many world-famous universities like the University of Sydney, the University of Melbourne, and the University of Queensland, etc. Australians love sport, which is an important part of Australian culture. Also, media outlets like ABC and SBS provide radio and television services not only to the locals but also to overseas audience; and almost all the people in Australia participate in the arts activities every year.

School Education

Generally, education in Australia follows the three-tier model which includes primary education, secondary education and tertiary education. Preschool, also known as kindergarten in some states and territories in Australia, is ***relatively***[1] unregulated, and is not compulsory. They're usually run by the state and territory governments, except in Victoria, South Australia and New South Wales where they are more often run by local councils, community groups or private organizations.

School education in Australia is compulsory between certain ages as specified by state or territory legislation. Depending on the state or territory, and date of birth of the child, school is compulsory from the age of five to six to the age of fifteen to seventeen. In recent years, over three quarters of students stay at school until they are seventeen.

Government schools, also known as public schools, are free to attend for Australian citizens and permanent residents, while independent schools usually charge attendance fees. In addition to attendance fees, however, stationery, textbooks, uniforms, school camps and other schooling costs are not covered under government funding.

Regardless of whether the schools are part of the government or independent systems, they are required to adhere to the same curriculum frameworks of their state or territory. The curriculum framework, however, provides some flexibility in the ***syllabus***[2]. Most school students wear uniforms, although there are varying expectations and some Australian schools do not require uniforms.

Students may be slightly younger or older than stated below, due to variation between states and territories. The name for the first year of primary school varies considerably between states and territories. For example, what is known as kindergarten in ACT and NSW may mean the year preceding the first year of primary school or preschool in other states and territories. Some states vary in whether Year 7 is part of the primary or secondary years, as well as the existence of a middle school system.

The academic year in Australia varies between states and institutions, but generally runs from late January or early February until mid-December for primary and secondary schools, and from late February until mid-November for universities with seasonal holidays and breaks for each educational institute.

The Melbourne Declaration on Educational Goals for Young Australians provides the policy framework for the Australian Curriculum. It includes two goals: Australian schooling promotes equity and excellence; all young Australians become successful learners, confident and creative individuals and active and informed citizens.

Higher education, also referred to as tertiary education, is generally provided by universities and by other higher education institutions such as Technical and Further Education institutes (TAFEs) and Registered Training Organizations (RTO). Tertiary education in Australia is primarily studying at a university or technical college in order to receive a qualification or further skills and training. A tertiary education institution is a body that is established or recognized by or under the law of the Commonwealth, or a state or territory. It has to be approved by the Australian Government before it can receive grants or its students can receive assistance from the Australian Government under the Higher Education Support Act 2003. After meeting the minimum requirements of being established, the institution carries on business in Australia with its central management and control in Australia; and its main purpose is to provide education and or to conduct research. A higher education provider either fulfills the tuition assurance requirements or is exempted from those requirements by the minister.

In Australia, higher education awards are classified as follows:

Certificates[3], diplomas and associate degrees, which take one to two years to complete, and consist primarily of coursework. These are primarily offered by TAFEs and other institutions as vocational training.

Bachelor's degrees, generally the first university degree undertaken, which take three to four years to complete, and consist primarily of coursework. Bachelor's degrees are sometimes awarded with honors to the best-performing students.

In some courses, honors is awarded on the basis of performance throughout the course, but normally honors consists of undertaking a year of research. If honors is undertaken as an extra year, it is known as an honors degree rather than a degree with honors. Generally, one must be invited by the university to do honors as an additional year of study, as opposed to being something a student can apply for and it is often only offered to the highest ranking students of that year group.

Australian Bachelor's degrees are usually three years in duration. The length of the degree usually depends on the field of study. Australian universities tend to have less of an emphasis on a liberal education than many universities in the United States, which is reflected in the shorter length of Australian degrees.

Master's degrees, which are undertaken after the completion of one or more Bachelor's degrees, deal with a subject at a more advanced level than Bachelor's degrees, and can consist either of research, coursework, or a mixture of the two.

Doctorates are undertaken after an Honors Bachelor's or a Master's degree, by an original research project resulting in a thesis or dissertation. Higher Doctorates, such as Doctor of Science or Doctor of Letters are awarded on the basis of a record of original research or of publications over many years.

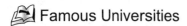
Famous Universities

The University of Sydney(Fig. 3-7) is an Australian public research university in Sydney, Australia. Founded in 1850, it was Australia's first university and is regarded as one of the world's leading universities. It is ranked in the top 20 universities in the world. The university comprises eight *faculties*[4] and schools, through which it offers Bachelor's, Master's and Doctoral degrees.

Fig. 3-7　The coat of arms for the University of Sydney

The university is colloquially known as one of Australia's sandstone universities. Its campus is ranked in the top ten of the world's most beautiful universities by the British *Daily Telegraph* and the *Huffington Post*, spreading across the inner-city suburbs of Camperdown and Darlington.

Seven Nobel and two Crafoord laureates have been affiliated with the university as graduates and faculties.

Fig. 3-8　The coat of arms for the University of Melbourne

The University of Sydney is a member of the Group of Eight, Academic Consortium 21, the Association of Pacific Rim Universities, the Association of Southeast Asian Institutions of Higher Learning, the Australia-Africa Universities Network, the Association of Commonwealth Universities and the Worldwide Universities Network.

The University of Melbourne(Fig. 3-8) is a public research university located in Melbourne, Australia. Founded in 1853, it is Australia's second oldest university and the oldest in Victoria.

Melbourne's main campus is located in Parkville, an inner suburb north of the Melbourne central business district, with several other campuses located across Victoria. Melbourne is a sandstone university and a member of the Group of Eight, Universitas 21 and the Association of Pacific Rim Universities.

The University of Melbourne has a number of prominent alumni in the community spanning many different areas including academics, architects, historians, poets, ***philosophers***[5], politicians, scientists, physicists, authors, industry leaders, corporate leaders and artists.

The University of Queensland (UQ)(Fig. 3-9) is a research university primarily located in Queensland's capital city, Brisbane, Australia. Founded in 1909 by the state parliament, UQ is Australia's fifth oldest university and is colloquially known as a sandstone university. The main St. Lucia campus occupies much of the riverside inner suburb of St Lucia, southwest of the Brisbane central business district. Other UQ campuses and facilities are located throughout Queensland, the largest of which are the Gatton campus and the Mayne Medical School. The University of Queensland's overseas establishments include the Brunei Clinical School and the UQ-Ochsner Clinical School in Louisiana, the United States.

Fig. 3-9 The coat of arms for the University of Queensland

The university offers Associate's, Bachelor's, Master's and Doctoral degrees. The University of Queensland incorporates over 100 research institutes and centers, such as the Boeing Research and Technology Australia Center, the Australian Institute for Bioengineering and Nanotechnology and the UQ Dow Center. Recent research achievements of the university include pioneering the invention of the HPV vaccine that prevents cervical cancer and the development of high-performance superconducting MRI magnets for portable scanning of human limbs. The University of Queensland is a founding member of online higher education consortium edX, Australia's research-intensive Group of Eight, and the global Universitas 21 network.

The University of Queensland is consistently ranked highly for business administration, mining engineering and life sciences in Australia. Over recent decades, UQ has produced notable alumni across a range of professions.

Cultural Life

Sports are a huge part of the culture in terms of spectating and participation in Australia. Even before Australia became a British colony, people were playing all kinds of sports, including cricket, horse racing, rugby, and football codes. Many Australians are passionate about sports.

Cricket is popular in the summer, and football codes are popular in the winter. It is generally agreed that cricket enjoys the most popularity in all parts of the country. Because of all of the excitement associated with sports in Australia, sports end up growing into part of Australia's national identity. Australians love sports. There are more than 95 National Sporting Organizations (NSOs) recognized by the Australian Sports Commission and thousands of local, regional and state sports bodies. Australia has hosted the summer Olympic Games twice (Melbourne 1956 and Sydney 2000). The world tennis circuit begins each year with the Australian Open in Melbourne.

Australia's warm climate and long coastline of sandy beaches and rolling waves provide ideal conditions for water sports such as swimming and surfing(Fig. 3-10). The majority of Australians live in cities or towns, on or near the coast, and so beaches are a place that millions of Australians visit regularly. Australians have a particular affinity for surf lifesaving, and surf lifesavers have a revered status in Australian culture. It forms part of a lifestyle in which millions participate and which millions more have an interest. The world's first surf lifesaving club, Bondi Surf Bathers' Life Saving Club, was founded at Bondi Beach, Sydney, in 1906.

Fig. 3-10 Surfing

Music: Australia is a music nation, and music has been woven into the fabric of this land through ceremony, celebration and culture. From the expression of Indigenous Australians to the contribution of migration, music is at the heart of how Australians come together and express themselves. It provides a soundtrack to what Australia tells the world. Many Australians listen to recorded music and more than half like to attend live music events.

Media: Australia has many media outlets. There are two national radio, television and online broadcasters that receive public funding—the Australian Broadcasting Corporation(ABC) (Fig. 3-11) and the Special Broadcasting Service(SBS). The ABC provides television, radio, online and mobile services across the country. Through its international charter, it also provides radio and television services to overseas audiences. The SBS broadcasts programs in English and a range of other languages, and covers news from all over the world. Australia also has three commercial free-to-air television networks, an indigenous commercial television station, hundreds of pay television channels, and many print, radio, digital and online media outlets.

Chapter Three Australia

Fig. 3-11 Logo of ABC

Arts: Australia has many publicly-run galleries, museums and performance spaces, from the World Heritage listed Opera House in Sydney and national galleries and museums in Canberra, to history museums and galleries in country towns. The Australia Council provides government funding to artists and arts organizations and Screen Australia supports Australia's film industry. Contemporary visual arts in Australia encompass photography, multimedia, sculpture, installations, drawings, paintings and performance art. Australia's performing arts groups, musicians, dance troupes and theatre performers display the energy and diversity of Australia's arts and many are involved in international exchanges. Opera Australia and the Australian Ballet regularly undertake world tours.

 Exercises

I. *Try to answer the following questions according to your understanding of the text.*

(1) Is school education in Australia all compulsory? Why or why not?

(2) What is the tertiary education in Australia like ?

(3) How is honors degree awarded to the students?

(4) What do the three universities introduced in the text have in common?

(5) Why are sports said to be huge part of culture in Australia? Which sport is the most popular?

II. *Read the following passage carefully, and make a comment on it at the end of the passage in no more than 100 words.*

Do you know Australia has the third highest number of international students in the world behind only the United Kingdom and the United States despite having a population of only 23 million? This isn't surprising when you consider Australia has seven of the top 100 universities in the world! With over 22,000 courses across 1,100 institutions.

These are strong academic credentials, but the institutions are just as highly rated as the cities that house them around the country. Australia has five of the 30 best cities in the world for students, based on student mix, affordability, quality of life, and employer activity—all important elements for students when choosing the best study destination. And with more than AUD$200 million provided by the Australian Government each year in international scholarships, they are making it easier for you to come and experience the difference an Australian education can make to your future career opportunities.

There is every chance Australia has students covered, with at least one Australian university in the top 50 worldwide across the study areas of Natural Sciences & Mathematics, Life & Agricultural Sciences, Clinical Medicine & Pharmacy and Physics.

Given this impressive education pedigree, it's not surprising there are now more than 2.5 million former international students who have gone on to make a difference after studying in Australia. Some of these students are among the world's finest minds. In fact, Australia has produced 15 Nobel prize laureates and every day, over one billion people around the world rely on Australian discoveries and innovations—including penicillin, IVF, ultrasound, Wi-Fi, the Bionic Ear, cervical cancer vaccine and Black Box Flight Recorder—to make their lives and the lives of others better.

Comments:

Each year, thousands of students study abroad. Some of the students would like to study abroad because they think they can acquire more advanced knowledge and technology; while others don't like it because they believe life is harder.

What is your opinion of studying abroad?

Reference:

Argument:

(1) Practicing the ability of independence and solving problems on one's own

(2) Learning how to allocate the time better

(3) Adapting oneself to a totally new environment and experiencing cultural differences

Counter-argument:

(1) Feeling homesick

(2) Being looked down upon

(3) Failing to cope with the problems that arise from cultural shock

Unit 4 Politics and Economy

Text Focus

1. Political System
2. Political Parties
3. Economy

3.5 Lecture5 Politics and Economy.mp4

Chapter Three Australia

Vocabulary

1. interpret	[ɪnˈtɜːprɪt]	v.	解释
2. bicameral	[ˌbaɪˈkæmərəl]	adj.	两院制的
3. ballot	[ˈbælət]	n.	投票
4. hierarchy	[ˈhaɪərɑːki]	n.	等级
5. coalesce	[ˌkəʊəˈles]	v.	合并
6. supplement	[ˈsʌplɪmənt]	v.	添加

The politics of Australia takes place within the framework of a federal parliamentary constitutional monarchy. Australia's system of government is based on the liberal democratic tradition. Its institutions and practices reflect British and North American models but are uniquely Australian. *The Constitution of Australia* sets out the rules and responsibilities of government and outlines the powers of its three branches—legislative, executive and judicial. The Labor Party and the Liberal Party are the two major political parties in Australia.

It's well known that Australia is one of the world's biggest producers of minerals and metals, and also a major exporter of agricultural products and energy. There are large companies like D'Arenberg, Barambah Organics.

Political System

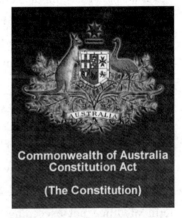

Fig. 3-12 *The Constitution of Australia*

The Constitution of Australia(Fig. 3-12) established a federal system of government, where powers are distributed between a national government and the six States. The Australian Capital Territory and the Northern Territory have self-government arrangements. Australia follows the British tradition of government. The Governor-General, representing The King/Queen, exercises the executive power of the Commonwealth. In practice, the Governor-General acts on the advice of the head of the Government, the Prime Minister, and other ministers. The Prime Minister leads a Cabinet of ministers, each of whom has responsibility for a portfolio of government duties. After a general election, the political party with the support of a majority of Members in the House of Representatives forms a government and its leader becomes the Prime Minister. Commonwealth ministers are appointed by the Governor-General on the advice of the Prime Minister. Similar systems operate in the states and territories.

The High Court of Australia and the Federal Court of Australia have the authority to *interpret*[1] constitutional provisions, with the Constitution vesting legislative power in federal parliament. The parliament makes laws, authorizes the Government to spend public money, scrutinizes government activities, and is a forum for debate on national issues.

The current Australian political system is not as old as that of Britain or the United States—elements of both of which have been borrowed.

The Constitution of Australia is the supreme law under which the Australian Commonwealth Government operates. It came into force when the six colonies federated to form the Commonwealth of Australia in 1901. *The Constitution* can be modified or changed only by referendum. Under Australia's common law system, the High Court of Australia and the Federal Court of Australia have the authority to interpret constitutional provisions. Their decisions determine the interpretation and application of the Constitution.

The Constitution follows two principles: the principle of federalism and the principle of responsible government. Federalism is necessarily associated with the principle of separation of powers. This separation of powers creates two tiers of government in Australia: the Commonwealth government and the state government. In this respect, the Australian system of government is based on the American model.

The Parliament of Australia, also known as the Commonwealth Parliament or Federal Parliament, is the legislative branch of the government of Australia. It is **bicameral**[2] and has been influenced both by the Westminster system and United States federalism. Parliament consists of three components: the Monarch, the Senate, and the House of Representatives. The Australian Parliament is the world's sixth oldest continuous democracy.

The Commonwealth Parliament was opened on May 9, 1901 in Melbourne by Prince George. On May 9, 1927, Parliament moved to the new national capital at Canberra. The new and permanent Parliament House was opened on May 9, 1988 by Queen Elizabeth II.

The Australian House of Representatives has 150 members, with each elected for a flexible term of office not exceeding three years, to represent a single electoral division, commonly referred to as an electorate or seat. The party or coalition of parties, which commands the confidence of a majority of members of the House of Representatives, forms government. The Australian Senate has 76 members. The six states return twelve senators each and the two territories two senators each, who are elected through the single transferable voting system. Senators are elected for flexible terms not exceeding six years, with half of the senators contesting at each federal election. The Senate is afforded substantial powers by *the Constitution*, and has the power to block legislation originating in the House as well as supply or monetary bills. The Queen of Australia is one of the components of Parliament. The constitutional functions of the Crown are given to the Governor-General, whom the Monarch appoints on the advice of the Prime Minister. Each of the two houses elects a presiding officer. The presiding officer of the Senate is called the President; that of the House is the Speaker. Elections for these positions are by secret *ballot*[3].

The principal function of the Parliament is to pass laws, or legislation. Any Senator or Member may introduce a proposed law, except for a money bill, proposing an expenditure or levying a tax, which must be introduced in the House of Representatives.

The High Court of Australia(Fig. 3-13) is the supreme court in the Australian court *hierarchy*[4] and the final court of appeal in Australia. It has both original and appellate jurisdiction, has the power of judicial review over laws passed by the Parliament of Australia and the parliaments of the States, and interprets the Constitution of Australia. It is composed of seven Justices: the Chief Justice of Australia and six other Justices. They are appointed by the Governor-General of Australia on the advice of

Fig. 3-13 The High Court of Australia

the federal government, and under the constitution must retire at the age of 70. The state supreme courts are also considered to be superior courts with unlimited jurisdiction to hear disputes, which are the pinnacle of the court hierarchy within their jurisdictions. The High Court has had a permanent home in Canberra since 1979. The majority of its sittings are held in the High Court building, which is situated in the Parliamentary Triangle overlooking Lake Burley Griffin.

Political Parties

Organized, national political parties have dominated Australia's political landscape since federation. The late 19th century saw the rise of the Australian Labour Party, which represented organized workers. Opposing interests *coalesced*[5] into two main parties: a center-right party with a base in business and the middle classes that has been predominantly conservative and moderate, now the Liberal Party of Australia; and a rural or agrarian conservative party, now the National Party of Australia.

Fig. 3-14 Australian Labor Party

Australian Labor Party(Fig. 3-14) is a social-democratic political party in Australia. It has been the governing party of the Commonwealth of Australia. In the state and territory parliaments, Labor governs in South Australia, Tasmania and the Australian Capital Territory. The party competes against the Liberal or National Coalition for political office at the federal and state level. It was founded as a federal party prior to the first sitting of the Australian Parliament in 1901, but was descended from Labor parties founded in the various Australian colonies by the emerging labor movement in Australia, formally beginning in 1891. Labor is thus the country's oldest political party.

Liberal Party of Australia(Fig. 3-15) is one of the two major Australian political parties. Founded a year after the 1943 election to replace the United Australia Party and its predecessors, the center-right Liberal Party competes with the center-left Australian Labor Party for political office. Federally, the Liberal Party runs in a coalition with the National Party, the Northern Territory Country Liberal Party, and Queensland Liberal branch, the Liberal National Party. Except for a few short periods, the Liberal Party and its predecessors have operated in similar coalitions since the 1920s.

Fig. 3-15 Liberal Party of Australia

Fig. 3-16 National Party of Australia

National Party of Australia(Fig. 3-16), also known as the Nationals or simply, the Nats, is an Australian political party. Traditionally representing graziers, farmers, and rural voters generally, it began as the Australian Country Party in 1920 at a federal level. It would later briefly adopt the name National Country Party in 1975, before adopting its current name in 1982. Federally, in New South Wales, and to an extent, in Victoria and historically in Western Australia, it has, in government, been the minor party in a center-right coalition with the Liberal Party of Australia, and its leader has usually served as Deputy Prime Minister.

While there are a small number of other political parties that have achieved parliamentary representation, these main three dominate organized politics everywhere in Australia and only on rare occasions have any other parties or independent members of parliament played any role at all in the formation or maintenance of governments.

Economy

Australia is one of the wealthiest Asia-Pacific nations and is a member of the APEC, G20, OECD and WTO. The economy of Australia is highly developed and one of the largest mixed market economies in the world. Trade is moderately important to Australia's economy; the combined value of exports and imports equals about 40% of GDP. Rich in natural resources, Australia is a major exporter of agricultural products, particularly wheat and wool(Fig. 3-17), minerals such as iron ore and gold, and energy in the forms of liquified natural gas and coal.

Fig. 3-17 Shaving wool

Chapter Three Australia

Australia has developed a wide edge in a range of goods and services, from high-technology products such as medical and scientific equipment through to wine and processed food. Major services exports include education, tourism, professional and technical services, and telecommunication,computer and information services. The wine industry is a significant contributor to the Australian economy through production, employment, export and tourism.

The beef industry is the largest agricultural enterprise in Australia, and it is one of the largest beef exporter in the world. Lamb has become an increasingly important product as the sheep industry has moved its focus from wool production to the production of prime lamb. The beef industry and the lamb industry are represented by Meat and Livestock Australia. Live export of cattle and sheep from Australia to Asia and the Middle East is a large part of Australian meat export. Domestic milk markets were heavily regulated until the 1980s, particularly for milk used for domestic fresh milk sales. This protected smaller producers in the northern states who produced exclusively for their local markets. Growth in the Australian dairy industry is dependent on expanding export markets. Exports are expected to continue to grow over time, particularly to Asia and the Middle East. Wool is still quite an important product of Australian agriculture. The Australian wool industry is widely recognized as producing the finest quality Merino wool. This is largely attributable to selective breeding and a superior genetic line.

Mining in Australia is a significant primary industry and contributor to the Australian economy. Historically, mining booms also encouraged immigration to Australia. Many different ores and minerals are mined throughout the country. Mining has had a substantial environmental impact in some areas of Australia.The minerals and fuels sector made the greatest contribution to Australia's exports.

D'Arenberg is an Australian wine company founded in 1912. All of its vineyards are located in South Australia's McLaren Vale wine region. It is now owned by the fourth generation of the Osborn family, headed by Chester-Osborn. D'Arenberg wines are known for the quirky names of their wines, and their specialism in the vines of the Rhône valley. They also produce many of their wines in a traditional manner, using basket pressing for both reds and whites and leaving the vast majority of the red wines unfiltered and unfined which can cause the wine to throw a sediment in bottle but leaves the flavour intact. The majority of their red wines are suitable for ageing as well as for drinking fairly young and even the cheaper wines show very well after a few years in bottle. Perhaps their best known wine is 'he Dead Arm Shira', made from fungus-infected shiraz grape vines.

Barambah Organics(Fig. 3-18) is an Australian-owned company based in South East QLD, producing high quality certified organic dairy products. Barambah Organics has two dairy farms located near Goondiwindi and Inglewood, 350

Fig. 3-18 Barambah Organics

kilometers southwest of Brisbane. The farms are well located on the Dumaresq River System and on the McIntyre Brook. Their cows graze on mixed pastures and are 80% grass fed. Their diet is **supplemented**[6] with grains and minerals during milking times. Barambah milk is always a pleasure to drink and use in the kitchen.

Exercises

I. *Try to answer the following questions according to your understanding of the text.*

(1) Is the Australian political system the same as that of Britain or the United States? Why?
(2) How many principles does the Australian Constitution follow? What are they?
(3) What is the role of the High Court of Australia and the state courts?
(4) What is a large part of Australian meat export? Why?
(5) What is D'Arenberg's traditional manner of producing wine?

II. *Read the following passage carefully, and make a comment on it at the end of the passage in no more than 100 words.*

Australia is strongly committed to building a rules-based international order which advances and protects the interests of nations and peoples. Australia plays an active role in a wide array of global and regional groups, including:

United Nations (UN)
Group of Twenty Major Economies (G20)
World Trade Organisation (WTO)
East Asia Summit (EAS)
Association of Southeast Asian Nations (ASEAN)
Asia-Pacific Economic Cooperation (APEC)
British Commonwealth
Organization for Economic Co-operation and Development (OECD)
Indian Ocean Rim Association (IORA)
Pacific Islands Forum (PIF)
Forum for East Asia-Latin America Cooperation (FEALAC)
International Climate Change Negotiations
Asia-Europe Meeting (ASEM)

Australia's foreign and trade policy focuses on strengthening its already significant engagement with countries in the dynamic Indo-Pacific region. As a founding member of APEC and an active participant in the East Asia Summit, Australia is helping to build regional institutions that foster stability, security and prosperity across the region.

Australia has close, longstanding bilateral ties with Indonesia, as well as strong ties with the other member nations of ASEAN. Australia also has significant relations with India and with the major states of Northeast Asia—China, Japan and the Republic of Korea—which are also major markets.

Beyond its region, Australia enjoys strong economic, security, political, social and cultural ties with the United States and Canada, and continues to build on its strong and longstanding political, cultural, trade, investment, and people-to-people links with the United Kingdom and Europe. Australia is committed to a broad-based, creative partnership with the European Union, addressing the contemporary challenges of economic management and international trade, development, security, and international governance.

Australia's connections with Latin American countries are expanding in a range of international forums, including in the WTO. Australia also has warm relations with Caribbean countries built on strong historical and cultural foundations.

Comments:

According to the passage and your information, what are Australia's strengths and weaknesses in developing its economy?

Reference:

Argument:

(1) Being one of the world's largest exporters of agricultural products, with abundant mineral resources

(2) Owning developed manufacturing and modern service industries

(3) Owning a vast market and a stable economic environment

Counter-argument:

(1) Being a relatively closed labor market

(2) Having relatively strict immigration policies

(3) Presenting a shortage of talents in the labor market

Unit 5   Culture and Customs

Text Focus

1. Traditional Culture
2. Literature Works
3. Food Customs

3.6 Lecture6 Customs.mp4   3.7 Lecture7 Culture.mp4

Vocabulary

1. diverge	[daɪˈvɜːdʒ]	v.	背离
2. enigmatic	[ˌenɪgˈmætɪk]	adj.	高深莫测的
3. wreath	[riːθ]	n.	花圈
4. designation	[ˌdezɪgˈneɪʃn]	n.	称号
5. lard	[lɑːd]	n.	烹调用的猪油

The culture of Australia is rich in both Indigenous and European tradition like the Aboriginal Dreamtime. The Australians celebrate a set of national holidays which are unique to their country and culture. There are many literature works written by Australian writers, who have obtained international renown, such as the Nobel winner Patrick White, the English-born Australian novelist Marcus Clarke, as well as author Peter Carey, etc. Whereas earlier food culture of modern Australia was influenced by British and Irish settlers, the 20th century food culture has been heavily influenced by Mediterranean and Asian cuisine.

Traditional Culture

The culture of Australia is essentially a Western culture influenced by the unique geography of the Australian continent, the diverse input of Aboriginal and Torres Strait Islander peoples, the British colonization of Australia, and the various waves of multi-ethnic migration. Since British settlement, however, Australian culture has ***diverged***[1] significantly, forming a distinct culture.

The Aboriginal Dreamtime, known as the mystical time when the aboriginal people established their world—prior to the invasion of the Europeans, is essentially the foundation of the aboriginal religion and culture. The myths are comparable to the American mythology and explain the creation of natural things such as the sun, the moon, etc. The Aboriginal Dreamtime explains the origins of the people and of the land, including a story of how things have happened, how the universe came to be, how humans were created, and how the Creator intended for humans to function in this world. It is believed that many of the Creators continued to live on the land or in the sky above watching over them. These supernatural ***enigmatic***[2] Creators were often referred to as men and women who had the ability to change shape into animals and other creatures such as the Rainbow Serpent.

Australia Day (Fig. 3-19) is the official national day of Australia. This holiday commemorates the anniversary of the day in 1788 when the English declared Australia a new colony. Although it was not known as Australia Day until over a century later, records of celebrations on January 26 date back to 1808, with the first official celebration of the formation of New South Wales held in 1818. It is presently an official public holiday in every state and territory of Australia and is marked by the presentation of the Australian of the Year Awards on Australia Day Eve, announcement of the Honors List for the Order of Australia and addresses from the Governor-General and the Prime Minister. With community festivals, concerts and citizenship ceremonies, the day is celebrated in large and small communities and cities around the nation. Australia Day has become the biggest annual civic event in Australia.

Fig. 3-19 Australia Day Celebration

Anzac Day, a day on which the country remembers those citizens who fell fighting or served the country in wars, is commemorated on April 25 every year. The tradition began to remember the Australian and New Zealand Army Corps soldiers who landed at Gallipoli in Turkey during World War I. It is probably considered the most important national occasion. Anzac Day is very special to Australians and commemorative services begin at dawn which feature marches by veterans and by solemn "Dawn Services". Veterans march through the streets of cities in the morning and share drinks and memories in the afternoon. During the day, the ceremonies always include an introduction, a hymn, a prayer, and address, laying of ***wreaths***[3], recitation, a period of silence, and the National Anthem. These ceremonies are held at war memorials around the country of Australia.

Literature Works

Australian literature is the written or literary work produced in the area or by the people of the Commonwealth of Australia and its preceding colonies. During its early Western history, Australia was a collection of British colonies, therefore, its literary tradition begins with and is linked to the broader tradition of English literature. However, the narrative art of Australian writers has, since 1788, introduced the character of a new continent into literature—exploring such themes as aboriginality, democracy, national identity, migration, Australia's unique location and geography, the complexities of urban living, and so on.

The Eye of the Storm(Fig. 3-20) is the 9th published novel by the Australian novelist and 1973 Nobel Prizewinner, Patrick White. It tells the story of Elizabeth Hunter, the powerful matriarch of her family, who still maintains a destructive iron grip on those who come to say farewell to her in her final moments upon her deathbed. It is regarded as one of White's best novels, largely owing to the reputation it received from the Swedish Academy when they specifically named it as the book that confirmed Patrick White's **designation**[4] as a Literature Laureate. In 2011, Fred Schepisi's film of *The Eye of the Storm* was released with screenplay adaptation by Judy Morris. This is the first screen realization of a White novel, fittingly the one that played a key role in the Swedish panel's choice of White as Nobel Prize Winner.

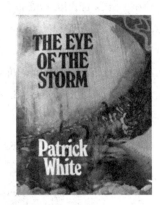

Fig. 3-20 The Eye of the Storm

For the Term of His Natural Life, written by Marcus Clarke, an English-born Australian novelist, was published in the *Australian Journal* between 1870 and 1872, appearing as a novel in 1874. It is the best known novelization of life as a convict in early Australian history. The book clearly conveys the harsh and inhumane treatment meted out to the convicts, some of whom were transported for relatively minor crimes, and graphically describes the conditions the convicts experienced. The novel is based on the research by the author as well as a visit to the penal settlement of Port Arthur, Tasmania. The novel is considered one of the first examples of Tasmanian Gothic literature. With its cruelty and systemic violence, this book, more than any other, has come to define the Australian convict past. Originally, Clarke wanted the shorter title to suggest that this story was about the universal human struggle and the future Australian race. He wanted to celebrate the survival of the human spirit in the direst circumstances.

Fig. 3-21 Oscar and Lucinda

Oscar and Lucinda(Fig. 3-21) is a novel by the Australian author Peter Carey. It was shortlisted for *The Best of the Booker*. It tells the story of Oscar Hopkins, the Cornish son of a Plymouth Brethren minister who becomes an Anglican priest, and Lucinda Leplastrier, a young Australian heiress who buys a glass factory. They meet on the ship over to Australia, and discover that they are both gamblers, one obsessive, the other compulsive. Lucinda bets Oscar that he cannot transport a glass church from Sydney to a remote settlement at Bellingen, some 400 kilometers up the New South Wales coast. This bet changes both their lives forever. The novel partly takes its inspiration from *Father and Son*, the autobiography of the English poet

Edmund Gosse, which describes his relationship with his father, Philip Henry Gosse.

 Food Customs

Australian food culture is heavily influenced by years of migration of people that took place from various locations of the world in the last four centuries. Settlers in this continental nation have developed mixed cuisines which represent a variety of men and women and their food habits.

Before colonization, aboriginal peoples were sustained by a diverse range of flora and fauna. The early settlers primarily consumed meat, bread, and vegetables, particularly potatoes. Nearly all regularly eaten foods—except seafood—were introduced after European settlement. However, there have been considerable changes in food preference patterns. In the 1940s, meat consumption began to decline, poultry consumption increased dramatically after the 1960s, and there has been a doubling of seafood consumption since the 1930s, in addition to a steady increase in fruit and vegetable consumption since the 1950s. Since World War II, the diet has become highly diversified. Each wave of immigrants has had an impact, including German, Italian, Greek, Lebanese, Jewish, and Southeast Asian foods and cooking styles. Olive and vegetable oils have replaced dripping and *lard*[5], and items such as garlic and Asian condiments are used more commonly.

Australian chefs are known worldwide for their "fusion cuisine", a blending of European cooking traditions with Asian flavors and products. Nevertheless, certain foods are recognized as national emblems, including Vegemite(Fig. 3-22), Milo, Anzac biscuit, and damper. Australians are among the world leaders in fast-food consumption. Burger and chicken chain stores are prominent in the suburbs, having displaced the traditional meat pies and fish and chips. While Australians were long known as tea drinkers, coffee and wine have become increasingly popular.

Fig. 3-22 Vegemite

Table manners generally follow the British tradition. If the food does not need to be cut with a knife, it is quite correct just to use a fork in the right hand; but otherwise, Australians do not cut up their food and then put the knife down and eat with the fork in the American way. The knife should be held with the handle covered by your hand, not like a pencil, while the fork facing down lifts the food. It is polite to put them both down on the plate while you chew your mouthful. At the end of the course, the knife and the fork are placed together in the center of the plate, with the fork facing upward, so that the waiter or your hostess will know that you have finished eating; but the table will be cleared only when everyone has finished. The knife and the fork laid separately on a plate where there is still some food indicate to the waiter that you have not finished.

Exercises

I. Try to answer the following questions according to your understanding of the text.

(1) What can you learn from the Aboriginal Dreamtime?

(2) How is Anzac Day celebrated in Australia?

(3) Why is *The Eye of the Storm* considered one of Patrick White's best novels?

(4) What are the changes in food preference patterns after European settlement?

(5) What are the table manners like in Australia?

II. Read the following passage carefully, and make a comment on it at the end of the passage in no more than 100 words.

Australia is a sophisticated, literate and multicultural market with extensive traditional ties to the United Kingdom and strong links to Asia. There are unique opportunities for the United Kingdom companies as Australia is a net importer of creative content. The main opportunity areas within the creative industries are creative services such as design, film and television production, e-publishing and the digital music market.

When looking at the Australian market, businesses are advised to consider the Internet as a primary method of connecting with customers. Australians rank the sixth in the world in terms of the total number of internet users. The Australian Federal Government is currently implementing the National Broadband Network, a high-speed broadband network which aims to connect all Australians in both regional and urban areas. This will increase the amount of broadband consumers as well as the level of usage per capita.

The Australian digital music market is one of the largest areas of growth and is anticipated to grow at an annualized 27.6% over the next five years through 2017 to 2018 to total AUD$281 million. Digital music downloads account for an increasing share of music sales, shifting the way Australians purchase music items, from whole albums to single tracks. Australians are avid cinema-goers. Online movie distribution is one of the fastest growing creative markets in Australia. Online shopping is a rapidly developing trend in Australia with more customers turning to the internet in search of bargains and variety. Revenue is expected to decrease in the traditional publishing industry over the next five years, although growth is expected in the e-book market. There are many opportunities in product design, particularly residential and commercial furniture, lighting, packaging and home accessories.

There are also great opportunities in the transference of print and broadcast media to digital media. There are several trade shows and conferences relating to the various Creative Industries sectors around Australia with increasing events in design related trade exhibitions and festivals, as well as music conferences. The Queensland University of Technology recently opened a "Creative Industries" Faculty which offers courses and undertakes research on Australia's creative economy.

Comments:

Since Australia has a long and sophisticated tie with the United Kingdom, what is your perspective on the relationship?

Reference:

Argument:

(1) Reforging the defence partnership

(2) Having more trade and business opportunities

(3) Enabling traders from both nations to benefit equally from the reduced tariffs

Counter-argument:

(1) Having historical controversies

(2) Interfered with some rules

(3) Adopting certain foreign policies that may cause disagreements between the two nations

Unit 6　Intercultural Communication

 Knowledge to Learn

What Is Verbal Communication?

Verbal communication refers to the use of sounds and language to relay a message. It serves as a vehicle for expressing desires, ideas and concepts and is vital to the processes of learning and teaching. In combination with nonverbal forms of communication, verbal communication acts as the primary tool for expression between two or more people.

What Are the Types of Verbal Communication?

Interpersonal communication and public speaking are the two basic types of verbal communication. Signs and symbols are the major signals that make up verbal communication.

 Cases to Study

Case 1

　　Sarah and Daniel are a young Australian couple who are teaching English at Nana University. Their new Chinese colleague, Lin Hua, invited them to her home for dinner at a weekend. When Sarah and Daniel arrived, Lin Hua introduced them to her husband Mr. Wang, asked them to sit down at a table containing eight plates of various cold dishes, and served them tea and then disappeared with her husband into the kitchen. Sarah offered to help in the kitchen but Lin Hua said she didn't need any help. Half an hour later, she came back and sat down and the three began to eat. Wang came in from time to time to put several hot dishes on the table. Most of the food was wonderful and there was much more than Sarah and Daniel could eat. They wanted Wang to sit down so that they could talk to him. Finally, he did sit down and eat a bit. Soon it was time for the Australian couple to go home. Sarah and Daniel felt slightly depressed by this experience.

How does Chinese understanding of the host-guest relationship influence Lin Hua and Wang's way of receiving Sarah and Daniel?

Analysis

(1) In China, it is traditional that hosts entertain guests by offering many courses of dishes to show their hospitality, and the Chinese like to serve guests with the best food they have. A Chinese banquet is made up of scores of dishes including cold dishes, hot fried dishes, salted dishes, sweet preserved fruit and fresh fruit.

(2) It is quite common that the husband helps a lot in cooking and serving food, especially in cities. Hosts treat guests, especially distinguished guests, very politely, and guests' offer of help in the kitchen is normally politely refused. These Chinese conventions help explain the way Lin Hua and Wang entertained Sarah and Daniel.

Case 2

Li Jun, a Chinese university lecturer, was teaching in an Australian university. One day he went to a party, Li Jun noticed that men and women touched each other a lot more than he was used to. One woman came to hug Li Jun, but he stiffened as she attempted to give him a hug. He had never hugged any women except his wife in his life. Other women noticed this, and no one else tried to hug him. However, Li Jun felt left out when people hugged each other but not him. He found himself in a very awkward situation: he did not want to be hugged, but nor did he want to be left out. He did not know what he wanted or how to resolve his conflicting emotions.

Can you explain the reason for his awkwardness?

Analysis

(1) Chinese people seldom hug each other, particularly in public places.

(2) In China, you will see senses of greeting and good-bye with all the feelings expressed in the eyes and the face, but it is unlikely that people will hug, with only the younger generation as an exception.

(3) In contrast, people of Australian culture touch each other in communication much more than people of Chinese culture.

(4) At a time of meeting a friend or upon departing, hugging each other is very natural for Australian people.

(5) One's discomfort at hugging in such situations may be interpreted by Australian as unfriendliness.

 Translations on Traditional Chinese Culture

Exercise 1

Translate the passage into English

港珠澳大桥全长 55 公里，是我国一项不同寻常的工程壮举。大桥将三个城市连接起来，是世界上最长的跨海桥梁和隧道系统。大桥将三个城市之间的旅行时间从 3 小时缩短到 30 分钟。这座跨度巨大的钢筋混凝土大桥充分证明中国有能力建造创纪录的巨型建筑。它将助推区域一体化，促进经济增长。大桥是中国发展自己的大湾区总体规划的关键。中国希望将大湾区建成在技术创新和经济繁荣上能与旧金山、纽约和东京的湾区相媲美的地区。

> **Translation Reference**
>
> With a total length of 55 kilometers, the Hong Kong-Zhuhai-Macao Bridge is an extraordinary engineering in China. As the longest cross-sea bridge and tunnel system in the world, the bridge connects Hong Kong, Zhuhai and Macao, shortening the traveling time among the three cities from three hours to 30 minutes. This reinforced concrete bridge with huge spans fully proves that China has the ability to build record-breaking huge construction. It will enhance regional integration and promote economic growth. The bridge is the key to China's development of its own master plan for the Great Bay Area. China hopes to build the Great Bay Area into an area comparable to the Bay Areas of San Francisco, New York and Tokyo in terms of technological innovation and economic prosperity.

Translate the passage into Chinese

The Potala Palace is a world-famous architecture complex. It is the highest ancient palace in the world, reaching an altitude of over 3,700 meters at the top point. Covering a total area of 360,000 square meters, the main building of the Potala Palace is 117 meters high in 13 storeys. The total palace is of distinct Tibetan style. The Potala Palace is called as a museum of various arts. It houses a collection of numerous treasures which is of great value for the study of politics, economy, history and culture in Tibet. In 1994, the Potala Palace was listed as a World Cultural Heritage Site.

Translation Reference

布达拉宫是一座举世闻名的建筑群。它是世界上最高的古代宫殿,最高点达到海拔3700多米。布达拉宫占地总面积为36万平方米,主楼高117米,共13层。整座宫殿具有鲜明的藏式风格。布达拉宫堪称是一座各种艺术的博物馆,它收藏的无数珍宝对于研究西藏的政治、经济、历史和文化都具有重大的价值。1994年,布达拉宫被列为世界文化遗产。

Exercise 2

Translate the passage into English

长江仅次于南美洲的亚马逊河与非洲的尼罗河,是世界第三大长河,亚洲第一大长河。辽阔的长江流域,资源极为丰富,自古以来是中国最重要的农业经济区。黄河为中国第二大长河,也是世界著名的长河之一。在中国历史上,黄河给人类文明带来很大的影响,是中华民族最主要的发祥地之一,因此中国人称其为"母亲河"。

Translation Reference

The Yangtze River ranks the longest river in Asia and the third longest river in the world, second only to the Amazon River in South America and the Nile in Africa. There are abundant resources in the vast Yangtze River basin. Since ancient times, the Yangtze River basin has been China's most important economic zone for agriculture. The Yellow River, the second longest river in China, is one of the most famous long rivers in the world. In China's history, the Yellow River has significant influence on human civilization and it's one of the most important birthplaces of the Chinese nation, so Chinese people call it "the Mother River".

Translate the passage into Chinese

Jinghang Canal is called the Canal for short. It is known as one of the greatest Chinese ancient projects. Since being founded in the fifth century BC, the canal has had two large-scale expansions within the Sui and Yuan Dynasties. Having the length of 1,794 kilometers, 15 times longer than Suez Canal, Jinghang Canal is the main waterway combining the north and the south in China. The Canal begins from Beijing and ends in Hangzhou, crossing six provinces or cities, linking not only the Haihe River, the Yellow River but also the Huaihe River, the Yangtze River and the Qiantang River. It is the second "prime channel" only following the Yangtze River in China. It has been playing a very important role in promoting the economic and cultural developments and exchanges between the northern and the southern areas in China.

Chapter Three　Australia

> **Translation Reference**
> 京杭大运河简称运河,为中国古代最伟大的工程之一。运河始建于公元前 5 世纪,后经隋、元两次大规模扩建。全长 1794 公里,是苏伊士运河的 16 倍,是中国一条重要的南北水上干线。它北起北京,南至杭州,经过六省市,连接了海河、黄河、淮河、长江、钱塘江五大水系,是中国仅次于长江的第二条"黄金水道"。它对中国南北地区经济、文化发展与交流起了巨大作用。

Exercise 3

Translate the passage into English

喜马拉雅山脉称为"雪的故乡",位于青藏高原南缘,西起帕米尔高原,东到雅鲁藏布江大拐弯处。喜马拉雅山脉由 110 多座海拔 7000 米以上的山峰组成。其中,珠穆朗玛峰海拔 8848.86 米,是世界第一高峰,位于中国与尼泊尔的边界处。喜马拉雅山脉是世界上最年轻的山脉,现在它还在不断地增长。

> **Translation Reference**
> The Himalayas, also known as "the Hometown of Snow", lie in the south of the Qinghai-Tibet Plateau and start from the Pamirs in the west to the Great Turning Point of the Yarlung Zangbo River in the east. The Himalayas consist of more than 110 mountains which are over 7,000 meters above sea level. Among them, Mount Qomolangma is the highest mountain in the world, with an altitude of 8848.86 meters, located on the border of China and Nepal. The Himalayas are the youngest mountain range in the world and they are still growing.

Translate the passage into Chinese

It is said that if there should be wonderlands on the earth, Jiuzhaigou Valley must be one of them. There is dreamlike scenery, like blue lakes, waterfalls, verdant forests and snow-covered mountains. More than the spectacular scenery, Jiuzhaigou Valley is also home to nine Tibetan villages, over 220 bird species as well as a number of endangered plant and animal species. Jiuzhaigou Valley was declared a World Heritage Site by UNESCO in 1992. It provides spectacular scenery throughout four seasons of the year, making it one of China's most well-known scenic sites.

> **Translation Reference**
> 据说如果地球上真有人间仙境,九寨沟一定是其中之一。这里有梦境般的风景:蓝色的湖泊、瀑布、翠绿的森林、白雪皑皑的山脉。九寨沟不仅有壮观的景色,还是九个藏族村寨的居住地,还有超过 220 种鸟类以及许多濒临灭绝的动植物

物种。它在 1992 年被联合国教科文组织宣布为世界文化遗产。九寨沟一年四季的美景使它成为中国最著名的景点之一。

 Culture to Know

Culture Note 1

The Imperial Palace, also called the Forbidden City, was the palace where the 24 emperors of the Ming and Qing Dynasties ruled China for nearly 500 years. The Imperial Palace is located in Beijing City, on the northern side of the Tian' anmen Square, rectangular in shape, about 960 meters long from north to south and 750 meters or so wide from east to west, with an area of around 720,000 square meters and a total floor area of about 150,000 square meters. It's the world's biggest and best-preserved palace made of wood in existence. The Imperial Palace is divided into two parts: the outer court and the inner court. In 1987, the Imperial Palace was listed by the UNESCO as one of the World Heritage Sites.

Culture Note 2

As the biggest waterfall in China and one of the famous waterfalls in the world, **Huangguoshu Waterfall** is watered from faraway rivers and brooks and turns into swift torrent at abrupt cliffs, thus creating a majestic sight composed of torrential waves, water bloom and mist with roaring sound. It is located in southwest of Anshun City, Guizhou province, with about 230 feet long and 266 feet wide.

Culture Note 3

The Yarlung Tsangpo Grand Canyon, also known as the Yarlung Zangbo Grand Canyon, is a canyon along the Yarlung Tsangpo River in Tibet Autonomous Region, China. It is the deepest canyon in the world, and is slightly longer than the Grand Canyon in the United States, making it one of the world's largest. The Yarlung Tsangpo originates near Mount Kailash and runs east for about 1,700 kilometers, draining a northern section of the Himalayas before it enters the gorge just downstream of Pei, Tibet, near the settlement of Zhibe. It is home to many animals and plants, barely explored and affected by human influence, while its climate ranges from subtropical to Arctic.

Chapter Three Australia

Culture Note 4

Traditional Chinese Medicine

Traditional Chinese medicine (TCM) has been passed down for thousands of years. With an extensive and profound culture, TCM is the treasure of Chinese civilization. It is not only widely used in Asia, but also has become increasingly popular in Europe and the United States. There are more than 60,000 acupuncturists in the United States right now. Chinese medicine has grown dramatically in the last 15 **years**. It is taking on a larger role in our medical system here as a safe and noninvasive method of treatment for a lot of problems that Western medicine has difficulty providing good outcomes or treatment options for. TCM, acupuncture and other TCM treatment methods are of great benefit to patients, especially those with some problems in Western medicine, or need surgery. TCM and acupuncture can relieve a patient's pain or eliminate the need for surgery.

 Further Reading

Passage 1

World Digital Education Conference

China must ensure an effective coordination of the strategy for invigorating China through science and education with the workforce development strategy and the innovation-driven development strategy, and promote the integration of the development of education, sci-tech innovation and personnel training to form a virtuous cycle. China must adhere to the unified design of original innovation, integrated innovation and open innovation to ensure that they are well coordinated. China must also realize the unified deployment of innovation, industrial and talent chains so that they can be deeply integrated.

Passage 2

IoT Wuxi Summit Sets Industrial Trends

In the World Internet of Things Wuxi Summit, a total of 20 projects were signed at the summit, covering areas such as artificial intelligence, IoT, integrated circuits, advanced manufacturing, industrial internet, and deep-sea equipment. These newly signed projects will help promote the industrial transformation and upgrading of Wuxi and further improved the quality and efficiency of the city's industrial development. Wuxi, the only national sensor network innovation demonstration zone in China, has seen its IoT industry valued over 300 billion yuan so far. The city is home to more than 3,000 IoT companies specializing in chips, sensors, and communications to undertake 23 major national application demonstration projects.

Chapter Four
Canada

Contents

1. Location and Resources
2. History and Symbols
3. Education and Recreation
4. Politics and Economy
5. Culture and Customs
6. Intercultural Communication

Banff National Park	班芙国家公园	**maple leaf**	枫叶
beaver	河狸	**maple syrup**	枫糖
Canada Day	加拿大国庆日	**Niagara Falls**	尼亚加拉大瀑布
Canadian Museum of Civilization	加拿大文明博物馆	**Parliament Buildings**	议会大厦
Canadian Rockies	加拿大落基山脉	**Peace Tower**	和平塔
CN Tower	加拿大国家电视塔	**Royal Ontario Museum**	皇家安大略博物馆
Confederation Bridge	联邦大桥	**Sky Dome**	天穹体育馆
Henry Norman Bethune	亨利·诺尔曼·白求恩	**the University of British Columbia**	不列颠哥伦比亚大学
hockey	冰球	**University of Toronto**	多伦多大学
ice wine	冰酒	**Vancouver Art Gallery**	温哥华美术馆

Chapter Four Canada

Unit 1 Location and Resources

Text Focus

1. Geographical Location
2. Weather and Climate
3. Natural Resources

4.1 Lecture1 Location.mp4

4.2 Lecture2 People.mp4

Vocabulary

1. stretch	[stretʃ]	v.	延伸
2. glacial	[ˈgleɪʃl]	adj.	冰川的
3. defensible	[dɪˈfensəbl]	adj.	可防卫的
4. hydroelectric	[ˌhaɪdrəʊɪˈlektrɪk]	adj.	水力发电的

Canada is located in the northern hemisphere and huge in size. Occupying the northern half of the North American continent, Canada's land mass is over 9.98 million square kilometers, making it the second-largest country in the world after Russia. From east to west, Canada encompasses six time zones. Most Canadians live within 150 miles of the country's long southern border and parts of northern Canada still have not been explored. There are four distinct seasons in most parts of Canada. Canada's climate is characterized by its diversity, as temperature and precipitation differ from region to region and from season to season. It is one of the few developed nations that is a net exporter of energy and the most important are the abundant oil and gas resources centered in Alberta and the Northern Territories.

Geographical Location

Stretching[1] from the Atlantic Ocean in the east to the shores of the Pacific Ocean in the west, and from its border with the United States in the south to the icy waters of the Arctic Ocean in the north, Canada is a huge and fascinating land. Canada is covered by wilderness, forest or frozen Arctic wasteland. Nearly 80% of Canadians live in large cities near the border with the United States. Canada shares a around 8,890-kilometer-long border with the United States that has not been fortified for over a hundred years and thousands of travelers cross the border every day.

Canada has an area of over 9.98 million square kilometers, which is about three fifths of that of Russia but larger than that of China. It covers about two fifths of the North American continent.

The regions of Canada are the Atlantic Region, Central Canada, the Prairie Provinces, the west coast and the North. Canada is composed of 10 provinces and three territories.

Canada(Fig. 4-1) is about 7,000 kilometers from east to west. The nation's only neighbor is the USA, which includes Alaska in the northwest. Since the end of the last **_glacial_**[2] period, Canada has consisted of eight distinct forest regions, including extensive boreal forest on the Canadian Shield. The highest point in Canada is Mount Logan in the Yukon. The two principal river systems are the Mackenzie and the St. Lawrence. Canada has around 31,700 large lakes, more than any other country, containing much of the world's fresh water. In addition to the Great Lakes on the United States border, there are nine others that are more than 161 kilometers long and 35 that are more than 80 kilometers long. Great Bear Lake is the largest lake entirely within Canada, the third largest in North America, and the seventh largest in the world. There are also fresh-water glaciers in the Canadian Rockies and the Coast Mountains. Canada is geologically active, having many earthquakes and potentially active volcanoes.

Fig. 4-1   Autumn in Canada

Ottawa(Fig. 4-2) is the capital of Canada. It is the 4th largest city in the country. The city is located on the south bank of the Ottawa River in the eastern portion of Southern Ontario. The name "Ottawa" is derived from the Algonquin word, meaning "to trade". On December 31, 1857, Queen Victoria was asked to choose a common capital for the province of Canada and she chose Ottawa. The Queen's advisers suggested she pick Ottawa for several reasons: Ottawa's position in the back country made it more **_defensible_**[3], while still allowing easy transportation over the Ottawa River. Ottawa was at a point nearly exactly midway between Toronto and Quebec City.

Toronto is the largest and the most populous city in Canada and also the provincial capital of Ontario. It is located on the northwestern shore of Lake Ontario. Toronto is at the heart of the Greater Toronto Area and is part of a larger combined region in Southern Ontario known as the Golden Horseshoe, making up the cultural entertainment, and financial capital of the nation. That is why Toronto abounds in investment and employment opportunities in such diverse fields as banking and financial services, film and television production, and fashion. As a multicultural city, Toronto offers a cosmopolitan mix of culture, art and entertainment.

Fig. 4-2 Ottawa Scenery

Montreal is the largest city in the province of Quebec, the second largest city in Canada. Originally called "City of Mary", the city takes its present name from Mount Royal, the triple-peaked hill located in the heart of the city. French is the city's official language, and is also the third largest French-speaking city in the world after Paris and Kinshasa. It remains an important center of commerce, aerospace, transport, finance, pharmaceuticals, technology, design, education, art, culture, tourism, food, fashion, gaming, films and world affairs.

Weather and Climate

Weather and climate of Canada vary in different seasons. Most of Canada has four distinct seasons, all of which occur right across the country although their arrival times vary. The most significant factor in climate, and even day-to-day weather, is latitude. In just a few hours travelling north by road, a drop in temperature is often felt.

Spring in most parts of Canada is a rainy season, when temperatures grow higher day by day, even though the nights remain cool. In southern Canada, spring generally begins as early as March. The first flowers begin to bloom, but the new leaves do not return to the trees until April or May, except for southern coastal British Columbia, which has the shortest, mildest winter in Canada.

In the summer months(Fig. 4-3), the weather in parts of southern Canada can be as hot as any tropical country. On the east and west coasts, the average high temperatures are generally below 20℃, while between the coasts, the average summer high temperature ranges from 25℃ to 30℃, with temperatures in some interior locations occasionally exceeding 40℃. City office buildings and shops are equipped with air conditioning.

Fig. 4-3　Summer in Canada

The autumn in Canada begins at about the time of the first frost. The shorter days and decreased light cause the leaves of many trees to change colors and then fall off. The weather tends to be rainy and changeable. In most places snow usually comes in November.

Winters can be harsh in many parts of the country, where daily average temperatures are near -15℃, but can drop to below -40℃ with severe wind chills. During the winter months, the temperature in Canada remains below freezing point most of the time, with the exception of parts of the Pacific and the Atlantic coasts. In non-coastal regions, snow can cover the ground for almost six months of the year, while in parts of the north snow can persist year-round. Almost all homes and offices are equipped with central heating. Public radio and television stations give weather forecasts regularly.

Natural Resources

Natural resources of Canada are distinctively rich and vast. Canada has many resources that are energy sources, including oil, natural gas, fossil and alternative fuels, uranium, and renewable.

The most important are the large oil and gas resources centered in Alberta and the Northern Territories. The vast Athabasca Oil Sands give Canada the world's third largest reserves of oil. In some provinces, like Quebec and Ontario, ***hydroelectric***[4] power is an inexpensive and relatively environmentally friendly source of abundant energy.

Water is one of the most important natural resources in Canada. Its waters such as the Great Lakes, St Lawrence River and the great rivers of western Canada have a very important effect on the exploration and settlement of the country and on its later industrial expansion. Canada has one of the longest coastlines in the world. The Atlantic and the Pacific waters are among the world's richest fishing grounds. What's more, almost half of the land area of Canada is covered by forests. Canadian wood products are among the finest in the world.

Chapter Four Canada

Exercises

I. *Try to answer the following questions according to your understanding of the text.*

(1) Where is Canada located?
(2) How big is Canada? Which country is larger than Canada in size?
(3) Which lake is the largest lake in Canada?
(4) How could you describe Canada's climate?
(5) What are the natural resources in Canada?

II. *Read the following passage carefully, and make a comment on it at the end of the passage in no more than 100 words.*

The Niagara Falls is located in the borderline between Canada and America in the east central North America, on a river that connected two of the five Great Lakes. The Niagara consists of two parts: the Horseshoe Falls on the Canadian side of the river, and the American Falls on the United States' side. They are about 50 meters high, 1,240 meters wide.

Niagara Falls comprises three distinct cataracts. The tallest are the American and Bridalveil Falls on the American side, separated by tiny Luna Island and plunging over jagged rocks; the broad Horseshoe Falls which curve their way over to Canada are probably the most impressive. They date back a mere 12 thousand years, when the retreat of melting glaciers allowed water trapped in Lake Erie to gush north to Lake Ontario. Back then the falls were seven miles downriver, but constant erosion has cut them back to their present site. The falls are colorfully lit up at night, and many say they're the most beautiful in winter, when the grounds are covered in snow and the waters turn to ice.

Since the falls were formed during the late Pleistocene period, about 12,000 years ago, they have been subject to the force of erosion. As they erode, the falls are moving upstream, so they will one day disappear into Lake Erie.

Like all waterfalls, Niagara erodes because water wears away the softer rock at the base of the cliff, where a turbulent pool forms below the waterfall. Because erosion affects the base of the cliff, the old cliff face will collapse and the new edge will be slightly upstream. The rate of erosion depends on factors like the volume of water going over the edge, the height of the drop, and the type of rocks that make up the base of the waterfall.

At Niagara, the volume of water is very high. In fact, one fifth of the world's fresh water empties from the Great Lakes Superior, Huron, Michigan, and Erie over the falls into Lake Ontario. Niagara is the second largest waterfall in the world.

Comments:

The scenery of Niagara Falls is spectacular and captivating. Every year, it attracts millions of tourists from all over the world. Tourists can enjoy the scenery of the waterfall from different perspectives, and also experience some exciting and interesting activities, such as crossing the waterfall and exploring caves, and so on. Some people prefer such kind of thrilling activities.

What's your opinion?

Reference:

Argument:

(1) Releasing stress

(2) Exercising the body

(3) Increasing courage and confidence

Counter-argument:

(1) Bringing physical exhaustion

(2) Bringing psychological pressure

(3) Having potential safety issues

Unit 2   History and Symbols

1. Historical Periods
2. Historical Figures
3. National Symbols

4.3 Lecture3 History and Education.mp4

Vocabulary

1. cede	[siːd]	v.		割让
2. exert	[ɪɡˈzɜːt]	v.		施加，产生
3. accretion	[əˈkriːʃn]	n.		添加
4. exploration	[ˌekspləˈreɪʃn]	n.		探索
5. acclaim	[əˈkleɪm]	n.		称赞
6. unaltered	[ʌnˈɔːltəd]	adj.		未改变的

The first inhabitants of Canada were native Indian peoples, primarily the Inuit, Eskimo. The European discovery of Canada can be traced back to the end of the 15th century. The first British settlers in Canada were American refugees who refused to fight against the British army in the War of American Independence. From the end of 19th century, the country was governed by the Conservative Party and the Liberal Party. Many well-known individual historical figures showed great influence on the history of Canada, such as Henry Hudson and Bethune. The typical national symbol of Canada is the maple leaf, which became the national symbol with the introduction of the Canadian flag in 1965 and now it is considered as the most internationally recognizable Canadian symbol.

 Historical Periods

The explorer Leif Eriksson probably reached the shores of Canada, Labrador or Nova Scotia, in 1000, but the history of the white man in the country actually began in 1497. French and British expeditions explored, and later settled, along the Atlantic coast.

On March 5, 1496, King Henry VII of England granted John Cabot the right to "seek islands and countries of the heathen towards the west, east, and north" sailing under the English flag. On May 2, 1497, John Cabot embarked on his ship to explore the lands across the Atlantic, hoping to find a North West passage to the India and China. John Cabot and his son Sebastian were the first Europeans to discover Canada, landing on the coast of Newfoundland.

In 1534, Jacques Cartier, a French explorer sailed along the St. Lawrence River. Almost 100 years later French colonists settled along the banks of the St Lawrence and near the Great Lakes. Nearly at the same time, the English established outposts around Hudson's Bay and along the Atlantic coast. Both England and France founded permanent settlements throughout 1600s.

In 1605, Samuel de Champlain established the first successful New France Colony at Port Royal, and in 1672, New France expanded into Canada. After the war known as the Seven Years War (1756—1763) in Canada, French colonists were driven out of the North American Continent. The French colony on the St. Lawrence was reorganized as the British province: Quebec in 1763. France *ceded*[1] nearly all of its colonies in North America to Britain in 1763 after the Seven Years' War.

The era after the War of 1812 marked the Canadian development and progress, population increased, transportation developed, especially shipping industry. There were two major events in the history of founding of Canada, which *exert*[2] foremost influence on modern Canada. The first one was the building of Canadian Pacific Railway and the second big event followed just after 1885. That was Louis Riel's execution.

In 1867, Canada was born when Quebec, Ontario, New Brunswick and Nova Scotia all joined together. As time passed, other provinces and territories also joined. In 1867, with the union of three British North American colonies through Confederation, Canada was formed as a federal dominion of four provinces. This began an *accretion*[3] of provinces and territories and a process of increasing autonomy from the British Empire, which became official with *the Statute of Westminster of 1931* and completed in *the Canada Act of 1982*, which severed the vestiges of legal dependence on the British parliament.

The huge west was deeply and largely explored. More immigrants moved to Canada from Europe, the United States and Asian nations. Canada became stronger and more powerful than before. With the economic development, Canada paid much attention to its identity of independence. It intensified the friendly foreign relations, in order to get rid of British control. World War I was the turning point for Canada as an independent nation. *The Statute of Westminster of 1931* recognized Canada as an equal member of the Commonwealth to Britain.

During World War II, Canada fought as an ally of Britain. Nearly one million men and women served in the armed forces. After the war, tremendous development took place in industries and agriculture in Canada. In 1949, Newfoundland became Canada's 10th province and in 1959 the opening of the Saint Lawrence Seaway saw a further growth in Canada's economy.

In the two decades after 1950, however, Canada enjoyed unprecedented growth and prosperity. Many urban dwellers abandoned the cities in favour of the new suburbs that appeared in the 1950s. The growth of the suburbs stimulated transportation construction, including new freeways and rapid transit systems. Canada's primary economic activities thrived, but the country also embarked on a new phase of industrial development, spurred by large-scale electronic, aeronautic, nuclear, and chemical engineering.

Under Trudeau, *the Canadian Constitution*, one of the last steps in full independence from Britain, came into being in 1982, along with *the Charter of Rights and Freedoms*.

In 1992, the Mulroney government adopted a different economic agenda. It weakened government intervention in the national economy. Canada survived the global economic downturn that began in 2008 better than most of its partners in the Group of Eight, partly because of the country's closely regulated banking system. Largely as a result of declining world oil prices, the Canadian economy stumbled into recession in 2015.

On October 19th, 2015, Justin Trudeau led his party to victory, winning a majority government with seats in every province and territory across the country. On October 21st, 2019, Justin led the Liberal Party to re-etection, earning a second mandate from Canadians.

As Prime Minister, Justin leads a government that works hard every day to continue moving Canada forward. His team is focused on creating good middle class jobs, making life more affordable, keeping Canada's communities safe, fighting climate change, and moving forward on reconciliation with Indigenous peoples.

Historical Figures

Henry Hudson(1565?—1611?) was an English explorer, during the early 17th century, best known for his ***explorations***[4] of present-day Canada and parts of the northeastern United States. In 1607 and 1608, Hudson made two attempts on behalf of English merchants to find a rumored Northeast Passage to Cathay, present-day China, via a route above the Arctic Circle. In 1609, he landed in North America and explored the region around the modern New York metropolitan area, looking for a Northwest Passage to Asia on behalf of the Dutch East India Company. He sailed up the Hudson River, which was later named for him, and thereby laid the foundation for Dutch colonization of the region.

Hudson discovered the Hudson Strait and the immense Hudson Bay on his final expedition, while still searching for the Northwest Passage. In 1611, after wintering on the shore of James Bay, Hudson wanted to press on to the west, but most of his crew mutinied. The mutineers cast Hudson, his son, and seven others adrift; the Hudson and their companions were never seen again.

Henry Norman Bethune(Fig. 4-4) (1890—1939) was a Canadian physician, medical innovator, and noted communist. Bethune came to international prominence first for his service as a front-line surgeon supporting the democratically elected Republican government during the Spanish Civil War. But it was his service with the Communist Eighth Route Army during the War of Resistence Against Japanese Aggression that earned him enduring ***acclaim***[5]. Dr. Bethune effectively brought modern medicine to rural China and often treated sick villagers as well as wounded soldiers. His selfless commitment made a profound impression on the Chinese people, especially

Fig. 4-4　Henry Norman Bethune

the Communist Party of China's leader, Mao Zedong. Mao Zedong wrote a eulogy to him, which was memorized by generations of Chinese people. While Bethune was the man responsible for developing a mobile blood transfusion service for front-line operations in the Spanish Civil War, he himself died of blood poisoning. As a prominent communist and veteran of the World War I, he wrote that wars were motivated by profits, not principles. Statues in his honors can be found in some parts of China.

Lester Bowles Pearson(1897—1972) was a Canadian professor, historian, civil servant, statesman, diplomat, and politician, who won the Nobel Peace Prize in 1957 for organizing the United Nations Emergency Force to resolve the Suez Canal Crisis, and he is considered the father of the modern concept of peacekeeping. During Pearson's time as Prime Minister, his minority government introduced a lot of good policies, such as universal health care, student loans, the Canada Pension Plan, etc. With these accomplishment, together with his ground-breaking work at the United Nations and in international diplomacy, Pearson is generally considered among the most influential Canadians of the 20th century.

National Symbols

The National Flag of Canada, also known as the Maple Leaf, is a red flag with a white square in its center, featuring a stylized 11-pointed red maple leaf. The two red borders refer to the Atlantic Ocean and the Pacific Ocean. The white square in the middle represents the vast land of Canada. But the 11 points on the maple leaf have no special significance. The adoption of the flag in 1965 marked the first time a national flag had been officially adopted in Canada to replace the Union Flag. The Royal Union Flag is also an official flag in Canada, used as a symbol of Canada's membership in the Commonwealth of Nations, and of its allegiance to the Crown.

"O Canada" is the national anthem of Canada. It was proclaimed national anthem on July 1, 1980. It was first sung on June 24, 1880. The song gained steadily in popularity. Many English versions have appeared over the years. The version on which the official English lyrics are based was written in 1908 by Mr. Justice Robert Stanley Weir. The official English version includes changes recommended in 1968 by a Special Joint Committee of the Senate and House of Commons. The French lyrics remain *unaltered*[6]. There are no regulations governing the performance of "O Canada", leaving citizens to exercise their best judgment.

The maple leaf is the most internationally recognizable Canadian symbol. At the beginning of the 18th century, the maple leaf had been adopted as an emblem by the French Canadian. It was one of numerous emblems proposed to represent the society in 1834. Speaking in its favour, the first mayor of Montreal, described the maple as "the king of our forest" and "the symbol of the Canadian people". The maple leaf finally became the central national symbol with the introduction of the Canadian flag in 1965, which uses a highly-stylized eleven-pointed maple leaf, referring to no specific species of maple.

Exercises

I. *Try to answer the following questions according to your understanding of the text.*

(1) Why are John Cabot and Jacques Cartier important in the early discovery of Canada?

(2) What was the consequence of the Seven Years' War between the British and the French?

(3) How many famous figures in Canada do you know? Who are they?

(4) What is the national flag of Canada like?

(5) What is the national anthem of Canada and when was it proclaimed to be the national anthem of Canada?

II. *Read the following passage carefully, and make a comment on it at the end of the passage in no more than 100 words.*

As questions about the future of work loom, Canada stands at a crossroads. Automation and technological advances pose unprecedented opportunities and challenges to workers across Canada's economy. Both men and women will need to navigate a wide-scale workforce transition, moving from lower-wage and lower-skilled jobs to higher-wage and higher-skilled jobs. For women, who already face inequalities in the workplace, this transition will be pivotal.

Today, commitment to gender equality is stronger than ever within Canadian organizations. Four of five Canadian organizations consider gender diversity a priority, and half of them have articulated a business case for gender diversity, a threefold increase since our 2017 survey. Although women and men now make up an equal split at the entry level, and women's representation across the talent pipeline has increased by two percentage points since 2017, women still face challenges in advancement and everyday discrimination at work. Only three women are promoted to manager for every four men who receive the promotion. These findings are based on a survey of more than one hundred Canadian organizations across all industries, which collectively employ more than half a million workers.

Canada is now at an inflection point, with an opportunity to narrow the gender gap: if between 8 to 30 percent of women can successfully transition across occupations to high-demand parts of the economy, they could maintain or even modestly increase their share of employment by one to two percentage points by 2030. However, if structural barriers and existing inequalities in the workplace prevent women from making these transitions and acquiring the skills needed to stay in the workforce, women could fall further behind, and gender inequality at work will persist.

In Canada, 24 percent of currently employed women could be at risk of their jobs being displaced by automation, compared with 28 percent of men. Women are also relatively well positioned to capture jobs in certain high-growth sectors—such as healthcare, where women account for 81 percent of employees. On the surface, this paints a positive picture for women—but they could also face more hurdles in navigating these transitions, presented by gender inequalities in today's workplace, the wage gap in existing occupations and sectors, and the double burden of unpaid care work. Supporting women in navigating these transitions could ensure that progress toward gender equality is not undermined.

Comments:

Nowadays, with the rapid development of our society and economy, there are many job opportunities. However, a problem persists: high-level positions are predominantly held by men, even though some women are equally competent.

What is your opinion?

Reference:

Argument:

(1) Being stronger and faster physically

(2) Being influenced by traditional concepts of gender roles

(3) Relating to some historical and social factors

Counter-argument:

(1) Recognizing and respecting the differences between men and women

(2) Creating an environment where both genders can fully realize their potential
(3) Considering the ability instead of the gender

Unit 3　Education and Recreation

Text Focus

1. School Education
2. Famous Universities
3. Cultural Life

Vocabulary

1. statute	[ˈstætʃuːt]	n.	法规
2. denounce	[dɪˈnaʊns]	v.	指责
3. secular	[ˈsekjələ(r)]	adj.	世俗的
4. affiliate	[əˈfɪlɪt]	v.	附属；隶属
5. sponsor	[ˈspɒnsə(r)]	v.	资助

Education in Canada is for the most part provided publicly, funded and overseen by federal, provincial, and local governments and it is within provincial jurisdiction and the curriculum is overseen by the province. The basic structure of provincial and territorial education systems across Canada has three tiers—elementary, secondary and post secondary, although start and end of the grades at each level are slightly different. A lot of famous universities exist in Canada, such as the University of Toronto, McGill University and the University of British Columbia. The transition of Canadian culture from European to authentically Canadian took place almost at the same time with the gradual settlement of the country. The bilingual, multicultural and North American elements of Canada's character have all influenced the formation of Canadian culture and the way Canadians express themselves through the arts.

School Education

Elementary, secondary and post-secondary education in Canada is a provincial responsibility and there are many variations between the provinces. Some educational fields are supported at various levels by federal departments.

Chapter Four Canada

All jurisdictions have kindergartens in various forms in Canada. Pre-elementary education may be compulsory and pre-school classes may be available at the age of 4 or even earlier based on jurisdictions. In elementary education, the age limits for compulsory schooling differ from one jurisdiction to another, but most schooling attendance is from Age 6 to Age 16. In some jurisdictions, compulsory schooling starts at the age of 5, and in others it extends to Age 18 or graduation form secondary school.

The elementary school curriculum emphasizes the basic subjects such as language, mathematics, social studies, science, health and physical education, and introductory arts.

Secondary schools include the final four to six years of compulsory education. In the first year, students mostly take compulsory courses, with some options. The students gradually increase options in the later years so that they may take specialized courses to make preparation for the job market or to meet different entrance requirements of post secondary institutions. Students who complete compulsory and optional courses are awarded to secondary school diplomas. National and academic programmes are offered within the same secondary schools in most cases; technical and vocational programmes are provided in separate and dedicated vocational training centers.

Since the adoption of *Section 23* of *the Constitution Act, 1982*, education in both English and French has been available in most places across Canada.

Private schools have historically been less common on the Canadian Prairies and were often forbidden under municipal and provincial ***statutes***[1] enacted to provide equality of education to students regardless of family income. This is especially true in Alberta, where successive Social Credit governments ***denounced***[2] the concept of private education as the main cause of denial of opportunity to the children of the working poor. These rules lasted longer than Social Credit, and it was only in 1989 that private K-12 schools were allowed to operate inside the boundaries of the City of Calgary.

Canada has a wealth of higher education options. There are life-enriching opportunities in its universities and university colleges which are located across Canada with at least one in every province.

As universities are no longer the only degree-granting institutions in some jurisdictions, post secondary system has evolved during the past few years. Post secondary education in Canada is provided by both government-supported and private institutions. Over 100 community colleges are included in post secondary system, which respond to the training needs of business, industry and the public service, as well as the educational needs of vocationally-oriented secondary school graduates.

Famous Universities

The University of Toronto is a public research university in Toronto, Ontario, Canada, situated on the grounds that surround Queen's Park. It has one of the strongest research and teaching faculties in North America, presenting top students at all levels with an intellectual environment unmatched in depth and breadth on any other Canadian campus. The University is Canada's most important research institution and has gained an international reputation for its research. The rankings make it clear that the University of Toronto stands among the best public universities in the world and recognized as Canada's top university. The University of Toronto was founded by royal charter in 1827 as King's College, the first institution of higher learning in Upper Canada. Originally controlled by the Church of England, the university assumed the present name in 1850 upon becoming a ***secular***[3] institution.

Academically, the University of Toronto is noted for influential movements and curricula in literary criticism and communication theory, known collectively as the Toronto School. The University has been the center of some major medical and scientific discoveries including insulin, the electric heart pacemaker, and the gene responsible for the more dangerous stream of Alzheimer's disease. Additionally, with over 15 million holdings and spanning 3 campuses, the University of Toronto is home to the second largest university libraries and one of the top 4 research libraries in North America.

McGill University(Fig. 4-5) is a public research university located in Montreal, Quebec, Canada . Founded in 1821, McGill was chartered during the British colonial era, 46 years before the Canadian Confederation, making it one of the oldest universities in Canada. The university is made up of 10 faculties and schools—agricultural and environmental sciences, arts, dentistry, education, engineering, law, management, medicine, music and science—that offer around 300 programs of study. Around two-thirds of the university's students study at the undergraduate level. The university is ***affiliated***[4] with multiple teaching hospitals, and its medical school is the oldest in Canada.

The University of British Columbia(Fig. 4-6), commonly referred to as UBC, is a public research university located in Vancouver, Canada. The university was established in 1908 and opened in 1915. It has two main campuses—the Vancouver campus and the Okanagan campus located in Kelowna. The Vancouver campus is the larger of the two, accommodating more than 85 percent of the students. The Vancouver campus offers more than two dozen academic divisions, while the Okanagan campus has eight. The university is the oldest in British Columbia and has the largest enrollment with over 54,000 students at its Vancouver and Okanagan campuses combined. The university library, which comprises 5.9 million books and journals, is the second-largest research library in Canada.

Fig. 4-5　McGill University

Fig. 4-6　University of British Columbia

Cultural Life

Canada has a well-developed media sector, but its cultural output—particularly in English films, television shows, and magazines—is often overshadowed by imports from the United States. Both the television broadcasting and publication sectors require a number of government interventions to remain profitable.

Canada is home to several film studios centers, primarily located in its three largest metropolitan centers: Toronto, Ontario; Montreal, Quebec and Vancouver, British Columbia. Industries and communities tend to be regional and niche in nature. Approximately 1,000 Anglophone-Canadian and 600 Francophone-Canadian feature-length films have been produced, or partially produced, by the Canadian film industry.

The music of Canada has reflected the multi-cultural influences that have shaped the country. Aboriginals, the French, and the British have all made contributions to the musical heritage of Canada. The music has subsequently been heavily influenced by American culture.

Sports in Canada consist of a wide variety of games. The most common sports are ice hockey, lacrosse, football, soccer, basketball, curling and baseball, with ice hockey and lacrosse being the official winter and summer sports, respectively.

Canada has had a thriving stage theater scene since the late 1800s. Theater festivals draw many tourists in the summer months. The Famous People Players are one of many touring companies that have also developed an international reputation. There are also two major theater venues in Ottawa, the government-owned and *sponsored*[5] National Arts Center and the privately owned Great Canadian Theater Company.

Canada has one of the largest video game industries in terms of employment numbers. Canada has grown from a minor player in the video games industry to a major industry player. In part, this is made possible by a large pool of university-educated talent and high quality of life, but favorable government policies towards digital media companies also play a role in making Canada an attractive location for game development studios.

Exercises

I. *Try to answer the following questions according to your understanding of the text.*

(1) Since when has education in both English and French been available in most places across Canada?

(2) What kind of initiatives have most schools in Canada introduced?

(3) What well-known universities do you know in Canada?

(4) What are the primary locations of film studio centers in Canada?

(5) What are the most common sports in Canada?

II. *Read the following passage carefully, and make a comment on it at the end of the passage in no more than 100 words.*

There are hundreds of thousands of international students in Canada today as part of a government strategy to reshape Canadian demographics by funneling well-educated, skilled workers through the university system. It is an answer to Canada's aging population and slowing birthrate, and an effort to shore up the nation's tax base.

The federal government changed its electronic immigration-selection system, called Express Entry, to make it easier for international students to become citizens. And a bill pending in the Senate would restore a rule that counts half of students' time spent studying in Canada toward the period of residency required for citizenship.

The country needs talented immigrants to backfill a thinly spread, aging population. According to Immigration, Refugees and Citizenship Canada, the country's immigration department, immigrants already make up 75% of the annual net growth in the country's work force and are expected to account for 100% within ten years.

Canada expects to have nearly half a million international students studying in the country within ten years. And more than half of its students from abroad hope to stay in the country and become Canadian citizens, according to a survey by the Canadian Bureau for International Education.

Internationalizing Canadian education promises a deep and lasting effect on the country, binding it to other nations and cultures through the family ties and the broader perspectives of international students who become citizens and may even rise to positions of national power. Canada's new immigration minister, for example, arrived in the country as a Somali refugee and earned a law degree at the University of Ottawa.

Comments:

The Canadian immigrant population exceeded 8.3 million until 2021, accounting for nearly 23% of the population, which is the highest proportion since the establishment of the Canadian

Federation in 1867.

What are the advantages and disadvantages of immigration?

Reference:

Argument:

(1) Filling job vacancies and skill gaps

(2) Promoting economic growth

(3) Increasing pensions and taxes for the economy

Counter-argument:

(1) Bringing about cultural conflicts

(2) Leading to resource allocation issues

(3) Increasing the security risks of cities

Unit 4 Politics and Economy

Text Focus

1. Political System
2. Political Parties
3. Economy

4.4 Lecture4 Politics and Economy.mp4

Vocabulary

1. fluctuate	[ˈflʌktʃʊˌeɪt]	v.	波动
2. prevail	[prɪˈveɪl]	v.	占优势
3. innovative	[ˈɪnəveɪtɪv]	adj.	创新的
4. multifaceted	[ˌmʌltiˈfæsɪtɪd]	adj.	多层面的
5. subsidiary	[səbˈsɪdiəri]	n.	子公司

The Constitution Act of 1867 is a major part of Canada's Constitution. It created a federal dominion and defined much of the operation of the government of the country including its federal structure, its bicameral legislature, the justice system, and the taxation system. Canadian political system comprises a group of political parties with the Liberal Party of Canada, the New Democratic Party and the Conservative Party of Canada. The economy of Canada is a highly developed mixed economy, which is dominated by the service industry, employing about three quarters of Canadians. Canada is also one of the largest agricultural producers and exporters in the world. There are a lot of top enterprises in Canada, such as IMAX and Air Canada, etc.

Political System

The Executive Branch: Canada is a constitutional monarchy, so the Head of State is the monarch of the United Kingdom. The monarch exercises power through a Governor-General at federal level plus Lieutenant Governors at provincial level and Commissioners at territory level. The Governor-General is advised by the Prime Minister and the Cabinet and by convention acts on this advice.

For all practical purposes, however, the head of the executive is the Prime Minister who by convention is the leader of the largest party in the House of Commons.

The Prime Minister's Office (PMO) is a key feature of the Canadian power structure and the Prime Minister appoints a Cabinet which by convention usually consists of at least one minister per province. As in the British model of government, Ministers generally come from one of the two chambers of the legislature and, if they are not already in the Commons or the Senate, they will be elected or nominated respectively. Again as in the British model, the size of the Cabinet is a matter for the Prime Minister and therefore *fluctuates*[1] from the lower 20 to almost 40.

The Cabinet is referred to either in relation to the prime minister in charge of it or, more formally, the number of ministries since Confederation in 1867. Like the United States, Canada is one of the few countries that locates its parliament and government in a political capital that is not its major city, so it is in Ottawa and not Toronto.

The House of Commons: In the Canadian political system, the lower chamber is the House of Commons which takes its name from the lower house in the British political system. The Commons consists of 308 members known as—like their British counterparts—Members of Parliament (MPs).

Members are elected by the first-past-the-post system in each of the country's electoral districts which are colloquially known as ridings. Seats in the House of Commons are distributed roughly in proportion to the population of each province and territory, but some ridings are more populous than others and the Canadian constitution contains some special provisions regarding provincial representation.

The House of Commons is more powerful of the two chambers. Although all legislation has to be approved by both chambers, in practice the will of the elected House usually *prevails*[2] over that of the appointed Senate. The processes and conventions of the Commons reflect very much those of its British namesake.

The Senate: In the Canadian political system, the upper chamber is the Senate which takes its name from the upper house in the American political system. The Senate consists of 105 members appointed by the Governor-General on the advice of the Prime Minister. Seats are assigned on a regional basis, with each of the four major regions receiving 24 seats, and the remaining nine seats being assigned to smaller regions. Senators may serve until they reach the age of 75. Although the approval of both chambers is necessary for all legislation, the Senate rarely rejects bills passed by the directly elected Commons.

The Judiciary: The Supreme Court of Canada is the highest court and final authority on civil, criminal and constitutional matters. The court's nine members are appointed by the Governor-General on the advice of the Prime Minister and Minister of Justice. In recent years, a real effort has been made to make the court geographically representative. Therefore the convention is that three judges come from Quebec, three from Ontario, two from Western Canada and one from the Atlantic provinces.

Each province operates its own individual court system. The country's legal system is based mainly on English common law but, in the province of Quebec, it is modeled on French civil law.

Political Parties

Canadian political system comprises a group of political parties with the Liberal Party of Canada, the Conservative Party of Canada and the New Democratic Party.

The Liberal Party is one of Canada's oldest and one of the most successful parties in Canada. The Party was in power in Canada for most of the 20th century. Its main areas of support lie in eastern and in urban areas, among middle-class professional and ethnic groups. It has been characterized by policies such as the welfare state, patriation of the constitution, multiculturalism, free trade, eliminating the national deficit and bilingualism.

The Conservative Party of Canada has gone by a variety of names over the years since Canadian Confederation. Initially known as the "Liberal-Conservative Party", and as a result of World War I, the Party joined with pro-conscription Liberals to become the "Unionist Party", and then the "National Liberal and Conservative Party". It then reverted to "Liberal-Conservative Party" until 1938, when it became simply the "National Conservative Party". The purpose of the Conservative Party was to "unite the right" and provide a viable alternative to the Liberal Party.

The New Democratic Party, which was founded on June 17, 1961, provides a democratic socialist political alternative in Canadian politics. In the Canadian House of Commons, it holds a center-left position in the Canadian political spectrum. The Party has never formed the federal government, but during federal minority government, it may wield considerable influence.

Some Political Parties without seats in the House of Commons are registered with Elections Canada. For the most part, these parties have not played a major part in Canadian politics. There are also parties without representation in the House of Commons and are not registered with Elections Canada.

Economy

Canada is one of the largest agricultural producers and exporters in the world. The proportion of the population and GDP devoted to agriculture fell dramatically over the 20th century, but it remains an important element of the Canadian economy. A wide range of agriculture is practiced in Canada, from sprawling wheat fields(Fig. 4-7) of the prairies to summer produce of the Okanagan valley. In the federal government, overview of Canadian agriculture is the responsibility of the Department of Agriculture and Agri-Food.

Fig. 4-7 Wheat Field

Canada has a well-established agriculture and agri-food industry with long-standing success in the global marketplace. It prides itself on its systems and policies that ensure world-class production standards. The industry's best practices and well-known reputation for ***innovative***[3] products and high-quality food have consistently positioned it as a cornerstone of the country's economy and a driving force in international trade.

Industry in Canada is to foster a growing, competitive, knowledge-based Canadian economy. The government works with Canadians throughout the economy and in all parts of the country to improve conditions for investment, improve Canadian's innovation performance, increase Canada' share of global trade and build a fair and competitive marketplace. Industry in Canada is responsible for regional economic development, investment and innovation and development.

The service sector in Canada is vast and ***multifaceted***[4], employing about three quarters of Canadians and accounting for about 78% of GDP. The service sector of the Canadian economy includes retail sector, financial services, real estate, education, health care, high-tech, entertainment and tourism. All these sectors are developing at a rapid rate with retail and health leading growth.

The education and health sectors are largely under the purview of the government. The health care industry has been quickly growing, and is the third largest in Canada. Its rapid growth has led to problems for governments who must find money to fund it.

Canada has an important high-tech industry, and also an entertainment industry creating content both for local and international consumption. Tourism is of ever increasing importance, with the vast majority of international visitors coming from the United States.

The IMAX Corporation is a Canadian theater company which designs and manufactures IMAX cameras and projection systems as well as performing film development, production, post production and distribution to IMAX affiliated theaters worldwide. Founded in 1968, it has operations in Toronto, as well as New York City and Los Angeles. In 2009, IMAX participated in the movie *Avatar*, to which the company credits its mainstream Hollywood success. In March 2011, IMAX noted that China's Wanda Cinema Line announced a 75-theater deal with IMAX Corporation. In 2012, IMAX opened its first location in Tianjin, China. In October, 2015, IMAX China, a ***subsidiary***[5] of the company, was listed on the Hong Kong Stock Exchange. According to *The Hollywood Reporter* and *The Wall Street Journal*, IMAX China raised $248 million in its initial public offering.

Air Canada(Fig. 4-8) is the flag carrier and the largest airline of Canada by fleet size and passengers carried. The airline, founded in 1937, provides scheduled and charter air transport for passengers and cargo to destinations worldwide. It is one of the world's largest passenger airline by fleet size, and is a founding member of the Star Alliance. Air Canada's corporate headquarters are in Montreal, Quebec, while its largest hub is at Toronto Pearson International Airport. The airline's regional service is Air Canada Express. Canada's national airline originated from the Canadian federal government's 1936 creation of Trans-Canada Airlines, which began operating its first transcontinental flight routes in 1938. In 2007, Air Canada was the first airline in North America to introduce electronic boarding passes for mobile check-in, and in 2016, Air Canada is the first Canadian airline to offer in-seat Wi-Fi access on select North American flights and across all narrow-body aircraft, boasting more Wi-Fi-enabled planes than any other Canadian airline.

Fig. 4-8　Air Canada

Exercises

I. *Try to answer the following questions according to your understanding of the text.*

(1) How many members are there in the Senate? And how are seats allocated?
(2) What are the major political parties in Canada?
(3) How much do you know about the service sectors in Canada?
(4) Can you list some top enterprises in Canada?
(5) What is Air Canada?

II. *Read the following passage carefully, and make a comment on it at the end of the passage in no more than 100 words.*

By the end of July, 2023, over 1,000 wildfires are burning more than 100,000 square kilometers of land in Canada, more than 600 of them out of control and growing rapidly, according to the Canadian Interagency Forest Fire Center (CIFFC). The burnt area is equivalent to the size of Iceland or South Korea. According to local media, more Canadians have been evacuated from their homes this year than in the last four decades, with more than 155,000 forced to leave due to fire and smoke.

Canada now has 5,500 damestie and some 3,300 international firefighters working together to put out the blaze, Reuters estimated based on a survey. However, the personnel deficit is still large compared to the scale of burning.

The enormous CO_2 emissions from the unprecedented fires raised concerns among scientists and the public as they hamper international efforts to mitigate climate change. The greenhouse gas emissions from the raging wildfires in Canada have exceeded one billion metric tons of carbon dioxide equivalent, according to a study by Chinese scientists led by Liu Zhihua, a researcher from the Institute of Applied Ecology, Chinese Academy of Sciences. The methane and nitrous oxide emissions are about 110 million metric tons of CO_2 equivalent, and the total greenhouse gas emissions are about 1.11 billion metric tons of CO_2 equivalent. A preliminary estimate suggests roughly 1.42 billion metric tons of CO_2 equivalent have been released from the fires so far, across Canada's managed and unmanaged forests. This is at least twice the emissions from all other sectors of the nation's economy combined.

Carbon emissions not only aggravate global warming but also create a dangerous feedback loop by creating conditions where forests are more likely to burn, further shrinking Earth's carbon sink capacities. The UN Environment Programme called for international and regional collaboration to tackle wildfires in its 2022 report on Rapid Response Assessment. For individual countries, effective measures should be taken to mitigate CO_2 emissions from natural processes, adding with regard to wildfires, strategies such as fuel treatment and improved forest management can be used to limit fire intensity and subsequently reduce CO_2 emissions.

Comments:

Some people think that the development of economy takes priority over environmental protection because it provides job opportunities and improves people's living standards; while others think it is wise of people to think that mankind has a long-term responsibility to protect the environment.

What is your opinion?

Reference:

Chapter Four   Canada

Argument:

(1) Being well-off and live a better life

(2) The current situation of China

(3) Non-contradiction

Counter-argument :

(1) Sustainable development

(2) Critical problems

(3) Future generations

Unit 5   Culture and Customs

Text Focus

1. Traditional Culture
2. Literature Works
3. Food Customs

4.5 Lecture5 Customs and Culture.mp4

Vocabulary

1. statutory	[ˈstætʃətri]	adj.	法定的
2. tendency	[ˈtendənsi]	n.	趋势
3. greasy	[ˈgri:si]	adj.	油腻的
4. contender	[kənˈtendə(r)]	n.	竞争者
5. syrup	[ˈsɪrəp]	n.	糖浆

The culture of Canada is a term that embodies the artistic, culinary, literary, humor, musical and social elements that are representatives of Canada and Canadians. Public holidays are legislated at the national, provincial and territorial levels, which represent traditional culture of Canada respectively. Obeying social rules and customs is a good way to adapt to Canadian society. A lot of popular literature works in Canada also reveal and unfold the specific culture of Canada, such as *the Handmaid's Tale*, *Life of Pi* and *Dear Life*. Canadian cuisine varies widely depending on the regions of the nation, with the roots of English, Scottish and French.

Traditional Culture

Throughout Canada's history, its culture has been influenced by European culture and traditions, especially British and French, and by its own indigenous cultures. Over time, elements of the cultures of Canada's immigrant populations have become incorporated into the mainstream Canadian culture. The population has also been influenced by American culture because of a shared language, proximity, television and migration between the two countries. Canada is often characterized as being "very progressive, diverse, and multicultural".

Canadian Aboriginals(Fig. 4-9) are categorized into three distinct groups. These are the First Nations, the Inuits, and the Metis people of Canada. Whilst the First Nations include members of all indigenous nations descending from Palaeo-Eskimos, the Inuits' ancestors were the Thule people, who originated in Alaska, from where they travelled to Canada and Greenland between 200 B.C. and 1,300 A.D. The Metis are descendants of both First Nations and European colonists, emerging in the 18th century, when French fur traders married Native women, but they are defined by their unique culture, taken from both Native and French customs, which may explain why they are called Metis, the French word for "mixed".

Fig. 4-9 Canadian Aboriginals

Holidays: Holidays in Canada represent Canadian traditional cultures a lot. Public holidays, known as "***statutory***[1] holidays", are legislated at the national, provincial and territorial levels. Nationwide statutory holidays in Canada, are New Year's Day, Canada Day on July 1, Labor Day on First Monday in September and so on. In addition to the nationwide holidays, the following holidays are statutory in some provinces and territories: Easter Monday, Victoria Day, Thanksgiving, Remembrance Day and Boxing Day.

Canada Day: On July 1, 1867, Canada became a self-governing dominion of Great Britain and a federation of four provinces: Nova Scotia; New Brunswick; Ontario; and Quebec. The anniversary of this date was called Dominion Day until 1982. Since 1983, July 1 has been officially known as Canada Day. In many towns and cities, municipal governments organize a range of events, often outdoors. These include pancake breakfasts, parades, concerts, carnivals, festivals, firework displays and citizenship ceremonies for new Canadian citizens. The celebrations often have a patriotic mood. Canada's national flag is widely displayed and a lot of people paint their faces red and white, which are Canada's national colors.

The Quebec Winter Carnival: For more than 56 years, the Quebec Winter Carnival has been the biggest winter festival in the world, offering 17 days of fun for all the family including over 300 shows and activities, an Ice Palace, two Magical Night Parades, a 400-foot-long Ice Slide, a Day Parade, and an outdoor stage with dance and music shows every Friday and Saturday night.

Literature Works

Canadian literature is often divided into French and English-language literature, which are rooted in the literary traditions of France and Britain, respectively. Canada's literature often reflects the Canadian perspective on nature, frontier life, and Canada's position in the world. Canadian is closely tied to its literature. Canada today is not the same Canada that was being written about in 1850, or 1930, so a historical distinction should be made: analysts of national literature often identify distinct periods which share particular characteristics, and this has been done in the Canadian case too.

The Handmaid's Tale is a dystopian novel by the Canadian author Margaret Atwood, originally published in 1985. The novel focuses on the journey of the handmaid Offred. Her name derives from the possessive form "of Fred"—handmaids are forbidden to use their birth names and must echo the male, or master, whom they serve.

Margaret Atwood(Fig. 4-10) is the most successful and internationally recognized current Canadian novelist. She is also a poet and critic. Atwood's works mainly focus on feminist themes, Canadian national identity and ecological catastrophes caused by blind developments of science and technology. She has published 14 books of poetry, 16 novels, ten books of non-fiction, eight collections of short fiction, eight children's books, and one graphic novel, as well as a number of small press editions in poetry and fiction. As a novelist and poet, Atwood's works encompass a variety of themes including the power of language, gender and identity, religion and myth, climate change, and "power politics". Many of her poems are inspired by myths and fairy tales which interested her from a very early age. Her best-known novels are *The Handmaid's Tale*, *Oryx and Crake*, and *The Year of the Flood*.

Fig. 4-10 Margaret Atwood

Fig. 4-11 Life of Pi

Life of Pi(Fig. 4-11) is a Canadian fantasy adventure novel by Yann Martel, published in 2001. The protagonist is Piscine Molitor Pi Patel, an Indian boy from Pondicherry who explores issues of spirituality and practicality from an early age. He survives 227 days after a shipwreck while stranded on a lifeboat in the Pacific Ocean with a Bengal tiger named Richard Parker. The novel has sold more than ten million copies worldwide. It was rejected by at least five London publishing houses before being accepted by Knopf Canada, which published it in September 2001. The UK edition won the Man Booker Prize for Fiction the following year. It was also chosen for CBC Radio's Canada Reads 2003, where it was championed by author Nancy Lee.

Life of Pi, according to Yann Martel, can be summarized in three statements: Life is a story. You can choose your story. A recurring theme throughout the novel seems to be believability. Pi at the end of the book asks the two investigators "If you stumble at mere believability, what are you living for?" According to Gordon Houser, there are two main themes of the book: "that all life is interdependent, and that we live and breathe via belief."

Dear Life is a short story collection by Canadian writer Alice Munro, published in 2012 by McClelland and Stewart. The book was to have been promoted in part by a reading at Toronto's International Festival of Authors, although the appearance was cancelled due to health concerns. Most of the stories collected in *Dear Life* had previously been published elsewhere. *Amundsen, Corrie, Dear Life, Gravel, Haven,* and *Leaving Maverly* were all originally published in *The New Yorker. Dolly* was first published in *Tin House*.

Alice Ann Munro(Fig. 4-12) is a Canadian short story writer who won the Nobel Prize in Literature in 2013. Munro's work has been described as having revolutionized the architecture of short stories, especially in its ***tendency***[2] to move forward and backward in time. Her stories have been said to "embed more than announce, reveal more than parade." Munro's fiction is most often set in her native Huron County in southwestern Ontario. Her stories explore human complexities in an uncomplicated prose style. Munro's writing has established her as "one of our greatest contemporary writers of fiction". Munro is the recipient of many literary accolades, including the 2013 Nobel Prize in Literature for her work as "master of the contemporary short story", and the 2009 Man Booker International Prize for her lifetime body of work.

Fig. 4-12 Alice Ann Munro

Chapter Four Canada

Food Customs

Canadian cuisine varies widely, depending on the regions of the nation. The three earliest cuisines of Canada have First Nations, English, Scottish and French roots, with the traditional cuisine of English Canada closely related to British cuisine, while the traditional cuisine of French Canada has evolved from French cuisine and the winter provisions of fur traders. With subsequent waves of immigration in the 19th and 20th century from Central, Southern, and Eastern Europe, South Asia, East Asia, and the Caribbean, the regional cuisines were subsequently augmented.

In terms of food, Canadians like sweet and sour, non-fat and not-too-hot food and not *greasy*[3] soup. They do not add spices while cooking, which are on the table for people to choose as they wish. Common *contenders*[4] as the Canadian national food include Poutine and Butter tarts. A noteworthy fact is that Canada is the world's largest producer and consumer of Maple *syrup*[5]. Aside from the fried or roasted beef, mutton, or chicken steak, they also like game, but they do not eat entrails or fat. Dinner is the most formal meal of the day, though they also enjoy afternoon tea and some wine.

Table manners are relatively relaxing and informal in Canada. Quebec does see a little more formality. The manners are generally Continental, i.e. the fork is held in the left hand and the knife in the right while eating. People usually wait before being shown to their seats and they do not begin eating until the hostess starts. People are not supposed to rest their elbows on the table, but they can feel free to refuse individual food or drink without offering an explanation. Leaving a small amount of tips at the end of the meal is generally acceptable. In formal situations, the host gives the first toast. An honored guest should return the toast later in the meal.

 Exercises

I. *Try to answer the following questions according to your understanding of the text.*

(1) What cultural elements influence Canadian culture in history?
(2) Could you give a brief introduction of Canadian literature?
(3) Could you introduce some major Canadian holidays and festivals?
(4) What roots did the earliest cuisines of Canada have?
(5) What flavor do Canadians like for their food?

II. *Read the following passage carefully, and make a comment on it at the end of the passage in no more than 100 words.*

Canada is a very interesting country, mainly due to its diversity. The weather in Canada can be both freezing and very hot. Some land is rocky and mountainous, while other places are composed of flat, rolling hills. And in Canada, you can find many different races, from Asian to

Latin, African to Indian.

Canada was the very first country in the world to introduce a multicultural policy. In 1969, the Royal Commission on Bilingualism and Biculturalism heard many ethnic spokespersons argue that Canada should adopt the idea of a "cultural mosaic", where different cultures would each contribute to Canada, making the country unified through each culture's uniqueness.

"Cultural mosaic" is a term used to describe the mix of ethnic groups, languages and cultures that co-exist within Canadian society. The idea of a cultural mosaic is intended to champion an ideal of multiculturalism, differently from other systems like the melting pot, which is often used to describe the neighboring United States' supposed ideal of assimilation.

The first use of the term mosaic to refer to Canadian society was by John Murray Gibbon. Gibbon clearly disapproved of the American melting-pot concept. He saw the melting pot as a process by which immigrants and their descendants were encouraged to cut off ties with their countries and cultures of origin so as to assimilate into the American way of life.

Since the beginning of the 20th century, Canada has been one of the world's major immigrant-receiving societies. Until the 1960s, immigrants were expected to assimilate into the mainstream society. The view of Canada as a mosaic of cultures became the basis for the Trudeau government's multiculturalism policies in the early 1970s. The Canadian government established *the Official Multiculturalism Act* in 1971 and appointed a minister responsible for multiculturalism in 1972.

Cultural mosaic in Canada is that people hold on to their own traditions, their own way of dress etc. This does not always work either. Most people in Canada would also like immigrants to blend and adopt Canada's way of life, so this is also a question for discussion and debate.

Comments:

The development of technology is on the move at an unprecedented speed nowadays. Some people think that traditional culture will be lost when technology gets developed; some disagree on it.

What is your opinion?

Reference:

Argument:

(1) Being more convenient to connect with traditional culture

(2) Protecting the traditional culture

Counter-argument:

(1) Doing harm to the traditional culture

(2) Losing some cultural heritages

Chapter Four Canada

Unit 6 Intercultural Communication

 Knowledge to Learn

What Is the Purpose of Verbal Communication?

Verbal communication encompasses everything from simple one-syllable sounds to complex discussions and relies on both language and emotion to produce the desired effect.

Why Is Verbal Communication Important?

We use verbal communication to inform, to clarify misunderstanding and to provide missing information. Verbal communication can also be used as a tool of persuasion. It creates an opportunity for debate, stimulates thought and creativity, and deepens and creates new relationships.

 Cases to Study

Case 1

> Lu was invited to a Christmas party organized by graduates. Most of the people there were Canadians. After a few drinks, Lu noticed that most students became more relaxed. The things they said to each other and their body language soon became very flirtatious. Men and women would lean against each other on the couch almost like boyfriends and girlfriends.
>
> One male graduate student sat behind Lu. She could feel that his hands were playing with her long hair. She turned around and wanted to stop him, but before she said anything, he said, "You look very seductive tonight."
>
> Lu felt terrible. "Do I? I'm sorry. I certainly didn't mean to seduce you." The student laughed, "Why are you feeling sorry? You're very attractive. It's a compliment!" Lu was confused. She did not know how to respond.
>
> What cultural information can we get from this conversation?

Analysis

(1) In China, flirting is associated with having a low moral standard. It usually arouses disgust. Flirting with another person can be the basis for a fight between spouses or a boy and girl friend.

(2) To Westerners, flirting is not necessarily seen as a serious expression of interest in another person. It is usually something done just for fun. It makes both persons feel attractive and special.

(3) Between strangers, flirting may take the form of discrete looks and smiles, perhaps some light-hearted words. Friends might be a bit bolder in their words, and might touch each other casually on the arm or hand.

Case 2

> Mr. Wang, Chairman of Board of a Chinese firm, told a story on CCTV program "Dialogue" of how he once almost lost a valuable Canadian employee working for him in Vancouver. He emailed every day to the Canadian, inquiring for the index number he was most concerned about. To his great astonishment, his Canadian employee turned in his resignation after a week. Mr. Wang was puzzled how he could do that to him as he gave such great attention to his job.
>
> Could you analyze the reasons behind the Canadian's resignation?

Analysis

(1) The resignation of the Canadian employee resulted from the communication barrier due to the preconception of Mr. Wang. Mr. Wang assumed unconsciously that the Canadian was more similar to his Chinese employees than he actually was and treated him just as he treated any Chinese employees.

(2) A Chinese employee would have been more than happy if his or her boss had showed such great concern for him or her. But Mr. Wang found out that, unlike Chinese employees, the Canadian took what meant great concern to Chinese as distrust.

(3) Preconceptions and biases can represent a barrier to communication. Prior interactions with people may have caused us to form opinions about them that may impact how closely you listen to them or how you view their comments and opinions.

(4) With strangers you may be impacted by the way they look or their manner of speech and may quickly form opinions that may be inaccurate. Being alert to your own potential for bias can help to avoid this common barrier in communication.

Translations on Traditional Chinese Culture

Exercise 1

Translate the passage into English

Tu Lou is a traditional dwelling for the Hakkas in the west of Fujian Province. It has an average of three or four storeys and a maximum of six storeys. Including the houses in the yard, Tu Lou can usually hold more than 50 families. Halls, storage houses, domestic animal houses, wells and other public houses are in the yard. The Hakkas created this special defensive building to protect themselves, and it's still in use now.

Translation Reference

土楼是福建省西部的客家传统住宅。它平均为三至四层，最高达六层。包括院子里的房屋在内，土楼通常可以容纳 50 多个家庭。大厅、储藏室、牲口圈、水井以及其他公共房屋都位于院子中。客家人建造这种特殊的防御性建筑是为了保护自己，而且现在依然在使用这种建筑。

Translate the passage into Chinese

The real culture of Beijing is the culture of Hutongs and courtyard. Hutong is the name given to a lane or small street that originated during the Yuan Dnasty. Hutongs in Beijing have various styles and different lengths. The longest one is Dongjiaominxiang Hutong, with a total length of about three kilometers. A standard courtyard usually consists of houses on its four sides with a yard in the center. The gates are usually painted red and have large copper door rings. Usually, a whole family lives in compound. The elder generation lives in the main house standing at the north end, the younger generations live in the side houses, and a house with a southern exposure is usually the family living room or study.

Translation Reference

真正的北京文化是胡同和四合院文化。胡同源于元朝时对小巷或小街的叫法。北京城的胡同风格各异，长短不一，最长的是东交民巷胡同，全长近 3 公里。标准的四合院通常由一个位于中心的院子和四侧厢房构成，门通常漆成红色，并有大的铜门环。通常全家人住在一处，北端的正房由长辈居住，年轻人生活在两侧厢房，朝南的房子，通常是家庭客厅或书房。

Exercise 2

Translate the passage into English

长城是世界上最伟大的奇迹之一，1987 年被列为联合国教科文组织世界文化遗产。它宛如一条巨龙，蜿蜒曲折，穿越草地、沙漠和高山，自西向东绵延 8,851.8 公里(明长城)。经过两千多年的沧桑，长城部分城墙已经被毁或湮灭。但是，由于建筑雄伟，历史悠久，长城现今依然是世界上最具吸引力的景点之一。长城始建于春秋战国时期的燕、赵、秦等国，作为防御工事。秦始皇将各段城墙连接起来，抵御北方部落的侵袭。

Translation Reference

The Great Wall, one of the greatest wonders of the world, was listed as a UNESCO World Cultural Heritage Site in 1987. Like a giant dragon, the Great Wall winds its way across grasslands, deserts and mountains, stretching approximately 8,851.8 kilometers (the Ming Walls) from west to east of China. With a history of more than 2,000 years, some of the sections are now in ruins or have disappeared. However, it is still one of the most appealing attractions all around the world owing to its architectural grandeur and historical significance. The Great Wall was originally built in the Spring and Autumn Period and the Warring States Period as a defensive project by states including Yan, Zhao, and Qin etc. Qinshihuang succeeded in his effort to have the walls joined together to fend off the invasions from tribes in the north.

Translate the passage into Chinese

The Summer Palace is situated in Haidian District, northwest of Beijing City, 15 kilometers from central Beijing. It is the largest and most well-preserved royal park in China. It also has long been recognized as "the Museum of Royal Gardens" with famous natural view and cultural landscape. The construction started in 1750 as a luxurious royal garden for royal families to rest and entertain. It became the main residence of royal members at the end of the Qing Dynasty. It not only ranks amongst the World Heritage Sites but also is one of the first national AAAAA tourist spots in China.

Translation Reference

颐和园位于北京市西北部的海淀区，距北京市中心15公里。它是中国最大、保存最完好的皇家园林。颐和园有著名的自然风景和人文景观，因此它也一直被公认为是"皇家园林博物馆"。颐和园始建于1750年，作为一座豪华的皇家花园供皇室成员休息和娱乐。清朝末期，颐和园成为了皇家成员的主要居住地。它位列世界遗产目录，也是中国第一批国家5A级旅游景区之一。

Exercise 3

Translate the passage into English

秦始皇是秦朝的开国皇帝，建立了中国历史上第一个中央集权的封建国家。兵马俑是秦始皇陵墓的一部分，是秦始皇为了在死后能继续他的统治而建造的。兵马俑大部分采用陶冶烧制的方法制成，真人一样大小的兵俑按战斗队形排列，依据不同的等级，他们的身高、制服和发型都不相同。他们生动、逼真的形象，显示了工匠们极高的雕刻水平，被誉为"世界第八大奇迹"。

Translation Reference

Qinshihuang is the first emperor of the Qin Dynasty and established the first centralized feudal state in Chinese history. The Terra-cotta Warriors and Horses is a part of

Qinshihuang's mausoleum. It was constructed for Qinshihuang to continue his reign in his afterlife. Most of them were made by means of pottery and firing. Varying in heights, uniforms and hairstyles in accordance with their ranks, the life-sized Terra-cotta Warriors are arranged in battle formation. The vivid and life-like images reflect the high engraving level of craftsmen. It was honored as "the Eighth Wonder of the World".

Translate the passage into Chinese

Between 1405 and 1433, Zheng He was ordered to command seven naval expeditions, known as "Zheng He's Voyages to the West Ocean". As the main activities were carried out in the area of today's Kalimantan Island, it is known as West Ocean in ancient times. His fleet was composed of more than 200 ships and carried over 20,000 men, including sailors, technical personnel, interpreters etc., and large amounts of gold and silk to be used for trade and as gifts. The round trip took two years. Zheng He's voyages were a great feat in the world's navigation history.

Translation Reference

从公元 1405 到 1433 年，郑和先后七次被派遣进行远航，称为"郑和下西洋"。这些主要活动区域在今天的加里曼丹岛以西海域，古时被称为西洋。他的舰队由 200 多艘船构成，所载人数超过 2 万人，包括水手、技师和译员等，还有大量黄金和丝绸，用于交易和作为礼品。往返用了两年时间。郑和下西洋是世界航海史上的一大壮举。

 Culture to Know

Culture Note 1

Chinese ancient architecture includes palaces, dwelling houses, temples, gardens, and so on. They are of distinctive characteristics in different regions, ethnic groups and times. More than a technical science, Chinese ancient architecture absorbs traditional arts, including Chinese painting and carving, etc. Many palaces and private gardens built in Ming and Qing are reserved today.

Culture Note 2

Beijing National Stadium, officially the National Stadium, also known as the Bird's Nest, is a 91,000-capacity stadium in Beijing with the building area of 258,000 square meters. Located at the Olympic Green, the stadium cost US $428 million. The stadium was designed for use throughout the 2008 Summer Olympics and Paralympics. The Bird's Nest sometimes has temporary large screens installed at the stands.

Culture Note 3

Wu Zhao, commonly known as Wu Zetian, is notable for being the only female monarch in the history of China. The importance of the history of Wu Zetian's period of political and military leadership includes the major expansion of the Chinese empire, extending it far beyond its previous territorial limits, deep into Central Asia. Wu Zetian also had a monumental impact upon the statuary of the Longmen Grottoes and the "Wordless Stele" at the Qianling Mausoleum, as well as the construction of some major buildings and bronze castings that no longer survive.

Culture Note 4

China Ushers in Golden Era of AI, Chatbots

AIGC-related technologies, including ChatGPT-like tools, drive content production for media, entertainment, education. Chinese tech companies are ramping up efforts to make a foray into the fast-growing artificial intelligence-generated content sector and roll out AI-powered chatbots or products similar to ChatGPT, which has taken the world by storm since its launch due to its advanced conversational capabilities. AI-generated content and ChatGPT-related technologies are likely to become a new engine driving innovation in content production and free human creators from tedious tasks, enabling them to focus on creative thinking, with immense application potential in a wide range of fields like culture, media, entertainment and education. Chinese enterprises possess the advantages of offering users AI-powered conversational results in the context of the Chinese language, and more efforts are needed to pool resources in improving algorithm models, computing power and natural language processing abilities.

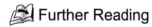
Further Reading

Passage 1

Smart Cars Set to Drive Auto Industry's Development

Sensors and software are becoming essential components of new vehicles. In China, such functions have become must-haves in newly launched models, including affordable compact cars priced at less than 100,000 yuan. Carmakers are also stepping up efforts to develop such capabilities and partnering with big-name technology companies. Electric car startup Nio joined with tech giant Tencent to work on high-precision mapping systems for drivers. The deal will allow Nio to use Tencent's cloud computing infrastructure for data storage and training for its driver-assistance and autonomous driving technology.

Passage 2

The Fast-Growing BeiDou Navigation Satellite Applications Industry

In terms of product manufacturing, breakthroughs have been made in a series of key BeiDou Navigation Satellite technologies such as chips and modules, which has effectively driven up the shipment volume. In terms of its applications, BeiDou Navigation Satellite System(BDS) has been widely applied to various industries and sectors, generating significant socioeconomic benefits. BDS-based applications have shown their growing relevance in scenarios closely related to daily life, notably in smartphones and smart wearable devices. BDS has been widely supported by products from international mainstream chip manufacturers, including smartphone device suppliers. Mass consumption has become one of the major sectors for BeiDou applications.

Chapter Five

New Zealand

Contents

1. Location and Resources
2. History and Symbols
3. Education and Recreation
4. Politics and Economy
5. Culture and Customs
6. Intercultural Communication

All Blacks	新西兰橄榄球国家队	**Maori**	毛利人
Auckland Harbour Bridge	奥克兰海港大桥	**Mount Cook**	库克山
Captain James Cook	詹姆斯·库克船长	**Museum of New Zealand**	新西兰国立博物馆
Dunedin Railway Station	达尼丁火车站	**rugby**	橄榄球
extreme sports	极限运动	**silver fern**	银蕨
Hongi	碰鼻礼	**Sky Tower**	天空塔
Kapa Haka	毛利族战舞	**the Beehive**	国会大厦
kohanga reo	语言巢	**the University of Auckland**	奥克兰大学
Kiwi	几维鸟；新西兰人	**Waitangi Day**	怀唐伊日(国庆节)
Manuka Honey	麦卢卡蜂蜜	**Waitomo Caves**	怀托莫溶洞

Chapter Five New Zealand

Unit 1 Location and Resources

Text Focus

1. Geographical Location
2. Weather and Climate
3. Natural Resources

5.1 Lecture1 Location.mp4   5.2 Lecture2 People.mp4

Vocabulary

1. scatter	[ˈskætə(r)]	v.	分散
2. moderately	[ˈmɒdərətli]	adv.	适度地
3. geothermal	[ˌdʒiːəʊˈθɜːml]	adj.	地热的
4. geyser	[ˈgiːzə(r)]	n.	喷泉
5. discharge	[dɪsˈtʃɑːdʒ]	v.	流出

New Zealand is an island country in the Southwestern Pacific Ocean. The country geographically comprises two main landmasses—the North Island and the South Island, and around 600 smaller islands. The country's varied topography, including volcanoes, waterfalls, rivers and glaciers, causes the mild temperature. New Zealand's capital city is Wellington, while the most populous city is Auckland.

Geographical Location

New Zealand is located in the Southwestern Pacific Ocean, and it is in the southern latitudes midway between the Equator and the South Pole. It is part of the Pacific Islands, or Oceania, which refers to a grouping of thousands of islands in the Pacific ocean. New Zealand has a total area of about 270,000 square kilometers, making it slightly smaller than Italy and Japan and a little larger than the United Kingdom. The country is very long and narrow. The nearest country to New Zealand is Australia, which is almost 2,000 kilometers away.

New Zealand was named, probably by a Dutch mapmaker, sometime after the Dutch explorer Abel Tasman made the first recorded European landfall in 1642. The commonly accepted Maori name for the country is Aotearoa, which means "land of the long white cloud".

On the map, New Zealand looks like a boot upside down. But if examined more closely, it is not hard to see that this "boot" is composed of two parts. They are the two main islands of New Zealand, namely the North Island and the South Island. Many small and widely scattered islands are also included in the territory of New Zealand. Some are tiny and uninhabited. Of the inhabited islands, Stewart Island is the largest and nearest, located about 30 kilometers off the southern shore of the South Island. The South Island and the North Island of New Zealand are respectively Oceania's second and third largest islands. They are separated by Cook Strait, a channel between the South Pacific Ocean on the east and the Tasman Sea on the west. Cook Strait is 20 kilometers across at its narrowest point. Apart from the North and South Islands, many small and widely *scattered*[1] islands are also included in the territory of New Zealand. Some are inhabited. Some are so tiny that nobody lives there.

The islands were created just 23 million years ago when the land was thrust out of the ocean by volcanic forces. New Zealand has more than 50 volcanoes, some of which are still active today. Sharp snowy peaks, rocky shores, and pastures create a majestic landscape.

Wellington is the capital city and the second most populous urban area of New Zealand after Auckland. Wellington is more densely populated than most other cities in New Zealand due to the restricted amount of land that is available between its harbour and the surrounding ranges of hills. It is at the southwestern tip of the North Island, between Cook Strait and the Rimutaka Range. Wellington also holds the distinction of being the world's southernmost capital city and the most remote capital city, the farthest away from any other capital city.

Wellington is New Zealand's political center, housing Parliament, the head offices of all Government Ministries and Departments and the bulk of the foreign diplomatic missions in New Zealand. Wellington's compact city center supports an arts scene, cafe culture and nightlife much larger than many cities of a similar size. It is an important center of New Zealand's film and theatre industry, and second to Auckland in terms of numbers of screen industry businesses.

Auckland is in the North Island of New Zealand and is the largest and most populous urban area in the country.

The city stretches over volcanic hills, sitting between the twin Waitemata and Manukau harbours. With so many bays, beaches and islands, glistening waters seem to beckon from every point.

Auckland is New Zealand's center of commerce and industry, and is perhaps the most vibrant, bustling and multicultural city in New Zealand. Auckland is the biggest Polynesian city in the world, and this cultural influence is reflected in many different aspects of city life. Auckland is a water lover's paradise, with some of the best beaches, swimming, diving, fishing, sailing, windsurfing and water sports in the country. It offers an eclectic mix of fashion, food and arts, and a host of activities to keep people entertained.

Christchurch is the largest city in the South Island of New Zealand, and the country's third-largest urban area. It lies one third of the way down the South Island's east coast, just north of Banks Peninsula. It is a place where its residents continue to enjoy a healthy, active lifestyle amidst a natural environment world-renowned for its beauty. A growing cosmopolitan ambience also adds a touch of excitement without overt flashiness.

It's a place where one can arrive at an international airport within two hours, one can ski at a world class alpine resort, play golf, go bungee jump, rafting, mountain biking, hot-air ballooning, wind surfing, whale watching and visit world-class wineries and gardens.

The city center is comfortingly compact and one of the most delightful central feature is the gently winding Avon River. On its grassy banks lined with poplars and weeping willows, office workers and visitors join street entertainers, seagulls and ducks for lunch in the sun.

Weather and Climate

New Zealand's location in the Southern Hemisphere, or south of the equator, means that its seasons are opposite to those in the Northern Hemisphere. New Zealand has a mild climate with four seasons. Inland areas have cooler winters and warmer summers than coastal areas, where the moderating influence of the ocean creates a more temperate climate. Temperatures tend to be warmer in the north than in the south; the warmest area is in the extreme northern end of the North Island, and the coldest area is on the southwestern slopes of the Southern Alps.

New Zealand has **moderately**[2] high rainfall, and many hours of sunshine throughout the country. Its climate is dominated by two main geographical features—the sea and the mountains. Seasons are reverse of those in the Northern Hemisphere. January and February are the warmest months, while July and August are the coolest. The far north of the country has an average temperature of about 15℃, while the deep south has a cooler 9℃ average.

Most places in New Zealand receive abundant sunshine, with an average of over 2,000 hours a year. As New Zealand observes daylight saving, during summer months daylight can last up until nine pm. New Zealand experiences little air pollution compared to many other countries, which makes the UV rays in the sunlight very strong during the summer. While its climate is generally a temperate one, New Zealand's weather is very changeable. A brisk rain shower can be expected even when the sun was shining a minute ago. The temperature can also change from quite warm to rather chilly during the same day. It is said that four seasons can occur in one day.

Natural Resources

New Zealand rivers and lakes are an important natural resource as the source of hydroelectricity. Mineral resources are limited, with some reserves of coal, gold, iron ore, and limestone. Significant stocks of natural gas and less plentiful reserves of oil are located both offshore and in the western regions of the North Island.

On the North Island elevations rarely exceed 1,000 meters, with the exception of several volcanic peaks. Mount Egmont is the best known extinct volcano in New Zealand, due to its symmetrical shape. It lies in Taranaki Province near the west coast. The mountain is 2,518 meters high and has one of the most perfect cone-shaped peaks in the world. Mount Ruapehu is the highest mountain in the North Island, which erupted with substantial clouds of ash in 1995 and 1996.

Closely related to the repeated volcanic activities are the rich resources—***geothermal***[3] power in the North Island. Here, plenty of hot springs and ***geysers***[4] can be found as a result of the underground heat. Most of the thermal region is located in the central and northern parts of the North Island. Some New Zealand geysers eject water columns more than 450 meters into the air. They have now become a popular tourist attraction.

Within the North Island, there are a large number of rivers. The longest river in New Zealand is also in the North Island. It is called Waikato and it is a typical mountain river which is 425 kilo meters long. Eight hydro-electric power stations have been built on the river banks. These power stations make an important contribution to the national power supply.

Lakes also abound in the North Island. Again, the reason for their formation has to do with volcanoes. The largest lake is Lake Taupo(Fig. 5-1). It is 46 kilometers long and 33 kilometers wide. Formed in the crater of an extinct volcano, Lake Taupo is one with many hot springs and spectacular scenery. The waters of Lake Taupo are also used to drive eight hydro-electric power stations on the Waikato River.

The South Island is home to the highest mountain peak in New Zealand, Mount Cook in the central Southern Alps, which rises to 3,754 meters and is called "Cloud Piercer" by the Maori people. The southern Alps extend about 500 kilometers, almost the entire length of the South Island. Apart from mountains, the South Island also has many other natural wonders, such as glaciers, lakes and rivers. Different from the volcanoes and hot springs in the North Island, the South Island is famous for its more than 360 glaciers(Fig. 5-2).

Fig. 5-1 Lake Taupo

Fig. 5-2 Glaciers

Most of the rivers of the South Island originate in the glacial lakes of the Southern Alps and flow generally southeastward to empty into the Pacific Ocean. The Clutha River is the largest river of the island. It ***discharges***[5] the largest volume of water of any river in New Zealand, and has been dammed in a number of places for hydroelectricity generation. Still another important river is the Waitaki River, which provides one of the most valuable hydroelectric power resources in the country.

New Zealand has an exceptionally long coastline compared to the size of the country. Its territorial waters stretch from the subtropical through to the sub-Antarctic. Both the North island and the South Island tend to have better swimming beaches on the east coast and the further north. The west coasts of both islands are rugged and have many cliffs, but there are still suitable swimming and bathing beaches here.

Exercises

I. *Try to answer the following questions according to your understanding of the text.*

(1) Where is New Zealand situated?
(2) How many major islands does New Zealand consist of? What are they?
(3) Which city is the largest in New Zealand?
(4) What is the climate like in New Zealand?
(5) What do you know about Lake Taupo?

II. *Read the following passage carefully, and make a comment on it at the end of the passage in no more than 100 words.*

Life in New Zealand is calm, sometimes too slow motion for someone from a big city like London, Paris, Tokyo, New York or Rio. Despite being quiet, New Zealand is not free from the day-by-day duties of the modern life. Anyway, what makes New Zealand calm and tranquil is the low concentration of population per square kilometer and its beautiful green pastures around the country.

With so many beautiful places, both the government and population take great care of their environment, keeping places and streets clean and free of garbage. Kiwis are very proud of the country they have in hands, despite the fact that some will look for better opportunities outside New Zealand. Kiwis are happy, informal but very well educated.

The New Zealand social system is based on the traditional family structure, despite the fact that it is becoming statistics the number of "Solo mothers in these days". The values of moral, character, study and work are still strongly present in New Zealand today. What a person does for a living or how much the person earns is not a matter of interest for a kiwi as soon as the person is acting legally, with a good character and manners. All kiwis are equal in law, and have the same obligations and rights. It is a country where the human rights are 100% respected.

Life in New Zealand is blessed, compared with other places in the world. There are no dangerous animals on land, diseases breakouts, terrorism fear or agricultural plagues. The country is clean, the sea water is very clear, beaches are pristine, and the air is also clean. The social security system is one of the best in the world, providing the basic support for those in need, not to mention the quality of hospitals and public schools which are top class. New Zealand is a great small country with nice people and one of the most beautiful landscapes in the world.

Comments:

Some people think that people are more dependent on each other in the modern world; while others think that people have become more independent.

What do you think of it?

Reference:

Argument:

(1) Modern life is more complex and interconnected

(2) Cooperating has become a key element in our daily work

(3) The increased need for friendship and communication

Counter-argument:

(1) Becoming more self-sufficient

(2) Allowing people to live alone with the rise of the Internet

(3) Cherishing more freedom and valuing less restrictions

Unit 2　History and Symbol

Text Focus

1. Historical Periods
2. Historical Figures
3. National Symbols

5.3 Lecture3 History and Education.mp4

Vocabulary

1. aware	[əˈweə(r)]	adj.	意识到的
2. treaty	[ˈtriːti]	n.	条约
3. cultivate	[ˈkʌltɪveɪt]	v.	开垦
4. expedition	[ˌekspəˈdɪʃn]	n.	探险
5. suffrage	[ˈsʌfrɪdʒ]	n.	选举权
6. initiative	[ɪˈnɪʃətɪv]	n.	方案

Chapter Five New Zealand

New Zealand has a shorter human history than any other country and Maoris(Fig. 5-3) were the first inhabitants. The current understanding is that the first arrivals came from East Polynesia in the 13th century. It was not until 1642 that Europeans became *aware*[1] that the country existed. The *Treaty*[2] *of Waitangi* symbolized that modern New Zealand was founded and that the United Kingdom established British sovereignty in New Zealand. Modern New Zealand is a developed country, and it is active in the world trade. Many well-known individual historical figures were in the history of New Zealand, such as Kate Sheppard, Donald McLean, Richard Seddon, etc. The national flag is called the Union Jack and the Stars of the Southern Cross.

Fig. 5-3   A Maori

Historical Periods

The arrival of Maori: According to Maori, the first explorer to reach New Zealand was Kupe. Using the stars and ocean currents as his navigational guides, he ventured across the Pacific on his voyaging canoe from his ancestral Polynesian homeland of Hawaiki. It is thought that Kupe made landfall at the Hokianga Harbour in Northland, around 1,000 years ago.

Maori were expert hunters and fishermen. They wove fishing nets from flax, and carved fishhooks from bone and stone. They hunted native birds, including moa, the world's largest bird, with a range of ingenious traps and snares. Maori *cultivated*[3] land and grew introduced vegetables from Polynesia, including the sweet potatoes. They also ate native vegetables, roots and berries. Weaved flax baskets were used to carry food, which was often stored in a pataka—a storehouse raised on stilts(Fig. 5-4).

Fig. 5-4   Maori People

The arrival of Europeans: Though a Dutchman was the first European to sight the country, it was the British who colonized New Zealand. The first European to sight New Zealand was Dutch explorer Abel Tasman. He was on an *expedition*[4] to discover a great Southern continent "Great South Land" that was believed to be rich in minerals. In 1642, while searching for this continent, Tasman sighted a "large high-lying land" off the West Coast of the South Island.

The arrival of the British: Captain James Cook(Fig. 5-5), sent to Tahiti to observe the transit of Venus, was also tasked with the search for the great southern continent thought to exist in the southern seas. Cook's cabin boy, Young Nick, sighted a piece of land near Gisborne in 1769. Cook successfully

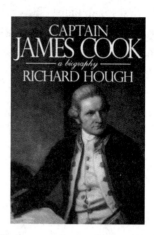

Fig. 5-5 Captain James Cook

circumnavigated and mapped the country, and led two more expeditions to New Zealand before being killed in Hawaii in 1779.

Prior to 1840, it was mainly whalers, sealers, and missionaries who came to New Zealand. These settlers had considerable contact with Maori, especially in coastal areas. Maori and Pakeha traded extensively, and some Europeans lived among Maori. The contribution of guns to Maori intertribal warfare, along with European diseases, led to a steep decline in the Maori population at this time.

The Treaty of Waitangi(Fig. 5-6): Signed in 1840, the *Treaty of Waitangi* is an agreement between the British Crown and Maori.

Fig. 5-6 The Signing of the Treaty of Waitangi

As more immigrants settled permanently in New Zealand, they weren't always fair in their dealings with Maori over land. A number of Maori chiefs sought protection from William IV, the King of England, and recognition of their special trade and missionary contacts with Britain. They feared a takeover by nations like France, and wanted to stop the lawlessness of the British people in their country.

As British settlement increased, the British Government decided to negotiate a formal agreement with Maori chiefs to become a British Colony. A treaty was drawn up in English and then translated into Maori.

The Treaty of Waitangi was signed on February 6, 1840, at Waitangi in the Bay of Islands. 43 Northland Chiefs signed it on that day. Over 500 Maori chiefs signed it as it was taken around the country during the next eight months.

It is the second and third articles that have caused controversy through the years, mainly because of translation problems. Successive governments believed the treaty enabled complete sovereignty over Maori, their lands and resources. But Maori believed that they were merely giving permission for the British to use their land.

Following its signing, many of the rights guaranteed to Maori in *The Treaty of Waitangi* were ignored. To help rectify this, the Waitangi Tribunal was set up in 1975. It has ruled on a number of claims brought by Maori tribes and in many cases, compensation has been granted. While disagreements over the terms of the treaty continue to this day, it is still considered New Zealand's founding document.

Growth of a nation: In 1852, under the United Kingdom Parliament's *New Zealand Constitution Act*, New Zealand was granted self-government, with a General Assembly consisting of an appointed Legislative Council and an elected House of Representatives. In 1867, the Maori won the right to a certain number of reserved seats in Parliament. In the year of 1907, New Zealand finally changed from being a colony to a separate dominion, equal in status to Australia and Canada.

As far as the nation's growth is concerned, the expansion of farming during the latter half of the 19th century served as the basis of New Zealand's growth as a nation. By the end of the 19th century, improved transportation facilities made possible a great overseas trade in wool, meat, and dairy products. Meanwhile, the 1860s discovery of gold mines in the South Island also contributed to a temporary economic boom.

It was not until 1947 that New Zealand gained its full independence from Britain. In 1951, the Legislative Council—the upper house of Parliament, was abolished as ineffectual, creating a unicameral legislature. In 1983, the term "dominion" was replaced with "realm". While retaining some ties to the British Crown, New Zealand has become a proud nation in its own right.

After World War II: While New Zealand is still heavily influenced by its colonial heritage, the country now has its own strong sense of identity. While still a member of the British Commonwealth, and maintaining close, friendly relations with the United States of America, New Zealand now has a far more independent trading and foreign policy. Since the mid-1980s, New Zealand has been a nuclear free zone, with its armed forces primarily focused on peacekeeping in the Pacific region.

The fifth Labor Government led by Helen Clark was elected in 1999. In power for nine years, it maintained most of the previous governments' economic reforms while putting more of an emphasis on social policy and outcomes.

John Key led the National Party to victory in November 2008. Key became Prime Minister of the fifth National Government which entered government at the beginning of the late 2000s recession. In February 2011, a major earthquake in Christchurch, the nation's second largest city, significantly impacted the national economy and the government formed the Canterbury Earthquake Recovery Authority in response.

Historical Figures

Kate Sheppard(Fig. 5-7)(1847—1934) was the most prominent member of the New Zealand's women's suffrage movement and was the country's most famous suffragette. Women's *suffrage*[5] in New Zealand was an important political issue in the late 19th century. In early colonial New Zealand, as in other European societies, women were excluded from any involvement in politics. Public opinion began to change in the latter half of the 19th century,

Fig. 5-7　Kate Sheppard

however, and after years of effort by suffrage campaigners, led by Kate Sheppard, New Zealand became the first self-governing colony in the world in which all women had the right to vote in

Fig. 5-8　Donald McLean

parliamentary elections. Since New Zealand was the first country to introduce universal suffrage in 1893, Sheppard's work has had a considerable impact on women's suffrage movements in several other countries. She also appears on the New Zealand ten-dollar note.

Donald McLean(Fig. 5-8)(1820—1877) was a 19th century New Zealand politician and government official. He was involved in negotiations between the settler government and Maori from 1844 to 1861, eventually as Native Secretary and Land Purchase commissioner. He was one of the most influential figures in Maori-Pakeha relations in the mid-1800s and was involved in the dispute over the "Waitara Purchase", which led up to the First Taranaki War.

Helen Elizabeth Clark(Fig. 5-9)(1950—) is a New Zealand politician who served as the 37th Prime Minister of New Zealand from 1999 to 2008, and was the Administrator

Fig. 5-9　Helen Elizabeth Clark

of the United Nations Development Programme from 2009 to 2017. She was New Zealand's fifth-longest serving Prime Minister, and the second woman to hold that office. Clark held numerous Cabinet positions in the Fourth Labor Government, including Minister of Housing, Minister of Health and Minister of Conservation. The Clark-led Fifth Labor Government implemented several major economic *initiatives*[6], and she advocated a number of free-trade agreements with major trading partners, including becoming the first developed nation to sign such an agreement with China. *Forbes* magazine ranked her the 22nd most powerful woman in the world in 2016.

National Symbols

The national flag of New Zealand(Fig. 5-10) is called the Union Jack and the Stars of the Southern Cross. Its royal blue background represents the blue sea and sky surrounding them, and the stars of the Southern Cross signify their place in the South Pacific Ocean. The Union Flag recognizes their historical foundations and that New Zealand was once a British colony and dominion.

Fig. 5-10 The national flag of New Zealand

The New Zealand coat of arms(Fig. 5-11) represents the sovereign nature of New Zealand and the Government's authority. It is for government use only and is found on a range of documents and papers of constitutional significance, from *Acts of Parliament* to passports.

The first quarter of the shield shows four stars that represent the Southern Cross, and three ships symbolize the importance of New Zealand's sea trade. In the second quarter a fleece represents the farming industry. The wheat sheaf in

Fig. 5-11 The New Zealand coat of arms

the third quarter represents the agricultural industry, and the crossed hammers in the fourth quarter represent mining. The supporters on either side of the shield are a Maori Chieftain holding a war weapon and a European woman holding the New Zealand flag. The Crown, shown above the shield, symbolizes Her Majesty Queen Elizabeth II as Queen of New Zealand. In the New Zealand coat of arms, two fern leaves provide a base for the supporters to stand upon.

There are two national anthems of New Zealand. They have equal status according to the law. The anthem has English and Maori lyrics, with slightly different meanings.

Exercises

I. *Try to answer the following questions according to your understanding of the text.*

(1) How did the first Maori arrive in New Zealand?

(2) Who is the first European to discover New Zealand? How did he find it?

(3) What is the contribution of Captain Cook to the discovery of New Zealand?

(4) What is the importance of *The Treaty of Waitangi*?

(5) What is the national flag of New Zealand?

II. *Read the following passage carefully, and make a comment on it at the end of the passage in no more than 100 words.*

The enduring story that women sent Anzac biscuits to New Zealand troops during World War I is a myth, according to an Auckland researcher.

"History is not an exact science—but there's no evidence to show that this actually happened," says Carmel Cedro, who's doing a PhD on baking, nostalgia and femininity at the Auckland University of Technology. Anzac biscuits, as we know, wouldn't have survived the journey to Europe because the coconut would have gone rancid on the way, she says.

Soldiers at the front were more likely to eat very hard biscuits made of water and flour, known as Anzac wafers that they'd have to dip into the tea to make them soft.

"They weren't very perishable—so you can still find them if you go to a museum."

The first Anzac biscuit recipe appeared some years after the war ended, Cedro says.

"The recipe that we are familiar with today, with the flour and the oats and the golden syrup or treacle and coconut, was showing up in cookbooks in Australia and New Zealand in the 1920s".

The story built up in Australia and New Zealand surrounding the Anzac biscuit represents a yearning for an idealized past. "Essentially, it continues because we like to buy into the myth that women show their love for their men through baking, and that by continuing to make and talk about the biscuits each year means the ritual is just repeated."

Aside from Anzac biscuits, Cedro's thesis looks at how baking is connected to contemporary femininity and nostalgic, with idealized concepts still present in modern cookbooks.

Comments:

Nowadays many classics are being adapted in many ways, which has aroused great concern. Some believe that the adaptation of the classics is creative; others think it does more harm than good.

What do you think of it?

Reference:

Argument:

(1) Readers' preference playing a critical role

(2) The concept of creativity being prevailing

(3) People pursuing more choices of entertainments

Counter-argument:

(1) The act of adaptation ruining its charm

(2) The adapted works confusing with history
(3) Real classics leading people to appreciate the real art

Unit 3 Education and Recreation

Text Focus

1. School Education
2. Famous Universities
3. Cultural Life

Vocabulary

1. integrated	[ˈɪntɪɡreɪtɪd]	adj.	综合的
2. synonymous	[sɪˈnɒnɪməs]	adj.	同义的
3. elevate	[ˈelɪveɪt]	v.	提高
4. nanoscience	[ˈnænəˌsaɪəns]	n.	纳米科学
5. blockbuster	[ˈblɒkbʌstə(r)]	n.	畅销片

New Zealand has an international reputation with a progressive education system. The passing of *the Education Act 1877* established the first free national system of primary education in New Zealand. Today education is nominally free for all primary, intermediate and secondary schooling.

State schools, private schools and state ***integrated***[1] schools are available in the whole country. Government provides funding for state schools and state integrated schools. Private schools receive about 25% of their funds from the government and rely on tuition fees for the rest. New Zealand has high levels of educational achievement: a third of New Zealanders have a tertiary qualification, and another 40% have qualifications from secondary school. New Zealand has many famous universities, such as the University of Auckland, Victoria University of Wellington, and Massey University.

School Education

Early Childhood Education, which is available for children aged from birth to five years, is non-compulsory in New Zealand. It is not owned, provided or managed by the state. About 60% of New Zealand children participate in early childhood education. It provides a variety of education programs for young children before they begin primary school. The programs include kindergartens, play centers, kohangareo, home-based services, and childcare centers. Pacific Island language programs have also been established recently, particularly in Auckland.

Primary and Secondary School Education is compulsory in New Zealand including both primary and secondary school education, which covers 12 years, usually from ages 6 to 16, although schooling is available to children from the age of five. Primary school education is the first level of compulsory education. All children in New Zealand must be enrolled at school from the age of six. Primary education starts at Year One and continues until Year Eight, with Years Seven and Eight mostly offered at either a primary or a separate intermediate school.

Secondary schools(Fig. 5-12), also known as high schools, colleges or area schools, are where the students get their second level of compulsory education in New Zealand. Secondary education covers Years Nine to 13, during which students are generally aged 13 to 17, and offers three levels of the National Certificate of Educational Achievement qualification. For university entrance, students are required to achieve a minimum number credits from an approved subject list, as well as the required literacy and numeracy credits.

Fig. 5-12 Secondary School Students

Primary and secondary schools provide subjects, such as languages, mathematics, sciences, technology, social studies, the arts, health and physical fitness. Most schools teach in English, but some schools use Maori as the teaching language. They are known as Kura Kaupapa Maori schools, in which the principal language of instruction is Maori, and education is based on Maori culture and values.

New Zealand now has over hundreds of primary schools and 2,477 secondary schools (until 2021), most of which are funded by the state. Most students attend public schools. Only a minority attend private or church-affiliated schools. The state-owned schools are managed by Boards of Trustees, which are made up of the school principal, a staff member and elected parent representatives. Private schools obtain their funds mainly from the tuition fees, though they do receive some government funding. Private schools are usually run by a church, and follow a particular philosophy.

Tertiary Education in New Zealand is used to describe all aspects of post-secondary education and training. Tertiary education institutions, therefore, include not only universities and colleges, but also other training organizations and establishments that provide vocational programs for school leavers.

There are several branches of tertiary education in New Zealand. State-owned tertiary institutions consist of universities, colleges of education, polytechnics and Wanangas. There are also numerous non-state-owned private training establishments. Each of these institutions provides a high level of tertiary education and internationally recognized degrees and diplomas. Qualifications are offered, ranging from levels two, three and four to level ten on the New Zealand Register of Quality Assured Qualifications.

There are currently more than 30 public tertiary education institutions, about 40 industry training organizations, and approximately 895 private training establishments in New Zealand. There are eight universities in New Zealand. The larger ones are the University of Auckland, and Massey University. The other six are the University of Waikato, the Victoria University of Wellington, the University of Canterbury, the University of Otago, Lincoln University, and the Auckland University of Technology. These eight universities constitute the national system of higher education, and are autonomous, self-governing and empowered to award their own degrees.

Entry to most universities is "open", that is to say, one only needs to meet the minimum requirements in the school-leaving examinations. Domestic students will pay fees subsidized by the government, and the student-paid portion of the fee can be loaned from the government under the government's Student Loan Scheme. The New Zealand Scholarship and the New Zealand University Bursary are awarded to school leavers by a competitive examination and provide financial support to school-leavers pursuing a university degree. International students pay full fees and are not eligible for Government financial assistance.

The universities in New Zealand generally award letter grades to students, with +/- variations. These letter grades correspond to percentage mark bands, though these vary between universities.

Although institute of technology and polytechnic are *synonymous*[2], the terms are confusing in the tertiary educational system in New Zealand, which may mean any institution of higher education and advanced research or vocational education. The term might also refer to a secondary school in vocational training. The term "institute of technology" is often abbreviated to IT, which may be the abbreviation of information technology as well. Polytechnics in New Zealand are established under *the Education Act of 1989* along with universities, colleges of education and Wanangas. Since then, there has been consolidation in the state tertiary education, for instance, Wellington Polytechnic being amalgamated with Massey University. The Auckland

University of Technology has been *elevated*[3] to university status.

All tertiary education in New Zealand receives around 70% of their fund from the government. Students' fees may compensate the balance. The government funds are provided according to the number of the enrolled students and the amount of time each course requires, but students pay about a quarter of the cost through fees. Student loans are available to assist with fees and living costs, and student allowances are available for students from lower-income families.

Famous Universities

The University of Auckland (Fig. 5-13) is New Zealand's leading university. Established in 1883, it is ranked 68th in the world by the QS World University Rankings 2024. It is an international centre of learning and academic excellence, situated in the heart of Auckland. The University provides an exciting and stimulating environment for more than 43,000 students, of which 8,200 are international students from more than 120 countries.

Fig. 5-13　The University of Auckland

The University of Auckland has comprehensive range of courses in the country with teaching and research conducted over eight faculties and two large-scale research institutes. There are opportunities for interdisciplinary studies and conjoint degrees. Some notable alumni are Philippa Boyens, the Academy Awards winner for the best screenwriter of *The Lord of the Rings* series; Jeffrey Grice, the world famous piano player; John Hood, the former president of the University of Oxford.

Victoria University of Wellington is a university in Wellington, New Zealand. It was established in 1897 by *Act of Parliament*, and was a constituent college of the University of New Zealand. The university is well known for its programmes in law, the humanities, and some scientific disciplines, and offers a broad range of other courses. Entry to all courses at the first year is open, and entry to the second year in some programmes is restricted.

Victoria had the highest average research grade in the New Zealand Government's

Performance-Based Research. In 2021/2022 it was ranked 241 in the QS World University Rankings, and is one of only 13 universities in the world to hold the maximum five Stars Plus in the QS Stars rating of excellence and five stars in each of eight categories—arts and culture, discipline ranking and accreditations, employability, facilities, inclusiveness, internationalization, research, and teaching.

Massey University is New Zealand's defining University and has a proud tradition of academic and research excellence. Massey University is one of New Zealand's largest universities.

Massey University has campuses in Palmerston North, Wellington and Auckland, with the largest in terms of student numbers being the Turitea site. Massey offers most of its degrees extramurally within New Zealand and internationally. It has the nation's largest business college. Founded in 1927, Massey University has grown from a small agricultural college in Palmerston North to become New Zealand's largest residential university spread over three cities. Massey University is the only university in New Zealand offering degrees in aviation, dispute resolution, veterinary medicine and ***nanoscience***[4]. Having been accredited by the American Veterinary Medical Association, Massey's veterinary school now has the distinction of having its degree recognized not only by New Zealand, but also the United States, Australia, Canada, and Britain, as well as most other countries in the world.

Cultural Life

Movies shot in New Zealand have captured the world fame. Towns and cities have cinemas, large and small screening family ***blockbusters***[5], international art house movies and the products of the local film-making industry that is achieving remarkable success around the world. New Zealand has produced some very talented actors and actresses in the 20th century, many of whom have gone on to star in comedies, dramas, horror movies and more. These Kiwi actors specialize in film, television or even theater.

Victoria Spence is a New Zealand stage and television actress most famous for her role as Salene in the Cloud nine television drama *The Tribe*. She made her acting debut in the 1993 film *Jack Be Nimble* and later appeared in the teen comedy series *Atlantis High*, in which she played the dual role of Antonia and Anthony, and William Shatner's *A Twist in the Tale* alongside *The Tribe* co-star Ryan Runciman.

Kevin Smith was born in Auckland, New Zealand and spent his early childhood there. His family moved to the small rural town of Timaru in New Zealand's South Island when he was 11. During high school, he began playing in rock-and-roll bands, but never aspired to a career as an actor.

Peter Jackson is a New Zealand film director, screenwriter and film producer. He is best known as the director, writer, and producer of *The Lord of the Rings* trilogy(Fig. 5-14) and *The*

Hobbit trilogy.

Fig. 5-14　The Lord of the Rings

　　Jackson has been awarded three Academy Awards in his career, including the Award for Best Director in 2003. He has also received a Golden Globe, four Saturn Awards and three BAFTAs amongst others.

　　Music of New Zealand has been influenced by blues, jazz, country, rock and roll and hip hop, with many of these genres given a unique New Zealand interpretation. A number of popular artists have gone on to achieve international success including Lorde, Split Enz, Crowded House, OMC, Bic Runga, Kimbra, Ladyhawke, the Naked and Famous, Fat Freddy's Drop, Savage, Flight of the Conchords, and Brooke Fraser.

　　Kiwi popular music is strong—from rock and reggae to dub and hip-hop—while world music fans flock to the World of Music Arts and Dance Festival held annually in New Plymouth's beautiful Bowl of Brooklands.

　　Pre-colonial Maori music consisted mainly of a form of microtonal chanting and performances on instruments called taonga pūoro: a variety of blown, struck and twirled instruments made out of hollowed-out wood, stone, whale ivory, albatross bone, and human bone. In the 19th century, European settlers brought musical forms to New Zealand including brass bands and choral music, and musicians began touring New Zealand in the 1860s. Pipe bands became widespread during the early 20th century.

　　New Zealand has a national orchestra, the New Zealand Symphony Orchestra, and many regional orchestras. A number of New Zealand composers have developed international reputations. The most well-known include Douglas Lilburn, John Psathas, Jack Body, Gillian Whitehead, Jenny McLeod, Gareth Farr, and Ross Harris.

　　TV in New Zealand was introduced in 1960. In addition to a legacy analogue network, there are three forms of broadcast digital television: satellite services provided nationwide by Freeview and Sky, a terrestrial service provided in the main centers by Freeview, and a cable service provided in Wellington and Christchurch by Telstra Clear. Programming and scheduling is done in Auckland where all the major networks are now headquartered.

Sports in New Zealand largely reflect its British colonial heritage, with some of the most popular sports, such as rugby union, rugby league, cricket, football, basketball and netball which are primarily played in Commonwealth countries. New Zealand is a small nation but has enjoyed success in many sports, notably rugby union, rugby league, cricket, America's Cup sailing, world championship, Olympics events and motor sport and softball.

Other popular sports include golf, hockey, tennis, cycling, rowing, and a variety of water sports, particularly sailing and surf sports. Winter sports such as skiing and snowboarding are also popular as indoor and outdoor bowls. Skateboarding is enjoyed amongst a small portion of the youth.

 Exercises

I. *Try to answer the following questions according to your understanding of the text.*

(1) What does "secondary schools" mean in New Zealand?
(2) What are branches of tertiary education in New Zealand?
(3) Why is the University of Auckland considered as the leading university in New Zealand?
(4) Why is Massey University regarded as New Zealand's defining university?
(5) Who is Peter Jackson in the field of movies in New Zealand?

II. *Read the following passage carefully, and make a comment on it at the end of the passage in no more than 100 words.*

China represents a key market for Education New Zealand(ENZ), thanks to the rich cultural exchange and connections for international students.

However, New Zealand is not the only country keen to entice Chinese students to study abroad, so Education New Zealand needed a way to engage directly with potential students and their parents.

Education New Zealand teamed with United Media Solution(UMS) to create a social media presence to communicate with students and their parents in China.

UMS created and implemented a social media strategy and created a content calendar for Education New Zealand, as well as adding local content and information from the China market.

Over the three and half years that UMS has worked with Education New Zealand, it has helped the brand build an engaged audience of potential students, parents and alumni, who are keen to follow ENZ news and information. As of January 2018, Education New Zealand had more than 19,588 WeChat fans and 34,715 microblog followers.

Olivia Silverwood, International Social Engagement Manager at Education New Zealand said, "One of the cool things for us, is that UMS CEO Jessica was an international student in New

Zealand so she really understands the experience and that has enabled UMS to really capture the experience."

"Quite a few members of the UMS team have been international students, so they have great insight into the customer service experiences and the perspective of what students want and respond to," says Silverwood.

In a bid to provide ENZ with a better understanding and more insights into its fans and followers. UMS created the welcome survey to provide a mechanism to interact with ENZ fans and to gain insights into their behaviours, interests and demographics.

The survey would also provide information about the status of followers, which stage of study they are in, their desired level of education, and most importantly, the reason they follow ENZ.

Comments:

Many scholars suggest that colleges should lay emphasis on vocational training by setting relative courses in the college curriculum so that graduates are more likely to be employed; while others believe that the vocational orientation does harm to the higher education.

What do you think of it?

Reference:

Argument:

(1) Developing students' professional qualities

(2) Cultivating students' comprehensive abilities

(3) Improving students' employment competitiveness

Counter-argument:

(1) Lacking the characteristics of the higher education

(2) Changing the goals of the course curriculum

(3) Causing utilitarianism in education

Unit 4 Politics and Economy

Text Focus

1. Political System
2. Political Parties
3. Economy

5.4 Lecture4 Politics and Economy.mp4

Chapter Five New Zealand

Vocabulary

1. transparency	[træns'pærənsi]	n.	透明度
2. prominent	['prɒmɪnənt]	adj.	卓越的
3. assent	[ə'sent]	n.	同意；赞成
4. expenditure	[ɪk'spendɪtʃə(r)]	n.	支出
5. flexibility	[ˌfleksə'bɪlətɪ]	n.	灵活性

New Zealand is a constitutional monarchy with a parliamentary democracy, although its constitution is not codified. The Head of the Government is the Prime Minister. The New Zealand Cabinet functions as the policy and decision-making body of the executive branch within the New Zealand government system. New Zealand is identified as a stable and well-governed state, with high government ***transparency***[1] and low perceived levels of corruption. There are two major political parties in New Zealand—the National Party on the right and the Labor Party on the left. New Zealand is a developed country and ranks highly in international comparisons of national performance. Since the 1980s, New Zealand has transformed from an agrarian, regulated economy to a diverse market economy. Agriculture in New Zealand is the largest sector of the tradable economy, thus it has a reputation as "world's largest farm".

Political System

Due to historical reasons, New Zealand has a political system that is closely patterned on that of the United Kingdom. Like Canada and Australia, the country is part of the British Commonwealth, with a parliamentary system of government.

Being a constitutional monarchy, New Zealand has a political system in which the head of state is a king or queen, ruling to the extent allowed by a constitution. However, New Zealand has no formal, written constitution. *The Constitution Act of 1986* is regarded as the principal formal statement of *New Zealand's Constitution*.

As its political system indicates, the head of state of New Zealand is the king or queen of New Zealand. The New Zealand monarchy has been distinct from the British monarchy since *the New Zealand Royal Titles Act of 1953*.

In recent years, there have occasionally been proposals to abolish the monarchy and establish a republic. However, New Zealand has not yet held a referendum on the matter, but a number of ***prominent***[2] politicians believe that an eventual move to republicanism is inevitable. Still, however, opinion polls have shown that unlike Australia, a majority of New Zealanders favor keeping the monarchy.

The legislature, or Parliament(Fig. 5-15) is composed of one chamber, the House of

Representatives. Parliament is vested with the power to make laws. The House of Representatives is composed of 120 members, known as "Members of Parliament" or MPs.

Fig. 5-15   The Beehive(Executive Wing of New Zealand Parliament Buildings)

Parliaments have a maximum term of three years, which means elections occur every three years. In New Zealand, all citizens over the age of 18 are entitled to vote. When a New Zealander turns 18, he or she must enroll on the Electoral Roll to become an eligible voter. Although enrollment is compulsory, voting is not.

New Zealand recognizes the British monarch as its sovereign, or formal head of state. The monarch is represented in New Zealand by a governor-general. This official is appointed by the monarch on the prime minister's recommendation to a five-year term. After national elections, the governor-general appoints the leader of the majority party in the legislature as prime minister and arranges for the prime minister to form a government, or cabinet of ministers. The governor-general formally appoints the ministers on the prime minister's recommendation. The governor-general must also give ***assent***[3] for parliamentary bills to become law. These duties are mostly ceremonial, the governor-general exercises little real power in New Zealand.

The prime minister heads the cabinet, which is the highest policy-making body of government. The cabinet is responsible for the day-to-day administration of government, and ministers all have specific responsibilities, including shaping government policies, initiating government-sponsored legislation, making decisions on government ***expenditure***[4], and organizing the administration. Ministers also convene in the Executive Council, a body that advises the governor-general. Constitutional convention requires the Governor-General to follow the council's recommendations.

The judiciary consists of the Supreme Court of New Zealand, the Court of Appeal of New Zealand, the High Court, the District Courts, and other courts and tribunals. The courts have a wide variety of functions, including enforcing the criminal law, resolving civil disputes amongst citizens, upholding the rights of the individual, ensuring that government agencies stay within the law, and explaining the law.

New Zealand law falls into two categories: statutes and the common law. The common law has been developed by judges over the centuries, and may be amended and developed by the courts to meet changing circumstances.

New Zealand is a unitary state rather than a federation. Local government in New Zealand has only the powers granted by Parliament. These powers have traditionally been distinctly fewer than those in some other countries. New Zealand can be divided into 16 regions, which form the highest level of local government and also can be divided into 73 territorial authorities, most of which are called districts. Regional councils administer the regions, and the territories are under the administration of territorial authorities. The territorial authorities include district and city councils, which have responsibility for most local administration. All members of these local governing bodies are directly elected.

Political Parties

There are two major political parties in New Zealand—the National Party on the right and the Labor Party on the left, which have dominated New Zealand political life since a Labor government came to power in 1935.

The National Party was formed in Wellington in May 1936. It grew out of the coalition government of the Reform and Liberal Parties in wartime. The name "National" was chosen as the new party sought to represent all parts of the community.

The National Party is a moderately conservative party, supporting a free-market economy, less legislative interference and lower taxation. It also advocates policies of promoting one standard of citizenship for all New Zealanders and reducing social welfare payment. In foreign policy, the party is less international and favors a large defense establishment. It believes that class and special-interest divisions should be minimized.

The Labor Party was founded in 1916 and is the longest established political party. Successive Labor Governments have introduced radical and progressive measures that have contributed to the steady improvement and ultimate transformation of New Zealand society.

When the current Labor-led Government, headed by Christopher John Hipkins gained power in 2023, it was necessary to restore balance to industrial actions through *the Employment Relations Act*. The government has become an active partner with the private sector in the pursuit of economic improvement.

Economy

New Zealand has a modern, prosperous, developed economy with an estimated Gross Domestic Product (GDP) of 249.9 billion dollars (2021). Previous to the 1980s, the country's economy was characterized by rigid regulations from the government. It was not until 1984 that the government began to engage in radical economic restructuring. The reforms were designed to promote economic *flexibility*[5] and competitiveness, while decreasing the government's role in the economy.

New Zealand's economy has been traditionally dependent on agriculture. With a favorable climate and rich soils, New Zealand has always been a major agricultural producer and exporter in the world and has a reputation as the world's largest farm. Today, agriculture remains the driving force of the economy. Farming industries produce more than half of New Zealand's export earnings.

Leading agriculture exports include meat, dairy products, fruit and vegetables, fish, and wool. Livestock accounts for three quarters of New Zealand's agricultural production. Sheep raising in New Zealand provides mutton and wool, woolen carpets and clothes are exported to many countries. New Zealand is also a major exporter of dairy products, including milk powders, butter and cheese. Its exported milk accounts for about a quarter of the world's international trade in dairy products.

Forestry plays another important part in New Zealand's economy. In New Zealand, forests cover nearly one third of the country. With such a vast coverage of forests, New Zealand has developed a well-established processing industry. The main forest products include logs, sawn timber, wood chips, and paper.

Equally worth mentioning is that New Zealand is a country with the tradition of fishing. New Zealand is an island country, which is an advantage for fishery industry. There are more than 100 kinds of sea fish in the south-western Pacific Ocean. When it comes to the criterion of the GDP, the manufacturing and service sectors rank much higher.

Similar in importance to the country's economy are industries producing machinery and equipment, metal products, processed timber, textiles, clothing, footwear, and leather. Most New Zealand wool is used for either carpet manufacture or clothing.

Still, the service sector is the most important to the economy in terms of its contribution to the GDP and employment. Services include tourism, transportation, education, health and banking.

The tourist industry is a fast-growing industry in New Zealand. In order to stimulate the tourist industry, the government decreases tax on services relating to the tourist market. The beautiful scenery, such as volcano, hot springs and natural livestock farms attracts lots of foreigners from all over the world.

Air New Zealand Limited is the national airline and flag carrier of New Zealand. Based in Auckland, New Zealand, the airline operates scheduled passenger flights to several domestic and international destinations in countries across Asia, Europe, North America and Oceania.

Air New Zealand's route network focuses on Australia and the South Pacific, with long-haul services to Asia, Europe and North America. The airline's main hub is Auckland Airport, located near Mangere in the southern part of the Auckland urban area. Air New Zealand is headquartered in a building called "The Hub", located 20 kilometers away from Auckland Airport, in Western Reclamation, central Auckland City.

The Fonterra Co-Operative Group Ltd. was created in October 2001. Responsible for about 20% of New Zealand's total exports, Fonterra operates as the world's largest exporter of dairy products, controlling over a third of international dairy trade. The Group is cooperatively owned by over 13,000 dairy farmers whose products are sold under such brands as Anchor, Anlene, Mainland, Anmum, and Chesdale, making their way to customers in approximately 140 countries. Over four million Fonterra cows produce over 20 billion liters of milk each year. The United States is Fonterra's largest single market by revenue while Asia is the Group's largest export region. Fonterra operates 24 manufacturing sites in New Zealand and has 60 additional locations throughout the world.

 Exercises

I. *Try to answer the following questions according to your understanding of the text.*

(1) In what way does the Parliament of New Zealand differ from that of the British Parliament?
(2) What's the function of the Cabinet of New Zealand?
(3) What's the principle of the National Party?
(4) What does leading agriculture exports in New Zealand include?
(5) Why does forestry play an important part in New Zealand's economy?

II. *Read the following passage carefully, and make a comment on it at the end of the passage in no more than 100 words.*

New Zealand's government recently announced it will help pay for poorer families to replace their old cars with cleaner hybrid or electric vehicles. The government said it plans to spend $357 million on the test program.

The move is part of a wider plan to reduce greenhouse gas emissions. Greenhouse gases are believed to cause warming temperatures in the Earth's atmosphere. New Zealand plans to provide aid for businesses to reduce emissions and have buses that run on environmentally safe fuel by 2035. The government also plans to provide food-waste collection for most homes by 2030.

Prime Minister Jacinda Ardern said in a statement, "We've all seen the recent reports on sea level rise and its influence right here in New Zealand. We cannot leave the issue of climate change until it's too late to fix." The plan is a step toward New Zealand's stated goal of reaching net-zero carbon emissions by 2050.

Reaching net-zero emissions means not creating more carbon in the atmosphere than oceans and forests can remove. Ardern said that reducing dependence on traditional fuels would help protect families from extreme price increases. The plan also sets a goal of reducing total car travel by 20 percent over the next 13 years. The programs will be paid for from a $2.8 billion climate emergency response fund.

Officials said that over time, money collected from polluters would pay for the programs rather than taxes from families. Some critics of the plan say it continued to be less restrictive on New Zealand's huge agriculture industry. Agriculture creates more than half of the nation's total greenhouse gas emissions. But the industry is also important to the economy as the nation's biggest export earner.

David Seymour is the leader of New Zealand's ACT political party. He said that some of the announced programs are proven to be ineffective and have been tried and failed overseas. Seymour added that people should be able to choose how they reduce emissions through the market-based emissions trading plan.

Comments:

New Zealand's government has introduced a series of policies to support the development of new energy vehicles and also promote consumers' awareness and acceptance of new energy vehicles.

What's your opinion on energy vehicles?

Reference:

Argument:

(1) Reducing air pollution and greenhouse gas emissions

(2) Offering lower operating and maintenance costs

(3) Reducing noise pollution

Counter-argument:

(1) Having limited driving ranges

(2) Lacking charging facilities

(3) Taking a longer time to recharge

Unit 5　Culture and Customs

Text Focus

1. Traditional Culture
2. Literature Works
3. Food Customs

5.5 Lecture5 Customs and Culture.mp4

Chapter Five New Zealand

Vocabulary

1. ancestor	[ˈænsestə(r)]	n.	祖先
2. communal	[kəˈmju:nl]	adj.	公共的
3. proficient	[prəˈfɪʃnt]	adj.	精通的
4. posture	[ˈpɒstʃə(r)]	n.	姿势
5. protocol	[ˈprəʊtəkɒl]	n.	礼仪
6. lament	[ləˈment]	n.	挽歌

The Maori people are the indigenous people of New Zealand, their language and culture have a major impact on all facets of New Zealand life. Maori culture is a rich and varied one, and includes traditional and contemporary arts. The British and Irish immigrants brought aspects of their own culture to New Zealand and also influenced Maori culture, particularly with the introduction of Christianity. The concept of a "New Zealand literature" originated primarily in the 20th century, and is produced predominantly in the English language. Beer is the most popular alcoholic drink in New Zealand. In summer, the barbecue is common, generally as a social event.

Traditional Culture

The Maori people are the indigenous people of New Zealand and first arrived here in voyaging canoes from their ancestral homeland of Hawaiki over 1,000 years ago. The Maori people are divided into a score or more tribes, each with its own well-defined lands, and tracing kinship to a common ***ancestor***[1]. A tribe is made up of several principle clans, each of which might in the old days have included about 1,000 fighting men. The clan was not a unilateral group. In other words, a person could belong to it through either his father or his mother; nor was it exogamous. Marriage within the group being favored provided that the parties were not first cousins. Within these major social units were lesser clan, tracing descent to more immediate ancestors, and these in turn were composed of family groups of near relatives who together often occupied a dwelling hut. Thus, the people of a tribe were the chief's relatives, their rank being broadly represented by the closeness of their kinship to him.

The Maori lived in villages, usually with a fort close at hand. Advantage was taken of the ***communal***[2] mode of life to secure cooperation in various tasks, and such labor was lightened by work songs. Division of labor was practiced, though in somewhat rudimentary form. The men did harder work, such as tree climbing, carving, fishing and fowling. The women weeded the crops, collected shellfish, plaited mats and wove garments from useful plants and attended to the cooking of the two daily meals.

Warfare was frequent and each man was trained in the use of weapons. Hand-to-hand fighting was preferred, and ambuscade and stratagem were frequent. In later warfare against Europeans, the Maori proved extraordinarily ***proficient***[3] in the military art. In time of peace, the social side of life was developed, visits were made, and neighboring tribes were invited to feasts at which dart throwing, wrestling, top spinning and ***posture***[4] dancing held the interest of people. Such receptions were held in the center of the village. Swimming and canoe racing were also popular sports.

Today the Maori people live throughout New Zealand, and many are actively involved with keeping their culture and language alive. In recent years, the re-introduction of the Maori language has revived it. Preschool children are encouraged to speak in Maori. Primary and secondary schools build on this early immersion by including Maori in the curriculum. Maori art and performance is deeply associated with New Zealand's landscape and environment, and Maori art draws heavily on Polynesian carving and weaving techniques.

For employment purposes, there are ten public holidays under *the Holidays Act 2018*: New Year's Day, Day after New Year's Day, Waitangi Day, Good Friday, Easter Monday, Anzac Day, Labour Day, Christmas Day and Boxing Day.

Waitangi Day is a public holiday, which is held each year on February 6, to celebrate the signing of *the Treaty of Waitangi*. In recent years, communities throughout New Zealand have been celebrating Waitangi Day in a variety of ways. These often take the form of public concerts and festivals. Some people use the day as an open day and an educational experience for their local communities, giving them the opportunity to experience the Maori culture and ***protocol***[5]. Others use the day as an opportunity to explain where the Maori are. Another popular way of celebrating the day is at concerts around the country. As the day is a public holiday and happens during the warmest part of the New Zealand summer, many people take the opportunity to spend the day at the beach, which is an important part of both the Maori and European cultures.

Labor Day is a public holiday on October 22 in New Zealand, and the origin can be traced back to the eight-hour-working-day movement that arose in the newly-founded Wellington colony in 1840, primarily because of Samuel Parnell's refusal to work more than eight hours a day. He encouraged other tradesmen to only work for eight hours a day and in October 1840, a workers' meeting passed a resolution supporting the idea. On October 28,1890, the 15th anniversary of the eight-hour day was commemorated with a parade. The event was then celebrated annually in late October as either Labor Day or Eight-Hour Demonstration Day. In 1899, the government legislated that the day be a public holiday. The day was celebrated on different days in different provinces, which led to ship owners complaining that seamen were taking excessive holidays by having one Labor Day in one port and then another in their next port. In 1910, the government "Mondayised" the holiday so that it would be observed on the same day throughout the nation.

Chapter Five New Zealand

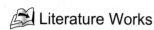 Literature Works

New Zealand literature is produced predominantly in English, as a sub-type of English literature. Like all Polynesian peoples, the Maori, who began to occupy the islands now called New Zealand about 1,000 years ago, composed, memorized, and performed **laments**[6], love poems, war chants, and prayers. They also developed a mythology to explain and record their own past and the legends of their gods and tribal heroes. As settlement developed through the 19th century, Europeans collected many of these poems and stories and copied them in the Maori language. The most picturesque myths and legends, translated into English and published in collections with titles like *Maori Fairy Tales*, were read to, or by, Pakeha children, so that some—such as the legend of the lovers Hinemoa and Tutanekai or the exploits of the man-god Maui, who fished up the North Island from the sea and tamed the sun—became widely known among the population.

The Maori language has survived to the present day although not widely spoken; it is used as medium of instruction in education in a small number of schools. As far as Maori literature can be said to exist, it is principally literature in English dealing with Maori themes and some writers are including Maori in their predominantly English-language work, and this may lead to independent works in Maori language, such as witnessed in works representing a revival of the suppressed Irish language in the 20th and 21st centuries.

New Zealand poetry is influenced by time and place and has been through a number of changes. Poetry has been part of New Zealand culture since before European settlement in the form of Maori sung poems or waiata. The first colonial non-Maori poetry was also predominantly sung poetry. Gregory O'Brien was among the more notable poets who marked out space for themselves in the 1990s. O'Brien, who was also a painter, sometimes illustrated his Semi-Surreal poems with matching iconography. Other poets were Jenny Bornholdt, a warmhearted, clever observer of the everyday; Andrew Johnston, also a witty poet, who gave language a degree of freedom to create its own alternative reality; and Michele Leggott, the most scholarly of this group and the one who took the most, and most directly, from American postmodernists such as Louis Zukofsky.

New Zealand has produced many world class writers—from Katherine Mansfield in the early 20th century to Eleanor Catton who won the 2014 Man Booker Prize for *the Luminaries*.

Novelists Janet Frame, Patricia Grace, Albert Wendt, Maurice Gee and children's author Margaret Mahy, are prominent in New Zealand. However, there is also a strong current of work written independently with little concern for international markets and having only a small readership, such as Ian Wedde's early novel *Dick Seddon's Great Dive*. Novelists such as Kirsty Gunn exemplify the shift to less parochial concerns.

Food Customs

Sharing food is a traditional Kiwi way of bringing people together in a relaxing atmosphere. Whether it's a picnic on the beach, a hāngi at your child's school or a barbeque with neighbours, you'll find that food and friendship go hand-in-hand in New Zealand. It's common to contribute to this hospitality, bringing food or wine to share. If the host says "don't bring anything", you can still bring a small gift. New Zealanders have a relaxed attitude to invitations. Sometimes people will say they are coming to a party but not turn up. Don't take it personally.

Coffee and tea are an important part of Kiwi socializing. If you visit someone's home, you'll usually be offered a coffee or tea, and "going out for coffee" is a regular event. The legal age for buying alcohol in New Zealand is 18. There are strict rules against providing alcohol for people under that age. Smoking is increasingly rare in New Zealand and prohibited in public buildings, including bars and restaurants. Generally, people are expected to smoke outside. If you want to smoke, it's polite to ask the people around you if they mind, even if you are outside.

Drinks after work on Friday are quite common in New Zealand too. This is mainly for work colleagues, and other family members don't normally come, although this depends on the workplace. At these events, it's best to keep talking about work to a minimum.

Exercises

I. *Try to answer the following questions according to your understanding of the text.*

(1) Why did the Maori people live in villages in the past?

(2) What did the Maori people do when there was no wars?

(3) What are the public holidays in New Zealand?

(4) Can you list some Maori fairy tales?

(5) Could you introduce the "bring a plate" occasion in New Zealand?

II. *Read the following passage carefully, and make a comment on it at the end of the passage in no more than 100 words.*

To celebrate International Hobbit Day on the 22nd of September 2018, Hobbiton Movie Set will be holding a special event to commemorate the day.

Hobbiton Movie Set is an experience to tantalise the senses as guests find themselves engulfed in the sights, smells, sounds and tastes of the Shire, at the home of *the Hobbits*, as featured in *The Lord of the Rings* and *The Hobbit Trilogies*. Your guide escorts you through the twelve-acre site recounting fascinating details of how the movie set was created.

You will then have the chance to spend the evening in our special event area created for Hobbit Day. With a drink in hand, you will have a chance to wander the Marketplace, a bustling, vibrant experience. Taste a real piece of the Shire from individually themed stalls bursting with traditional Hobbit fare. The market stalls consist of New Zealand cheeses, freshly baked artisan breads, cured meats, smoked fish, and of course fresh products from the Hobbiton gardens. Throughout the evening, there will be roaming entertainment mingling amongst the guests.

Inside The Green Dragon Inn, you will have ample time to relax in front of the open fires. The Green Dragon Inn was the meeting place for all residents of Hobbiton, who would gather in the warm surroundings of the bar to chatter about the day's events. Indulge in a few beverages from our Hobbit Southfarthing range, which encompasses two traditional ales, an apple cider and non-alcoholic ginger beer, all handcrafted and exclusive to Hobbiton Movie Set.

To conclude this premium Hobbiton Movie Set experience, after dinner, the guests will rejoin their guide to make their way back through the wandering paths of Hobbiton. The trails will be illuminated by path lighting and guests will receive an authentic handheld lantern to light the way. This stunning journey under moonlight will travel through the village breathtakingly lit up with Hobbit hole chimney's smoking and lanterns glowing against the darkness. Prizes for best dressed will be awarded on the night.

Comments:

Some people think that celebrating western festivals has become much more influential in people's lives today and that this is a negative development. To what extent do you agree or disagree?

Reference:

Argument:

(1) Making the lives of young people more colorful and exciting

(2) Getting involved in the global world

(3) Providing young people with more opportunities to comprehend different cultures

Counter-argument:

(1) Endangering the inheritance or development of traditional culture

(2) Being harmful to traditional Chinese values

(3) Causing money worship or other bad ideas

Unit 6   Intercultural Communication

Knowledge to Learn

What Is Culture Shock?

Culture shock is the personal disorientation a person may feel when experiencing an unfamiliar way of life due to immigration or a visit to a new country, or to a move between social environments. It is a feeling of frustration, uneasiness, or uncertainty that many people experience in unknown settings.

What Are the Four Phases of Culture Shock?

Honeymoon phase.

Negotiation phase.

Adjustment phase.

Mastery phase.

Cases to Study

Case 1

> In New Zealand, a Chinese was trying to make his way through the crowded train, but his way was blocked by a lady carrying several large packages.
>
> "Excuse me, make a way please."
>
> The lady's response was to ignore him and not move.
>
> What cultural phenomenon can be reflected?

Analysis

(1) The above sentence "Excuse me…" is acceptable to Chinese because Chinese learners are taught that imperative sentences can be used to make a request.

(2) In fact, English-speaking people seldom use imperatives to express requests. This kind of request threatens the hearer's face. Instead, a native speaker would say "Excuse me, do you think you could let me pass?" which sounds polite.

(3) The English language is full of these little formalities which can definitely determine whether you're going to make a good first impression on someone or not. In a lot of situations, people expect a sort of indirect way of speaking to each other, which might be a little silly.

(4) Being polite may differ from culture to culture, as there are linguistic and paralinguistic means of conveying politeness. We should do more things with this language—ranking, labeling, matching, analyzing, using, etc. in order to avoid sounding aggressive and abrupt in interactions.

Case 2

> Mr. Richardson, an engineer from Auckland, works in a company in Shenzhen. One day, Mr. Wong, who works with Mr. Richardson in the same office, had a conversation with him. Mr. Wong enjoyed this conversation and he said to Mr. Richardson that they really should get together to have lunch sometime. Mr. Richardson said that he would enjoy that. After a few weeks, Mr. Richardson began to feel that Mr. Wong had been rather insincere

because he had not followed up his invitation to lunch with a specific time and place.

Why does Mr. Wong say to Mr. Richardson, "We should get together to have lunch some time"?

Analysis

(1) Asian speakers of English and Western speakers of English have different discourse patterns which are the sources of the problem between Mr. Wong and Mr. Richardson.

(2) The pattern which we have mentioned above of displacing important points until the end of a conversation, which is often found in East Asian discourse, has led Mr. Richardson to think that this mention of lunch at the end of the conversation is of some importance to Mr. Wong.

(3) Mr. Richardson believes that Mr. Wong is seriously making an invitation to lunch. Mr. Wong, on the other hand, has made this mention of having lunch together sometime at the end of his conversation because it is of little major significance. For him it does not signify any more than that he has enjoyed his conversation with Mr. Richardson. It is not a specific invitation, but just a conventional way of parting with good feelings toward the other.

 Translations on Traditional Chinese Culture

Exercise 1

Translate the passage into English

京剧被视为中国的国剧，源于 18 世纪晚期安徽和湖北的当地剧种。集传统音乐、舞蹈、诗歌、杂耍、武术于一身，京剧由生、旦、净、丑四个主要角色组成。京剧表演者主要应用四种技能：唱、念、做、打。京剧脸谱是一种具有民族特色的特殊化妆方法，脸谱上每一种图形和亮丽的颜色都有象征意义：红色表示忠诚，蓝色表示有勇有谋，黑色表示正直。

Translation Reference

Peking Opera is regarded as the national opera in China. It originated in the late 18th century from the basis of some local operas in Anhui and Hubei Provinces. Peking Opera is a synthesis of traditional music, dancing, poetry, acrobatics and martial arts, consisting of Sheng, Dan, Jing, Chou. During the performance, the performers mainly utilize four skills: singing, speaking, acting and acrobatic fighting. Peking Opera facial makeup is a kind of special makeup method with national characteristic. Each of the patterns and brilliant colors on the painted face has a symbolic meaning: red suggests loyalty; blue suggests courage and resourcefulness; black suggests honesty.

Translate the passage into Chinese

Acrobatics is the performance that shows excellent skills of balance and action coordination. Acrobatics is most often associated with activities that make extensive use of gymnastic skills, such as circus and gymnastics, but many other activities, such as martial art, ballet and diving may also adopt elements of acrobatics. Wuqiao is well known as the hometown of acrobatics in China. People practice the art during the breaks from work. Many families have their unique skills handed down through generations. There are acrobats from Wuqiao throughout China, even the world.

> **Translation Reference**
> 中国杂技是展现高超的平衡技巧和动作协调能力的表演。杂技常和广泛使用体操技能的活动相联系，比如马戏、体操，但许多其他运动，如武术、芭蕾和跳水也可能采用杂技元素。吴桥是中国众所周知的杂技之乡，人们在工作间隙练习杂技，许多家庭都有独特的技艺代代相传。中国乃至世界都有很多来自吴桥的杂技演员。

Exercise 2

Translate the passage into English

筷子是中国古人发明的一种具有鲜明民族特色的进食工具，是反映中国饮食文化特色的重要组成部分。中国人使用筷子的历史可追溯到商代，距今已有三千多年。筷子可谓是中国国粹，既轻巧又灵活，在世界各国餐具中独树一帜，被西方人誉为"东方的文明"。凡是使用过筷子的人，不论中国人或是外国人，都因其使用方便、物美价廉而赞叹不绝。

> **Translation Reference**
> Chopsticks, a kind of tableware with distinct national features, invented by ancient Chinese people, is an important component that reflects the characteristics of Chinese diet culture. The history of using chopsticks in China dates back to the Shang Dynasty, more than 3,000 years ago. Chopsticks, the quintessence of Chinese culture, whose lightness and flexibility develop a school of its own among various tableware all over the world, are praised as "Oriental Civilization" by the Westerners. All those people who have ever used chopsticks, no matter Chinese or foreigners, marvel at their convenience, excellent quality and reasonable price.

Translate the passage into Chinese

The abacus is a great invention in ancient China. In the old times, people used small rods to count. With the social development, numbers needed calculating were increasingly greater, which made it impossible for the rods to fulfill the task. Thus, people invented a more advanced calculating device—the abacus. Since it was convenient to use and easy to learn, the abacus was widely used in China. On the basis of the abacus, there came the mental abacus with the image of an abacus in mind to calculate the figures.

Translation Reference

算盘是中国古代的一项伟大发明。在古代，人们用小木棍进行计算，随着社会的发展，需要计算的数目越来越大，用小木棍已无法完成，于是，人们发明了更为高级的计算工具——算盘。由于算盘操作方便、简单易学，因此在中国被广泛使用。在算盘的基础上，有人发展了珠心算，即把算盘的形象描绘在脑海中来计算数字。

Exercise 3

Translate the passage into English

刺绣是用针和线在织物或其他材料上进行装饰的手工艺。苏绣因其精致的拼接，生动的图片，美丽的图案和色彩淡雅而著名。广东和四川刺绣流行的图案有孔雀开屏，鹊上枝头等。中国记载的最古老的刺绣可追溯至商朝。在当时，刺绣象征着社会地位。随着经济的发展，刺绣走进普通人的生活。

Translation Reference

Embroidery is the handicraft of decorating fabric or other materials with needle and thread. Suzhou embroidery is famous for its sophisticated stitching, vivid pictures, beautiful patterns and elegant colors. Guangdong and Sichuan embroideries' popular motifs are a peacock spreading its tail and a magpie on the branch of a plum tree etc. The oldest embroidery on record in China dates from the Shang Dynasty. Embroidery in this period symbolized social status. With the development of economy, embroidery entered the life of the common people.

Translate the passage into Chinese

Chinese painting distinguishes itself from Western paintings since it is drawn on Xuan paper with the Chinese brush and Chinese ink. According to different means of expression, Chinese paintings can be divided into two categories which are the Xieyi school and the Gongbi school. The Xieyi school is characterized by free expressions and exaggerated forms, while the Gongbi school attaches importance to details with fine brush work. Landscape painting is widely regarded as the highest level of Chinese painting. To attain proficiency in this art, it is necessary to have a good control of the brush, and certain knowledge of Xuan paper and Chinese ink besides repeated exercises. Before painting, the painter must have a draft in his mind and paint according to his imagination and experience.

Translation Reference

国画不同于西方画，它是用毛笔和墨汁在宣纸上作画的。根据表现手法，国画可分为写意派和工笔派两大类，写意派以自由表达和形式夸张为特点；工笔派则注重以精细的笔法描绘细节，山水画被公认为是国画的最高境界。精通这门艺术需要不断重复的练习，需要控制好毛笔，需要对宣纸和墨汁有一定的认识。绘画前，画家必须在脑海里构思一个草图，然后根据他的想象力和经验进行绘画。

Culture to Know

Culture Note 1

Kun Opera originated in the Kunshan region of Jiangsu. It is one of the oldest existing forms of Chinese operas with a history of more than 600 years. Kun Opera has a complete system of acting characterized by its own distinctive tunes. During the early Ming Dynasty, Kun Opera got developed and it dominated Chinese theatre from the 16th to the 18th century. In addition, Kun Opera has influenced many other Chinese theatre forms. Today, Kun Opera is still played in some major cities of China and enjoys popularity among many people.

Culture Note 2

Kites were also called "Yuan (a hawk)". In ancient China, in the Spring and Autumn Period, Mocius, a philosopher in the Eastern Zhou Dynasty, spent three years making a wooden hawk that could fly in the sky. That wooden hawk Mocius made has a history of over 2,400 years, which is claimed to be the first kite in the world. In the Tang Dynasty, kites were introduced to Korea, Japan and other neighboring countries. Now Weifang is called the "Home of Kites of the World". It has a long history of making kites, and kites made here are well-crafted, beautifully shaped and smooth when flying and easy to fly away. Every year, Weifang International Kite Festival is held from April 20 to 25.

Culture Note 3

Ink wash painting is a type of brush painting. Only black ink is used for the painting of basic ones, in various concentrations. During the Tang Dynasty, ink wash painting got developed. The goal of ink wash painting is not simply to reproduce the appearance of a subject, but to capture its soul. To paint a horse, the ink wash painting artist must understand its temperament better than its muscles and bones. To paint a flower, there is no need to perfectly portray its petals and color, but it is essential to convey its liveliness and fragrance.

Culture Note 4

WHO Declares China Malaria Free

Following a 70-year effort, China has been awarded a malaria-free certification from WHO—a notable feat for a country that reported 30 million cases of the disease annually in the 1940s. The success was hard-earned and came only after decades of targeted and sustained action. China is the first country in the WHO Western Pacific Region to be awarded a malaria-free certification in more than 3 decades. China's achievement takes us one step closer towards the vision of a malaria-free Western Pacific Region.

Further Reading

Passage 1

Chinese Brands Bet on Sponsorships at Qatar World Cup

In terms of the global industrial supply chain, "made in Yiwu" has already become a worldwide commercial symbol originating in China, which indicates reliance and trust. Lusail, Qatar's biggest stadium to hold the World Cup final, was built by China Railway Construction Corp International, at a cost of $770 million. CCTV News reported that Chinese companies, mainly from Guangdong and Zhejiang provinces, have also provided more than 10,000 container houses for the World Cup, used as accommodation for tourists and football fans. The World Cup sponsorship by a large number of Chinese companies is a demonstration of China's economic power, and makes the globe feel the power of Chinese brands.

Passage 2

Watching the Flag-raising Ceremony in the Tian'anmen Square

People secure a place in the front row to watch the flag-raising ceremony in the Tian'anmen Square, which over the years has been watched by countless people from China and elsewhere. Everyone wants to watch the ceremony in the front row to see the national flag being raised as the sun comes up, which makes Chinese people feel proud. This daily event sends a powerful signal that a strong nation is always behind its people. In addition to feeling proud of China, they feel a strong sense of security while watching the ceremony. The flag-raising is considered by many Chinese to be an event they must attend at least once in their lifetime, especially since the number of honor guards was greatly increased and additional ceremony was introduced to the occasion on May 1, 1991.

Chapter Six

The Republic of Ireland

Contents

1. Location and Resources
2. History and Symbols
3. Education and Recreation
4. Politics and Economy
5. Culture and Customs
6. Intercultural Communication

Abbey Theatre	艾比剧院	**National University of Ireland**	爱尔兰国立大学
Antony Strokes	安东尼·斯托克斯	**Norman Ireland**	诺曼爱尔兰
Blarney Castle	布拉尼城堡	**Oscar Wilde**	奥斯卡·王尔德
Celtic	凯尔特人	**the Republic of Ireland**	爱尔兰共和国
Dublin Castle	都柏林城堡	**the Cranberries**	小红莓乐队
Enya	恩雅	**the Irish tricolour**	爱尔兰三原色
George Bernard Shaw	乔治·伯纳·萧	**the River Shannon**	香农河
Irish Whisky	爱尔兰威士忌	**Trinity College Dublin**	都柏林三一学院
James Joyce	詹姆斯·乔伊斯	**U2**	U2 乐队
Kingdom of Ireland	爱尔兰王国	**William Butler Yeats**	威廉·巴特勒·叶芝

Chapter Six The Republic of Ireland

Unit 1   Location and Resources

Text Focus

1. Geographical Location
2. Weather and Climate
3. Natural Resources

6.1 Location and Resources.mp3

Vocabulary

1. sovereignty	[ˈsɒvrənti]	n.	主权
2. isles	[aɪlz]	n.	群岛
3. inlet	[ˈɪnlet]	n.	水湾
4. partition	[pɑːˈtɪʃ(ə)n]	n.	分裂
5. garrulous	[ˈɡærələs]	adj.	唠叨的
6. insular	[ˈɪnsjələ]	adj.	海岛的
7. craggy	[ˈkræɡi]	adj.	陡峭的

The island of Ireland is located in the north-west of Europe and the Republic of Ireland covers ***sovereignty***[1] over five-sixths of it, and Northern Ireland, a part of the United Kingdom, covers the remainder and is located in the northeast of the island. Dublin is the capital city and it is a historical and contemporary cultural centre for the country, as well as a modern centre of education, arts, administration, economy, and industry. Cork and Limerick are also large and populous cities in Ireland. The Republic of Ireland(Ireland) consists of a mostly flat low-lying area in the midlands, ringed by mountain ranges. It has a mild but changeable oceanic climate with few extremes. Due to its rainy climate, Ireland is very green and with lots of trees and grasslands, suitable for farming.

Geographical Location

The island of Ireland is located in the northwest of Europe, between latitudes 51° and 56° N, and longitudes 11° and 5° W. It is separated from the neighbouring island of Great Britain by the Irish Sea and the North Channel, which has a width of 23 kilometers at its narrowest point. To the west is the northern Atlantic Ocean and to the south is the Celtic Sea. Ireland and the Great Britain, together with nearby islands, are known collectively as the British ***Isles***[2]. As the term

British Isles is controversial in relation to Ireland, the alternate term "Britain and Ireland" is often used as a neutral term for the islands.

Politically, the island of Ireland is divided between the Republic of Ireland, which covers just under five-sixths of the island, and Northern Ireland, a part of the United Kingdom, which covers the remainder and is located in the northeast of the island.

A ring of coastal mountains surround low plains at the centre of the island. The highest of these rises to 1,038 meters above sea level. The most arable land lies in the province of Leinster. Western areas can be mountainous and rocky with green vistas. The River Shannon, the island's longest river at 386 kilometers long, rises in County Cavan in the northwest and flows 113 kilometers to Limerick city in the midwest.

Ireland has a wide range of physical features. Much of the centre of the country is flat, with areas of bog land. Around the coasts are where most of the mountains are found. The western part of the country is particularly rugged with lots of mountains and rocky land. The west coast has a large amount of bays and ***inlets***[3] and small islands. Being on the eastern edge of the Atlantic Ocean, Ireland gets a lot of rain and so it has many lakes and rivers. Another consequence of so much rain is that Ireland is very green and with lots of trees and grasslands, suitable for farming. Ireland doesn't have any really hot and dry areas of land, so there are no deserts in Ireland.

Dublin is the capital and most populous city of Ireland, also the capital of the province of Leinster. The English name for the city is derived from the Irish name Dubhlinn, meaning "black pool". Dublin is situated near the midpoint of Ireland's east coast, at the mouth of the River Liffey and the centre of the Dublin Region.

Originally founded as a Viking settlement, it evolved into the Kingdom of Dublin and became the island's principal city following the Norman invasion. The city expanded rapidly from the 17th century. Following the ***partition***[4] of Ireland in 1922, Dublin became the capital of the Irish Free State and later the Republic of Ireland.

Similar to the cities of Cork, Limerick, Galway and Waterford—Dublin is administered separately from its respective County with its own City Council. The city is listed by the Globalization and World Cities Research Network as a global city, among the top 30 cities in the world. It is a historical and contemporary cultural centre for the country, as well as a modern centre of education, arts, administration, economy and industry.

Cork is located in the southwest region of Ireland and is part of the province of Munster, which is the second largest city in the Republic of Ireland.

The city is built on the River Lee which divides into two channels at the western end of the city. The city centre is located on the island created by the channels. Its streets are built over waterways where ships would have been anchored. Cork Harbour is one of the world's largest natural harbors.

Chapter Six The Republic of Ireland

The city is said to be the friendliest city in Ireland and its citizens the most talkative in a generally *garrulous*[5] country. The city's nickname "the rebel city" originates in its support for the Yorkist cause during the War of the Roses. The city is often referred to as "the real capital" in reference to the city's role as the centre of anti-treaty forces during the Irish Civil War.

Limerick is known to be Ireland's third biggest city. Yearly, millions of people visit this place because of its vigorous nightlife, countless shopping spots and many business opportunities. But behind all the glamour, Limerick also has one more thing to offer its locals and tourists—a showcase of its meaningful history and rich culture.

Tourist attractions in the city centre include King John's Castle, Hunt Museum, several seasonal tours, the University of Limerick, Georgian House and gardens and the Treaty Stone. Adare village and the Foynes Flying Boat Museum are also popular attractions. The Limerick City Museum is next to King John's Castle. It contains displays on Limerick's history and manufactures.

Weather and Climate

The island's lush vegetation, a product of its mild climate and frequent rainfall, earns it the name of Emerald Isle. Overall, Ireland has a mild but changeable oceanic climate with few extremes. The climate is typically *insular*[6] and temperate, avoiding the extremes in temperature of many other areas in the world at similar latitudes. This is a result of the moderating moist winds which ordinarily prevail from the southwest of Atlantic.

The influence of the North Atlantic Current also ensures the coastline of Ireland remains ice-free throughout the winter. The climate in Ireland does not experience extreme weather, with tornadoes and similar weather features being rare. Summers are generally warm and winters are mild. There is a regional variation, with inland areas being cooler in winter and warmer in summer than their coastal counterparts.

The warmest areas are found along the southwest coast. The coldest areas are found inland. Extreme heat and cold are both rare throughout the country. The sunniest months are May and June. During these months sunshine duration averages between five and six point five hours per day over most of the country. The Southeast gets the most sunshine, averaging over seven hours a day in early summer. December is the dullest month with an average daily sunshine ranging from about one hour in the north to almost two hours in the Southeast. Over the year as a whole most areas get an average of three and a half hours of sunshine each day. Irish skies are completely covered by cloud roughly half of the time.

Rainfall is the most common form of precipitation on the island, and is extremely common throughout Ireland, although some parts of the west coast receive over four times as much rain as the east coast. Rainfall in Ireland normally comes from Atlantic frontal systems which travel northeast over the Island, bringing cloud and rain.

Severe cold weather is uncommon in Ireland with the majority of winter precipitation coming in the form of rain. Although hills and mountainous regions in the country can see up to 30 days of snowfall annually, most low lying regions of the island only see a few days of lying snow per year, or may see no snow at all during some winters.

Due to the volatility of Ireland's weather, weather during the winter months is very variable and difficult to predict, with the aforementioned factors making both extremely low temperatures and relatively mild temperatures possible.

Natural Resources

Ireland consists of a mostly flat low-lying area in the midlands, ringed by mountain ranges. Some mountain ranges are further inland in the south of Ireland. The highest peak is 1041 meters high. The mountains in Ireland are not high—only three peaks are over 1000 meters. Moulded by the Ice Age into a land of *craggy*[7] peaks and deep valleys, Ireland is a hillwalker's delight.

The main river in Ireland is the River Shannon, 386 kilometres, the longest river in either Ireland or Britain, which separates the boggy midlands of Ireland from the west of Ireland, and develops into three lakes along its course. The River Shannon enters the Atlantic Ocean after Limerick city. Other major rivers include the River Liffey, River Lee and River Blackwater, etc. Lough Neagh, in Ulster is the biggest lake in Ireland.

Ireland's main mineral resources include natural gas, peat, copper, lead, graphite, zinc, silver, barite, gypsum, limestone, dolomite, etc.

Exercises

I. *Try to answer the following questions according to your understanding of the text.*

(1) Where is Ireland located?
(2) Why has Ireland got the name of Emerald Isle?
(3) What is the capital city of Ireland and what's the weather like there?
(4) What's the nickname of the City Cork? And why?
(5) What natural resources does Ireland have?

II. *Read the following passage carefully, and make a comment on it at the end of the passage in no more than 100 words.*

Ireland Entices Chinese Tourists with Trade Show

Ireland's tourism authority kicked off its annual road show in Beijing on April 24, 2017. The five-day event also included stops in Shanghai, Guangzhou and Hong Kong.

Niall Gibbons, CEO of Tourism Ireland said "Our annual sales mission is an important event

Chapter Six The Republic of Ireland

in our marketing calendar."

Its purpose was to enhance and widen networking and business ties between the island's tourism industry and leading Chinese travel trade partners and airlines. The goal was to get a bigger slice of the Chinese market; roughly 4 million Chinese visit Europe every year, Gibbons added.

More than 300 Chinese travel trade and airline partners were expected to participate in this year's event, according to the tourism authority.

"Our green island has magnificent natural landscape scenery, dynamic cities and unique Irish culture and history—and of course, there are world-renowned golf courses," said Gibbons.

Approximately 55,000 Chinese paid visits to the country in the past five years, and the number was expected to hit 100,000 in the 2020s, he said.

The country welcomed a total of 9.3 million overseas travelers, and raked in 4.7 billion euros ($5.1 billion) in tourism income.

Comments:

With the rapid development of Chinese economy, more and more countries in the world would like to strengthen cooperation with China, including the field of tourism. Through the exchange and collaboration, cultural communication and understanding are enhanced in various aspects.

What do you think of the link between China and Ireland in the field of tourism?

Reference:

Tourism Ireland and partners worked on a China Ready training program. Several Irish tourism providers learned about the Chinese language, culture, cuisine and specific requirements and needs, which will surely attract more tourists from China and promote the communication between two countries.

Unit 2 History and Symbols

Text Focus

1. Historical Periods
2. Historical Figures
3. National Symbols

6.2 History and Symbols.mp3

Vocabulary

1. buoyant	[ˈbɔɪənt]	*adj.*	繁荣的
2. vibrant	[ˈvaɪbrənt]	*adj.*	充满活力的
3. peninsula	[pəˈnɪnsjələ]	*n.*	半岛
4. execution	[ˌeksɪˈkjuːʃ(ə)n]	*n.*	执行

With the history of Ireland dating back as far as 8,000 BC, the past has truly paved the way for the island's ***buoyant***[1] present and future. Ireland has experienced mid-Stone Age culture, high Neolithic culture and Viking culture. Ireland was struck by the Great Famine at the latter half of the 19th century. Modern Ireland enjoys more immigration than emigration. Thanks in large part to the boom of the Celtic Tiger economy in the 1990s, the Ireland of the 21st century is a ***vibrant***[2], culturally rich and ethnically diverse country with an entirely youthful and optimistic outlook. A lot of Irish figures in the filed of politics, literature and science have played important roles in the development of Irish history, such as Edmund Burke, Oscar Wilde, James Joyce, George Bernard Shaw, William Butler Yeats, Earnest Thomas Sinton Walton etc. The national flag of Ireland is the Irish tricolour and the official symbol or coat of arms of Ireland is the harp.

Historical Periods

Prehistoric Ireland: Most of Ireland was covered with ice until the end of the last ice age over 9,000 years ago. Mesolithic stone age inhabitants arrived sometime after 8,000 BC and agriculture followed with the Neolithic Age around 4,500 to 4,000 BC when sheep, goats, cattle and cereals were imported from the Iberian ***peninsula***[3]. The Celts were commonly thought to have colonized Ireland in a series of invasions between the 8th and 1st centuries BC.

Early Christian Ireland: Irish pirates struck all over the coast of western Britain in the same way that the Vikings would later attack Ireland. The first English involvement in Ireland took place in this period. In the summer of 684 AD, an English expeditionary force invaded Ireland.

Early Medieval and Viking Era: The first recorded Viking raid in Irish history occurred in 795 when Vikings from Norway looted the island. The Battle of Clontarf in 1014 began the decline of Viking power in Ireland. However the towns which Vikings had founded continued to flourish, and trade became an important part of the Irish economy.

Norman Ireland: The Normans consolidated their presence in Ireland by building hundreds of castles and towers. The Normans initially controlled the entire east coast, from Waterford to eastern Ulster, and penetrated a considerable distance inland as well. Throughout the 13th century the policy of the English Kings was to weaken the power of the Norman Lords in Ireland.

Chapter Six The Republic of Ireland

Early Modern Ireland: It took nearly a century to extend the control of the English Kingdom of Ireland over all of its claimed territory. During the 17th century, Ireland suffered an eleven-year warfare. Cromwell's conquest was the most brutal phase of the war. Ireland became the main battleground after the Glorious Revolution of 1688, when the Catholic James II left London and the English Parliament replaced him with William of Orange.

Protestant Ascendancy: By the late 18th century, many of the Anglo-Irish ruling class had come to see Ireland as their native country, but Catholics could not yet become members of the Irish Parliament, or become government officials. Some were attracted to the more militant example of the French Revolution of 1789. The Great Famine of the 1840s caused the deaths of one million Irish people and over a million more emigrated to escape it. The 19th and early 20th centuries saw the rise of modern Irish nationalism, primarily among the Roman Catholic population.

Contemporary Era: The republican movement was divided into anti-Treaty and pro-Treaty supporters. Between 1922 and 1923 both sides fought the bloody Irish Civil War. The new Irish Free State government defeated the anti-Treaty army, imposing multiple *executions*[4].

Global economic problems in the 1970s caused the Irish economic crisis. This period came to be known as the Celtic Tiger and was focused on as a model for economic development in the former Eastern Bloc states, which entered the European Union in the early 2000s. Irish society adopted relatively liberal social policies during this period.

Census data in 2022 shows that the population of Ireland rises to more than 5 million, which is the highest level in the past 170 years.

Historical Figures

Edmund Burke(Fig. 6-1)(1729—1797), an Irish politician, writer, political theorist, and philosopher, served as a member of the Whig Party in the House of Commons of the United Kingdom for several years. His most well-known deeds include his position against King George III and the British government, his support for the American colonies and the later American Revolution, and his later criticism of the French Revolution. Reflecting on the French Revolution, he became the main conservative figure in the Whig Party. Burke also published many works related to aesthetics and founded a political journal called Annual Register. He is often regarded as the founder of British and American conservatism.

Fig. 6-1 Edmund Burke

George Bernard Shaw(Fig. 6-2)(1856—1950) was an Irish playwright. In 1925, he won the

Nobel Prize for Literature for his idealism and humanitarianism in his works. He is an outstanding realistic dramatist in modern Britain, a world famous language master of humor and satire, and an active social activist and a propagandist of Fabian socialism. He supported women's rights, called for fundamental changes in the electoral system, advocated income equality, and advocated the abolition of private property. His life was closely related to the socialist movement. He studied Das Kapital carefully and declared publicly that he was "an ordinary proletarian" and "a socialist". His ideas were deeply influenced by German philosophers Schopenhauer and Nietzsche.

Fig. 6-2　George Bernard Shaw

Fig. 6-3　Earnest Thomas Sinton Walton

Earnest Thomas Sinton Walton(Fig. 6-3)(1903—1995) was an Irish physicist, the winner of the 1951 Nobel Prize for Physics, the only Irishman to win a Nobel Prize for any science. He was born in Dungarvan, County Waterford, Ireland, graduated from Cambridge University. He became the first person in history to split the atom artificially because he and John Clough did the "atomic collision" experiment in Cambridge University, thus creating the nuclear era and winning the Nobel Prize in Physics.

National Symbols

The national flag of Ireland is vertical and frequently referred to as the Irish tricolour—green, white and orange. It is a simple flag but says a lot of the culture. The green symbolizes Nationalism, the white symbolizes Peace and the orange symbolizes Unionism, therefore the national flag of Ireland represents peace between Nationalists and Unionists.

The official symbol or coat of arms of Ireland is the harp(Fig. 6-4) and has been since medieval times. The current design is based on the "Brian Boru harp" of the 14th century, which can be found in the museum of Trinity Colleges in the heart of Dublin. The harp is used by the Government, its agencies and representatives in Ireland and abroad. The harp is also featured on the reverse side of all Irish Euro coins. The National Anthem of Ireland is called *Amhrán na bhFiann* which means "The Soldiers Song", which became the official state anthem in 1926.

Fig. 6-4　The harp

Chapter Six The Republic of Ireland

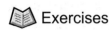 Exercises

I. *Try to answer the following questions according to your understanding of the text.*

(1) What great changes took place in Ireland during the middle centuries of the first millennium?

(2) When did the first recorded Viking raid in Irish history occur and what was brought to Ireland?

(3) What was the republican movement divided into?

(4) Who is George Bernard Shaw?

(5) What colors are the national flag of Ireland?

II. *Read the following passage carefully, and make a comment on it at the end of the passage in no more than 100 words.*

The Museum of Science and Art, Dublin was founded in 1877 by Act of Parliament. The decision to establish a state-run museum arose from requests by the Royal Dublin Society (RDS) for continued government funding for its expanding museum activities. The Science and Art Museums Act of 1877 had the effect of transferring the buildings and collections of the RDS to state ownership. The collections were further enhanced by the transfer of other notable collections from institutions such as the Royal Irish Academy (RIA) and Trinity College Dublin (TCD).

State support for the institution was manifested in the construction of a new building on Kildare Street, which opened to the public in 1890. The new museum housed coins, medals and significant Irish antiquities from the RIA including the Tara brooch and Ardagh chalice, ethnographical collections with material from Captain Cooke's voyages from TCD, and the collections of the Geological Survey of Ireland. These were joined by material from the decorative arts and ethnographical collections of the RDS along with their Irish collections of antiquities, minerals and plants. State involvement in the running of the Museum allowed for steady funding and a connection with other state museums in London and Edinburgh which was of considerable benefit. The name of the institution was changed in 1921 to the 'National Museum of Ireland'.

The Dublin Writers Museum was opened in 1991 in Dublin. The museum occupies an original 18th century house, which accommodates the museum rooms, library, gallery and administration area.

The Museum was established to promote interest, through its collection, displays and activities, in Irish literature as a whole and in the lives and works of individual Irish writers. Through its association with the Irish Writers' Centre, it provides a link with living writers and the international literary scene. On a national level it acts as a centre, simultaneously complementing the smaller, more detailed museums devoted to individuals like James Joyce, George Bernard Shaw, William Butler Yeats and Patrick Pearse. It functions as a place where people from Dublin, Ireland and abroad experience the phenomenon of Irish writing both as history and as actuality.

The writers featured in the Museum are those who have made an important contribution to Irish or international literature or, on a local level, to the literature of Dublin. It is a view of Irish literature from a Dublin perspective.

The Irish Museum of Modern Art also known as IMMA, is Ireland's leading national institution exhibiting and collecting modern and contemporary art. The museum opened in May 1991 and is located in a 17th century building to the west of Dublin's city centre.

The Museum concentrates on acquiring contemporary art by living artists. It also accepts donations of art dating from 1940 onwards and through some generous gifts has made progress towards a representative collection of art of that period. It concentrates on hosting exhibitions and has a very active exhibition programme.

The museum is limited its ability to house large works of art, but it is a striking location for displaying modern art. Modelled on Les Invalides, the setting of the museum is very fine: the courtyard, the noble facades, a restored baroque formal garden and a lovely old dining room and chapel.

Comments:

Museums have become vital parts of our lives. It is where people go to get their education and entertainment. Nowadays, more and more people are energetic to visit history museums or art museums, because they find the collections and antiques displayed in museums can stimulate their curiosity and enlarge their scope. Some people think museums should be free, while others think it is reasonable for museums to charge some fees to sustain better service.

What do you think of it?

Reference:

Argument:

(1) Having been funded by government through taxes

(2) Needing to visit museums on a regular basis, not just once in a lifetime

(3) Conveying the national history to the young people

Counter-argument:

(1) Maintaining, repairing and developing the museums

(2) Attracting more international visitors and spreading the cultural uniqueness to the world

(3) Encouraging visitors to use facilities maximally

Chapter Six The Republic of Ireland

Unit 3 Education and Recreation

Text Focus

1. School Education
2. Famous Universities
3. Cultural Life

6.3 Education and Recreation.mp3

Vocabulary

1. potential	[pəˈtenʃ(ə)l]	*n.*	潜能
2. delegated	[ˈdelɪɡeɪtɪd]	*adj.*	授权的
3. consolidate	[kənˈsɒlɪdeɪt]	*v.*	使加固
4. quadrille	[kwəˈdrɪl]	*n.*	四对方舞
5. infrastructure	[ˈɪnfrəstrʌktʃə(r)]	*n.*	基础设施

The levels of education in Ireland are primary, secondary and higher education. Growth in the economy has driven much of the change in the education system. Education in Ireland is free at all levels, including colleges. The Department of Education and Skills, under the control of the Minister for Education and Skills, is in overall control of policy, funding and direction, while other important organizations are the National Qualifications Authority of Ireland, the Higher Education Authority, and on a local level the Vocational Education Committees are the comprehensive system of government organization. There are many other statutory and non-statutory bodies which have a function in the education system.

School Education

Primary education: The present Irish primary school system consists of eight years: Junior and Senior. Most children attend primary school between the ages of 4 and 12 although it is not compulsory until the age of 6. The primary education seeks to celebrate the uniqueness of the child. As it is expressed in each child's personality, intelligence and ***potential***[1] for development. It is designed to nurture the child in all dimensions of his or her life—spiritual, moral, cognitive, emotional, imaginative, aesthetic, social and physical.

Secondary education: Most students attend and complete secondary education, with approximately 90% of school-leavers taking the terminal examination, the Leaving Certificate, at the age of 16—19. Secondary education is generally completed at one of the four types of school: voluntary secondary schools, owned and managed by religious communities or private organizations; vocational schools, owned and managed by Vocational Education Committees; comprehensive schools or community schools, fully funded by the state, and run by local boards of management; Gaelcholáistes, the second-level schools for Irish language medium education sector.

Besides, Grind Schools are fee paying privately run schools outside the state sector, who tend to run only Senior Cycle 5th and 6th year as well as a one-year repeat Leaving Certificate programme. In urban areas, there is considerable freedom in choosing the type of school the child will attend. The emphasis of the education system at second level is as much on breadth as on depth; the system attempts to prepare the individual for society and further education or work.

Higher Education: Higher education awards in Ireland are conferred by more than 38 Higher Education Institutions including the famous Trinity College Dublin, National University of Ireland, Dublin City University, Dublin Institute of Technology and etc. These are the degree-awarding authorities approved by the Government of Ireland and can grant awards at all academic levels.

Some colleges are "linked" colleges of universities, whilst others are designated institutions of the Higher Education and Training Awards Council. The latter include the Institutes of Technology, Colleges of Education, and other independent colleges. Some colleges have "*delegated*[2] authority" from the Higher Education and Training Awards Council, which allows them to confer and validate awards in their own name.

Famous Universities

Trinity College Dublin(Fig. 6-5), formally known as the College of the Holy and Undivided Trinity of Queen Elizabeth near Dublin, is the sole constituent college of the University of Dublin in Ireland. The college was founded in 1592 and it is one of the seven ancient universities of Britain and Ireland, as well as Ireland's oldest university.

Originally established outside the city walls of Dublin, Trinity College was set up in part to *consolidate*[3] the rule of the Tudor monarchy in Ireland, and it was seen as the university of the Protestants for much of its history.

Fig. 6-5 Badge of Trinity College Dublin

Trinity College is now surrounded by Dublin and is located on College Green, opposite the former Irish Houses of Parliament. Academically, it offers degree and diploma courses at both undergraduate and postgraduate levels.

National University of Ireland was founded in 1845 as one of three Queen's Colleges located in Belfast, Cork, and Galway. It became University College, Cork, under *the Irish Universities Act of 1908*. *The Universities Act 1997* renamed the university as National University of Ireland, Cork, and a *Ministerial Order of 1998* renamed the university as University College Cork—National University of Ireland, Cork, though it continues to be almost universally known as University College Cork.

The original site chosen for the College was particularly appropriate in that it is believed to have had a connection with the patron saint of Cork, Saint Finbarr. And the mill attached to the monastery is thought to have stood on the bank of River Lee, which runs through the College lower grounds.

 Cultural Life

Music: The Irish are known for their love for music. Irish Music is the generic term for music that has been created in various genres on the island of Ireland.

The indigenous music of the island is termed Irish traditional music. It has remained vibrant through the 20th, and into the 21st century, despite globalizing cultural forces. Irish music in many different genres has been very successful internationally. However, the most successful genres have been rock, popular and traditional fusion, with performers such as U2, Enya, Westlife, Boyzone, Van Morrison and The Cranberries.

Irish traditional music includes many kinds of songs, including drinking songs, ballads and laments, sung unaccompanied or with accompaniment by a variety of instruments. In the 19th century folk instruments would have included the flute and the violin.

Dances: The beauty of the Irish dance is such that it can mesmerize even those who have no particular interest in dance. Step dancing remains to be the most popular till date. Sean-nós dancing, old step dancing and the modern versions of step dancing are popular all over the world.

Irish dancing or Irish dance is a group of traditional dance forms originating in Ireland which can broadly be divided into social dance and performance dances. Irish social dances can be divided further into céilí and set dancing. Irish set dances are ***quadrilles***[4], danced by four couples arranged in a square, while céilí dances are danced by varied formations of 2 to 16 people. In addition to their formation, there are significant stylistic differences between these two forms of social dance. Irish social dance is a living tradition, and variations in particular dances are found across the Irish dancing community.

Movies: The Irish film industry has grown somewhat in recent years thanks partly to the promotion of the sector by the Irish Film Board (IFB) and the introduction of heavy tax breaks.

IFB is a body that has supported the indigenous industry of Irish film making, helping produce such films as *The Wind That Shakes the Barley*, *Intermission* and *Man About Dog*. These films and more have helped Ireland's best on-screen talent break through to the international stage. The support of indigenous film making is important for Irish culture and Irish identity, and this should not be ignored, but its economical effect is interesting. This is a positive growth industry with real talent and firm *infrastructure*[5].

Exercises

I. *Try to answer the following questions according to your understanding of the text.*

(1) How many years does the present Irish primary school system consist of?

(2) How is Ireland's secondary education level compared with other EU countries?

(3) Please give a brief introduction to one of the famous universities in Ireland.

(4) What is considered Irish traditional music and how is it accepted today?

(5) Please give a brief introduction of dance in Ireland.

II. *Read the following passage carefully, and make a comment on it at the end of the passage in no more than 100 words.*

How this BLAST Residency Initiative Will Operate?

The Department of Education is announcing the launch of the 2022 Arts-in-Education BLAST Residency Programme, which will enable up to 425 new Arts-in-Education residencies in schools each year.

This initiative aims to support the integration of the principles and key skills outlined in the Arts-in-Education Charter and the Creative Ireland Programme (2017—2022), Pillar One Creative Youth. The aim of this scheme is to give students in schools all over the country the opportunity to work with a professional artist on unique projects to be planned and developed between the artist, the teacher and the school under the co-ordination of the Education Support Centers Ireland ESCI network of 21 full-time education centers.

This initiative supports children and young people for the future, where skills like the ability to connect and collaborate with others, engage in creative and critical thinking and practice exclusivity at every level which will be paramount to peace, stability, sustainable economic growth and equality.

What is proposed is a unique streamlined process whereby schools apply for an artist on the Online Register of Approved Artists who are already trained for the new BLAST Arts-in-Education Residency Programme, managed by the local education centre. The education centre will also pay the artist which will further remove the administrative burden on teachers and schools.

Comments:

Now there are increasing people going study abroad. Some people think studying abroad has many advantages, while others think there are lots of disadvantages.

Chapter Six The Republic of Ireland

What is your attitude towards studying abroad?

Reference:

Argument:

(1) Getting access to advanced science and technology

(2) Improving language and cultural communication ability

(3) Being independent

Counter-argument:

(1) Costing a large amount of money

(2) Having to adapt to the new environment

(3) Missing home

Unit 4 Politics and Economy

Text Focus

1. Political System
2. Political Parties
3. Economy

6.4 Politics and Economy.mp3

Vocabulary

1. parliamentary	[ˌpɑːləˈmentri]	adj.	议会制的
2. nominate	[ˈnɒmɪneɪt]	v.	提名
3. coalition	[ˌkəʊəˈlɪʃ(ə)n]	n.	联合政府
4. livestock	[ˈlaɪvstɒk]	n.	牲畜
5. surplus	[ˈsɜːpləs]	n.	顺差
6. venture	[ˈventʃə]	n.	商业

Ireland is a ***parliamentary***[1], representative democratic republic and a member state of the European Union. While the head of state is the popularly elected President of Ireland, this is a largely ceremonial position with real political power being in the indirectly elected prime minister who is the head of the government. Executive power is exercised by the government which consists of no more than 15 cabinet ministers, inclusive of the prime minister and the deputy prime minister. Legislative power is in the bicameral national parliament and the President of Ireland. The judiciary is independent of the executive and the legislature. The head of the judiciary is the Chief Justice who presides over the Supreme Court. There are a number of political parties in the state, the political landscape has been dominated for decades by two opposed and competing parties, which both occupy the traditional centre ground.

Political System

Executive authority is exercised by a cabinet known simply as the Government. The Taoiseach is appointed by the President, after being **nominated**[2] by the lower House of Parliament. The remaining ministers are nominated by the Taoiseach and appointed by the President following their approval by the Dáil. The Government must enjoy the confidence of Dáil Éireann and, in the event that they cease to enjoy the support of the lower house, the Taoiseach must either resign or request the President to dissolve the Dáil, in which case a general election follows.

Ireland is a common law jurisdiction. The judiciary consists of the Supreme Court, the High Court and other lower courts established by law. Judges are appointed by the President after being nominated by the Government and can be removed from office only for misbehavior or incapacity, and then only by resolution of both houses of the Oireachtas. The final court of appeal is the Supreme Court, which consists of the Chief Justice, seven ordinary judges. The Supreme Court rarely sits as a full bench and normally hears cases in chambers of three, five or seven judges. Both the Supreme Court and the High Court have the power of judicial review and may declare to be invalid both laws and acts of the state.

The Government, through the civil and public services and state-sponsored bodies, is a significant employer in the state. Management of these various bodies vary, for instance in the civil service there will be clearly defined routes and patterns whilst among public services a sponsoring minister or the Minister for Finance may appoint a board or commission. Commercial activities, where the state involves itself, are typically through the state-sponsored bodies which are usually organized in a similar fashion to private companies.

The civil service of Ireland consists of two broad components, the Civil Service of the Government and the Civil Service of the State. Whilst these two components are largely theoretical, they do have some fundamental operational differences. The civil service is expected to maintain the political impartiality in its work, and some sections of it are entirely independent of Government decision making.

The constitution of Ireland provides a constitutional basis for local government. The Oireachtas is empowered to establish the number, size and powers of local authorities by law. Members of local authorities must be directly elected by voters at least once every five years.

Political Parties

Coalition[3] governments are common. The Irish electoral system has been characterized by the two and a half party system, with two large catch all parties dominating.

Fine Gael, which is the largest party in the state, is associated with strong belief in pro-enterprise and reward. Despite expressions of Social Democracy by its previous leader, it remains a Christian democratic, economically liberal party along European lines, with a strongly pro-European outlook.

Labour Party, the second largest party in the state, was founded in 1912. Labour have formal links with the trade union movement and have governed in seven coalition governments. This role as a junior coalition partner has led to Labour being classed as the half party of Ireland's two and a half party system.

Fianna Fáil, a traditionally Irish republican party founded in 1927, are the third largest party. It first formed a government on the basis of a populist programme of land redistribution and national preference in trade and republican populism remains a key part of its appeal.

Economy

The economy of the Republic of Ireland is a modern knowledge economy, focusing on services and high-tech industries and dependent on trade, industry and investment.

With fertile soils, a temperate climate and abundant rain water, Ireland has enviable natural advantages for farming the land to produce food, fibre and fuel. Aided by the moderating influence of the Gulf Stream, Ireland's climate is particularly suited for the growth of ryegrass, an excellent and inexpensive feed for *livestock*[4]. This simple comparative advantage is the basis for much of Ireland's farming.

The country also has a rich tradition of crop husbandry, with farming skills handed down through at least 200 generations. Research has shown that they were a highly organized community of farmers who worked together on clearing hundreds of acres of forestry and dividing the land into fields for cattle rearing.

Beef and milk production are the two most important farming sectors in Ireland. Ireland exports some of its net beef output, making Ireland the largest beef exporter in Europe and one of the largest in the world. Similarly, dairy output is exported.

Given Ireland's geographical position, fishing has been a naturally important economic activity, particularly in rural coastal areas where there are few other industries. The fishing industry has evolved to incorporate more diverse forms of activity such as fish farming. Full and part-time workers together accounted either directly or indirectly connected to the fishing industry and the value of exports increased considerably.

Ireland posts regular trade *surpluses*[5]. Helped by trade and attractive policies, Ireland's economy has made the intelligent transition from an agriculture based economy to a more trade based one. Although Ireland's trade, especially the export sector, remains dominated by foreign multinationals, exports contribute significantly to the national income.

Ireland's trade has been the reason for the nation's prosperity. Although the recession forced the government to implement various strategies, foreign companies, have kept the exports alive through their wide range of products.

Irish's computers and office products have become some of Ireland's most profitable export products. Other export items include chemicals, data processing equipment, software machinery and equipment, live animals and animal products.

CRH is one of the world's leading building materials businesses. It manufactures and distributes a diverse range of superior building materials, products and solutions, which are used extensively in construction projects of all sizes, across the world. CRH ***ventures***[6], its venture capital unit, supports the development of new technologies and innovative solutions to meet the increasingly complex needs of customers and evolving trends in construction.

DCC is a leading international sales, marketing and support services group with a focus on performance and growth. It operates through three divisions: energy, healthcare and technology. It is an entrepreneurial business supplying products and services, which builds routes to market, drive for results, focuses on cash conversion and generates superior returns on capital employed enabling it to reinvest in business creating value for stakeholders.

Exercises

I. *Try to answer the following questions according to your understanding of the text.*

(1) Who is the real head of the Irish government?

(2) Who exercises the executive power in Ireland?

(3) Who are entitled to participate in elections to the Irish national parliament?

(4) What natural advantages for farming does Ireland have?

(5) What have become some of Ireland's most profitable export products?

II. *Read the following passage carefully, and make a comment on it at the end of the passage in no more than 100 words.*

More than 60 countries and regions, as well as six international organizations, were exhibiting at the 2021 China International Fair for Trade in Services, according to organizers. Ireland, the guest country of honor for this year's China International Fair for Trade in Services(CIFTIS), was showcasing a variety of sectors including tourism, agricultural products, and culture to healthcare and education. At its agricultural booth, it displayed dairy products, pork and shellfish. Ireland's whiskey and cream liqueur were also on show, which had been certified by the European Union as geographical indication products.

The signing of the China-EU agreement on GI had helped Ireland bring more brands to

Chapter Six The Republic of Ireland

China. China had been developing fast in the consumer goods sector and the development of new channels such as e-commerce, new retail and cold-chain logistics were helping Ireland export more products. Media reported that Ireland's service trade with China reached a new level and China had become Ireland's fifth-largest trading partner in the world and its largest trading partner in Asia.

Ireland has a very rich services tradition—about two-thirds of global trade all over the world is in services. The service trade in China is very much opening-up across the board in terms of China's dual circulation strategy. Ireland's trade in services with China has increased by 30 percent year-on-year.

International organizations had also set up exhibits at the event and the United Nations Industrial Development Organization was showcasing technologies and projects that feature artificial intelligence and sustainable development.

Comments:

Nowadays, with the developments in the economy and society, more and more joint ventures are being formed. These ventures bring both advantages and disadvantages to the countries involved.

What is your opinion?

Reference:

Argument:

(1) Benefiting a lot from foreign investment

(2) Providing a large number of employment opportunities for locals

(3) Promoting multi-cultural communication

Counter-argument:

(1) Depriving of equal trade opportunities

(2) Bringing challenges and pressure to state owned enterprises

(3) The outflow of talents

Unit 5 Culture and Customs

Text Focus

1. Traditional Culture
2. Literature Works
3. Food Customs

6.5 Culture and Customs.mp3

Vocabulary

1. parade	[pəˈreɪd]	n.	游行
2. awe	[ɔː]	n.	敬畏
3. satire	[ˈsætaɪə(r)]	n.	讽刺
4. mead	[miːd]	n.	蜂蜜酒
5. stew	[stjuː]	n.	炖煮的菜肴
6. exotic	[ɪgˈzɒtɪk]	adj.	异国风情的

The United Kingdom Bank Holidays Act 1871 established the first Bank holidays in Ireland. There are some famous public holidays observed in Ireland. Public holidays in Ireland may celebrate a special day or other event, such as Saint Patrick's Day. On public holidays, most businesses and schools close. Other services, for example, public transport, still operate but often with reduced schedules. Ireland boasts the finest writers of all times and has produced some of the Western world's most acclaimed writers and they create lots of works, such as *The Midnight Court*, *The Real Charlotte*, *Ulysses* etc. Most traditional Irish foods use simple, basic and cheap ingredients.

Traditional Culture

St. Patrick's Day is celebrated with **parades**[1] in the large cities, the wearing of the green and drinking Guinness. On St. Patrick's Day, Irish families would traditionally attend church in the morning and celebrate in the afternoon. Prohibitions against the consumption of meat were stopped and people would dance, drink and feast—on the traditional meal of Irish bacon and cabbage.

The Irish government held a national campaign to use interest in St. Patrick's Day to drive tourism and show Ireland and Irish culture to the rest of the world. Lots of people annually take part in Ireland's St. Patrick's Festival in Dublin, a multi-day celebration featuring parades, concerts, outdoor theater productions and fireworks shows.

Bloomsday is a commemoration and celebration of the life of Irish writer James Joyce during which the events of his novel *Ulysses* are relived. It is observed annually on June 16 in Dublin and elsewhere. Joyce chose the date as it was the date of his first outing with his wife-to-be; they walked to the Dublin suburb of Ringsend. The name was derived from Leopold Bloom, the Ulyssean protagonist. Bloomsday was invented in 1954, on the 50th anniversary of the events in the novel, when John Ryan, an artist, critic, publican and founder of Envoy magazine and the novelist Brian O'Nolan organized what was to be a daylong pilgrimage along the Ulysses route.

Chapter Six The Republic of Ireland

📖 Literature Works

Ireland's literature is the third oldest in all of Europe, second only to Greek and Latin. One of the hallmarks of Irish literature includes an ***awe*²** of nature and a love of the homeland, particularly prevalent in its poetry. Ireland's literature also includes a rich and imaginative folklore. But perhaps the most distinguishing quality of Irish literature is its mastery of the satirical.

Ireland boasts the finest writers of all times and has produced some of the Western world's most acclaimed writers: James Joyce and George Bernard Shaw.

Cúirt an Mheán Oíche (The Midnight Court), a vigorous and inventive ***satire*³** by Brian Merriman from County Clare, is a famous long poem. The copying of manuscripts continued unabated, and one such collection was in the possession of a teacher of County Kilkenny who kept a unique diary in vernacular Irish covering local and international events, with a wealth of information about daily life.

The Real Charlotte was published in 1894. The novels and stories, mostly humorous, of Edith Somerville and Violet Florence Martin, are among the most accomplished products of Anglo-Irish literature, though written exclusively from the viewpoint of the "big house".

Ulysses, considered to be one of the 20th century's greatest literary achievements. It has been described as "a demonstration and summation of the entire Modernist movement". James Joyce also wrote *Finnegans Wake*, *Dubliners*, and the semi-autobiographical *A Portrait of the Artist as a Young Man*. He is often regarded as the father of the literary genre "stream of consciousness", best exemplified in his famous work.

📖 Food Customs

Stories related to the old Irish culture have the mention of honey being widely used especially to make ***mead*⁴**. Meat was widely eaten along with poultry products. The food habits have influences from all over the world. Although meat has always been the main item in Irish food, fast food has also taken over. New Irish dishes aim at some healthy eating habits among the Irish people. These focus mainly on fresh vegetables.

Almost everyone when asked about Irish food mentions two things—Irish ***Stew*⁵** and Corned Beef with Cabbage. And almost every visitor to Ireland is surprised to find neither features commonly on restaurant menus. In fact, Corned Beef is not traditionally Irish at all—but Bacon and Cabbage is. Most traditional Irish foods use simple, basic and cheap ingredients, and this should be no surprise—they do not have a huge range of ***exotic*⁶** ingredients.

Irish people are still extremely fond of their fried breakfast, which always includes pork sausages, bacon and black pudding.

Summer is berry time and wild blackberries are abundant throughout Ireland as are rose hips and wild strawberries. The wet warm weather of late summer and early autumn is mushroom time and wild mushroom can be found everywhere, especially following a good rain shower. A little later there are plenty of nuts.

Irish people are very fussy about their potatoes(Fig. 6-6). Typically a supermarket will stock at least five or six different varieties, often many more, with the varieties changing depending on the season and each suited to a particular method of cooking.

Fig. 6-6　Beef potatoes

Of all foods, the humble spud is certainly the most traditional. The Irish may not be dependent on them in the way they were in the past but there are a lot of Irish people for whom a dinner without potatoes is not a dinner at all.

Exercises

I. *Try to answer the following questions according to your understanding of the text.*

(1) When is St. Patrick's Day?

(2) What is Bloomsday and how is it celebrated?

(3) How has Ireland made a significant contribution to the world of literature?

(4) Please say something about the traditional Irish foods.

(5) How potatoes are welcomed to the Irish people?

II. *Read the following passage carefully, and make a comment on it at the end of the passage in no more than 100 words.*

Music has no boundaries. That's how the Turkish businessman Erdem Ozturk felt when he listened to a remix of Yongju Opera, a traditional opera originating from Ningbo, Zhejiang province. Ozturk participated in a cultural exchange activity in the city's Yinzhou district on Monday during which musicians from China, Spain and Ireland performed and shared their opinions about music.

Wang Leting, a Chinese remix musician, shared one of his arrangements, an adaptation of a piece of Yongju Opera. "He has blended Chinese traditional music with electronic music. For me, he's like blending some coffee from Colombia with coffee from Arabic regions to create a new flavor." Terence Needham, a teacher at Ningbo Tech University and an Irish musician, also attaches great importance to renewing the music. "I think it's very interesting to use modern music to revitalize traditional culture," Needham said. "If you don't keep renewing, it will become something for a museum. But for culture, it has to be adapted to the new generation and continue to grow."

He Zhenbiao, a professor at NingboTech, has been taking the Chinese music to the world for years. He was a part-time DJ in a radio station in the United States in the past and shared different kinds of Chinese music with local DJs. "I introduced Butterfly Lovers for a classical channel and also introduced Chinese rock music, such as *Dream Back to the Tang Dynasty*," He said. "They cannot understand Chinese very well, but they can enjoy them as we do." The activity was held at Demohood, a creative park in Yinzhou district. The park, which was renovated from a former factory, is now home to catering, shopping and cultural and creative stores and has become popular with young residents.

Comments:

Music plays an important part in our daily lives. Some suppose that they like pop music, while others prefer classical music.

What is your point of view?

Reference:

Argument:

(1) Pop music is lively, modern, and more related to our daily life

(2) Pop music is more catering to young people's taste

(3) Classical music is too long and complicated to understand

Counter-argument:

(1) Classical music has been passed down from generation to generation

(2) Classical music is the heritage of mankind

(3) Pop music is just popular for short time before they are replaced

Unit 6   Intercultural Communication

 Knowledge to Learn

What Is Non-verbal Communication?

Non-verbal communication includes body language, such as gestures, facial expressions, eye contact and posture. Touch is a non-verbal communication that not only indicates a person's feelings or level of comfort, but illustrates personality characteristics as well. A firm handshake or warm hug indicates something very different than a loose pat on the back or a timid handshake does. The sound of our voice, including pitch, tone and volume are also forms of non-verbal communication. The meaning behind someone's words is often entirely different than the literal translation, as is seen in instances of sarcasm and mockery. The clothing we wear and the way we design our living space are also forms of non-verbal communication that frequently shape people's judgments about others, regardless of whether or not the perceptions are true.

How to Improve Verbal and Non-verbal Communication?

Verbal communication is enhanced when a person is an effective listener. Watching other people's body language, facial expressions and intonations, and being conscious of your own physicality and feelings can enhance non-verbal communication.

Cases to Study

Case 1

Peter is the general manager of a British company in China. Li Jun is one of the Chinese managers in the company, who made a serious mistake at work. Li Jun was very upset about what had happened and came to Peter to apologise. Here is the conversation:

Li Jun: "Peter, I've been so sorry about the trouble I've caused to the company. I'm here to apologise. I'm terribly sorry about it and I want you to know that it will never happen again." (He smiles.)

Peter: "Are you sure?"

Li Jun: "I'm so sorry and I promise it won't happen again." (He smiles, too)

Peter: "I'm sorry but I cannot accept your apology. You don't feel sorry at all."

Li Jun's face turned red: "Peter, please trust me; no one could feel sorrier than I do about it." (He still smiles.)

Peter was furious now.

Why didn't Peter accept Li Jun's apology and even became furious? Is there anything wrong with what Li Jun said?

Analysis

(1) Nothing is wrong with Li Jun's words. What goes wrong is his smile on the face.

(2) When apologising, Li Jun always wore a smile on his face, which caused the misunderstanding. For Li Jun, the smile was an important part of the apology. As a result, he couldn't understand why Peter got angry when he made such a sincere apology.

(3) For Americans, smiling when apologising means the apologiser was not really sorry for the mistake, and it is seen as a sign of disrespect.

Case 2

Kathy and David, a couple from Australia, signed a one-year contract to work in China. Both were extroverts and soon made some Chinese friends.

Before long, people started calling them at home. David was sometimes away on business trips for a few days. If someone called looking for him, Kathy often would find

Chapter Six The Republic of Ireland

the conversation awkward.

"Where did he go?" the caller typically would ask.

"Can I pass on any message?" Kathy asked politely, trying to avoid the question.

"Is he out of town?" the caller was usually very persistent.

"Yes, can I help you in any way?" Kathy tried to be polite, but she could not help feeling uncomfortable.

What is the cultural reflection we could get from the conversation?

Analysis

(1) In China, when someone calls a person who is not at home, "Where is he/she?" and "Where did he/she go?" are natural questions. Usually, the questions are asked simply as a way to carry on the phone conversation which is a kind of typical Chinese courtesy when calling.

(2) In Australia, information about one's daily actions is private and is not generally shared with others.

(3) If the caller needs to speak with David before a certain date or time, that person could say so by stating something like, "Yes, I'd like to leave a message." and could indicate the date before he/she needs to talk with David.

 Translations on Traditional Chinese Culture

Exercise 1

Translate the passage into English

中国最盛大的节日就是春节,也就是中国年。节日是以中国农历而不是公历确定的,因此春节可能是公历1月底或2月初。一般说来,春节真正开始于新年除夕,而于正月十五结束。春联是中国特有的一种文学形式,历史悠久,春联上的文字简洁、精巧,象征着人们对未来的巨大期盼,表达人们对新年的美好愿望。

> **Translation Reference**
>
> The most important holiday in China has long been the Spring Festival, also known as the Chinese New Year. The dates for this annual celebration are determined by the lunar calendar rather than the Gregorian calendar, so the timing of the holiday varies from late January to early February. Generally speaking, the festival actually begins on the eve of the lunar New Year's Day and ends on the fifteenth day of the first month of the lunar calendar. The Spring Festival couplet is a unique Chinese literary form with a long history. The text of couplets is concise and delicate, which symbolizes the great expectation of Chinese for the future and conveys people's good wishes for the New Year.

Translate the passage into Chinese

The 24 solar terms reflect the climate change, guide agriculture farming and also affect people's life. It was in 104 BC that the 24 solar terms were finally set down. As we all know, China is a country with a long history of agriculture. Agricultural production is largely influenced by the laws of nature. In ancient times, farmers arranged their agricultural activities according to the solar terms.

Translation Reference

24 节气反映了天气变化，指导农业耕作，也影响着人们的生活。公元前 104 年 24 节气最终确立。众所周知，中国是个有着悠久农业发展史的国家，农业生产受自然规律影响极大。在古代，农民根据节气安排农业生产活动。

Exercise 2

Translate the passage into English

中医有五千多年的历史，是中国古代劳动人民几千年来对抗疾病的经验总结。中医将人体看成是气、形、神的统一体，以"望、闻、问、切"为其独特的诊断过程。中医使用中药、针灸以及许多其他治疗手段，使人体达到阴阳调和。阴阳和五行是中医的理论基础。五行是自然界中的五种基本物质，即金、木、水、火、土。

Translation Reference

Traditional Chinese Medicine (TCM) has a long history of more than 5,000 years. It is a summary of the experience of the working people over many centuries of struggle against diseases. TCM considers human body as a unity of Qi, Xing and Shen. The diagnostic process of TCM distinguishes itself by "observation, auscultation, inquiry and pulse diagnosis". TCM uses traditional Chinese medicine, acupuncture and many other treatments to bring human body into harmony between Yin and Yang. The theory of Yin and Yang and the theory of Five Elements are the theoretical basis of TCM. The Five Elements are the five basic substances in nature, that is, metal, wood, water, fire, and earth.

Translate the passage into Chinese

The Compendium of Materia Medica is written by Li Shizhen, a famous medical scientist in the Ming Dynasty. With almost two million Chinese characters, the book lists 1,892 kinds of medical substances. Besides Chinese herbal medicines, it includes animals and minerals used as medical substances. The Compendium of Materia Medica is regarded as the most complete medical book in the history of traditional Chinese medicine. Detailed introductions of all the medical substances are given in the book, including name, smell, appearance etc. It has been

Chapter Six The Republic of Ireland

translated into more than 20 languages and spreads all over the world. Even now it is still often used as a reference book in medicine.

> **Translation Reference**
> 《本草纲目》是明代著名的医学家李时珍所著。这部著作近 200 万字，记载药物 1892 种。除了中草药，该书也包含了动物和矿物质作为药物的记载。《本草纲目》堪称中医史上最完整的医书，对各种药物的名称、气味、形态等都做了详尽的介绍。它被翻译成 20 多种语言并在全世界广为流传。即便现在，人们还常常将它用作医学参考书。

Exercise 3

Translate the passage into English

气功是以调心、调息、调身为手段的身心锻炼方法。气功包括一些简单的动作和姿势，是一种能量锻炼法，也强调呼吸的技巧。气功能解乏并改善睡眠质量，从而提高工作效率。气功分为医疗气功和健身气功两类：医疗气功用于治疗身体疾病；健身气功主要用于强健体魄，延缓衰老。

> **Translation Reference**
> Qigong is to exercise both the body and the mind through the regulation of the mind, the breath and the body. Qigong is an energy practice, generally encompassing simple movements and postures. It also emphasizes breathing techniques. Qigong relieves fatigue and improves sleep quality so as to improve work efficiency. There are two kinds of Qigong practices, that is, healing Qigong and fitness Qigong. The former serves as a treatment for diseases while the latter is used for strengthening the body and delaying aging.

Translate the passage into Chinese

The Five-animal Exercise, as a means of physical training in ancient China, was created by Hua Tuo, an eminent doctor in the late Eastern Han Dynasty. He summarized the traditional practice of our predecessors' building up their physical strength by imitating the animal movements, and created a set of healthcare gymnastics—the Five-animal Exercise, which consisted of five groups of actions, imitating the movements and manners of the tigers, deer, bears, apes and birds. Not only is the Five-animal Exercise good for health and longevity, but for the eradication of illnesses.

Translation Reference

五禽戏是我国古代体育锻炼的一种方法,创始人是东汉末年名医华佗。华佗总结了前人模仿鸟兽动作以锻炼身体的传统做法,创编了一套保健体操,包括虎、鹿、熊、猿、鸟的动作和姿态,也就是五禽戏。五禽戏不仅具强身延年之功,还有祛疾除病之效。

Culture to Know

Culture Note 1

12 Chinese Zodiac Signs are the 12 kinds of animals which Chinese people customarily use to mark the year in which a person is born. They are Rat, Ox, Tiger, Rabbit, Dragon, Snake, Horse, Goat, Monkey, Rooster, Dog and Pig. It is based on a 12-year cycle. Each year in that cycle corresponds to an animal sign. For a long time, there has been a special relationship between humans and the 12 zodiacal animals. It is believed that the year represented by the animal affects one's character. A cultural sidelight of the animal signs in Chinese folklore is that horoscopes have developed around the animal signs.

Culture Note 2

Mafeisan is the first anesthetic in the world and was invented by Hua Tuo, an outstanding doctor in the late Eastern Han Dynasty. Although Hua Tuo's ancient prescriptions were lost, the ingredients are thought to have included cannabis and datura, which is a hallucinogenic plant and was later recorded as an anesthetic during the Song Dynasty. Some specific cases of abdominal operations were dilated upon in Hua Tuo's biography.

Culture Note 3

Taijiquan sometimes colloquially known as "Shadowboxing", is an internal Chinese martial art practiced for defense training, health benefits, and meditation. The term "Taiji" is a Chinese cosmological concept for the flux of Yin and Yang, and "quan" means fist. Etymologically, Taijiquan is a fist system based on the dynamic relationship between polarities (Yin and Yang). Today, Taijiquan has enthusiastic practitioners worldwide. Most modern styles of Taijiquan trace their development to one or more of the five traditional schools: Chen, Yang, Wu (Hao), Wu, and Sun. All trace their historical origins to Chen Village.

Chapter Six The Republic of Ireland

Culture Note 4

The Significance of Red Envelopes in Chinese Culture

A red envelope is simply a long, narrow, red envelope. Traditional red envelopes are often decorated with gold Chinese characters, such as happiness and wealth. Variations include red envelopes with **cartoon** characters depicted and red envelopes from stores and companies that contain coupons and gift certificates inside. During Chinese New Year, money is put inside the red envelopes which are then handed out to younger generations by their parents, grandparents, relatives, and even close neighbors and friends. At some companies, workers may also receive a year-end cash bonus tucked inside a red envelope. Red envelopes are also popular gifts for birthdays and weddings. Unlike a Western greeting card, red envelopes given at Chinese New Year are typically left unsigned. For birthdays or weddings, a short message, typically a four-character expression, and signature are optional.

Further Reading

Passage 1

Photos from Space

An Italian astronaut posted a group of photos taken from space and attached several lines from a famous ancient Chinese composition, demonstrating her outstanding Chinese language ability that amazed Chinese internet users and language experts. "Looking up, I see the immensity of the cosmos; bowing my head, I look at the multitude of the world. The gaze flies, the heart expands, the joy of the senses can reach its peak, and indeed, this is true happiness." The text she quoted is from the Preface to Poems Composed at the Orchid Pavilion, a Chinese calligraphy masterpiece by Chinese calligrapher Wang Xizhi (303—361) of the Eastern Jin Dynasty (317—420). Exploring the universe has been mankind's dream since ancient times. Thanks to scientific and technological progress, reaching beyond the moon has become a reality. Humanity will continue to benefit from the noble endeavor of exploration and peaceful use of space.

Passage 2

Shenzhou XV Astronauts Take Their First Spacewalk

The Shenzhou-15 taikonauts on board the orbiting Chinese Tiangong space station completed their first spacewalk. During the extravehicular activities (EVAs) lasting about seven hours, they completed several tasks, including the installation of the extension pumps outside the Mengtian lab module. China have grown stronger in basic research and original innovation, made breakthroughs in some core technologies in key fields, and boosted emerging strategic industries. China has witnessed major successes on multiple fronts, including manned spaceflight, lunar and Martian exploration, deep sea and deep earth probes, supercomputers, satellite navigation, quantum information, nuclear power technology, new energy technology, airliner manufacturing, and biomedicine. China has joined the ranks of the world's innovators.

Reference

[1] 常俊跃，吕春媚，赵永青. 跨文化交际(第 2 版)[M]. 北京：北京大学出版社，2021.

[2] 约翰·吉布尼. 爱尔兰简史[M]. 潘良，译. 桂林：广西师范大学出版社，2021.

[3] 冯建明. 当代爱尔兰教育概况[M]. 上海：上海三联书店，2020.

[4] 兰冬秀. 中国特色政治术语翻译研究[D]. 福建：福建师范大学，2017.

[5] 凯伦·史密斯. THIS IS AUSTRALIA：澳大利亚[M]. 天津：天津人民出版社，2017.

[6] 王恩铭. 新编英美文化教程[M]. 北京：清华大学出版社，2016.

[7] 董晓波. 美国历史文化概况[M]. 北京：对外经贸大学出版社，2016.

[8] 常俊跃，李莉莉，赵永青. 英国国情：英国社会与文化(第 2 版)[M]. 北京：北京大学出版社，2016.

[9] 海因里希·伯尔. 爱尔兰之旅[M]. 刘兴华，译. 上海：上海文艺出版社，2015.

[10] 赵晓寰，乔雪瑛. 新西兰：历史、民族与文化[M]. 上海：复旦大学出版社，2009.

[11] 常俊跃. 美国社会与文化[M]. 北京：北京大学出版社，2009.

[12] 何自然. 语用三论[M]. 上海：上海教育出版社，2007.

[13] 夏廷德. 翻译补偿研究[M]. 武汉：湖北教育出版社，2006.

[14] 许渊冲. 翻译的艺术[M]. 北京：五洲传播出版社，2006.

[15] 张柏然，许钧. 面向 21 世纪的译学研究[M]. 北京：商务印书馆，2002.

[16] 马林，李洁红. 放眼看天下加拿大卷[M]. 哈尔滨：哈尔滨工程大学出版社，2009.

[17] 吴斐. 加拿大社会与文化[M]. 武汉：武汉大学出版社，2011.

[18] 隋铭才. 英语国家概况(下)[M]. 北京：高等教育出版社，2009.